Robert Pech

Innovation: Pathway to Growth

Robert Pech

Innovation: Pathway to Growth

A case-study approach

LAP LAMBERT Academic Publishing

Impressum/Imprint (nur für Deutschland/ only for Germany)
Bibliografische Information der Deutschen Nationalbibliothek: Die Deutsche Nationalbibliothek
verzeichnet diese Publikation in der Deutschen Nationalbibliografie; detaillierte bibliografische
Daten sind im Internet über http://dnb.d-nb.de abrufbar.
Alle in diesem Buch genannten Marken und Produktnamen unterliegen warenzeichen-, marken-
oder patentrechtlichem Schutz bzw. sind Warenzeichen oder eingetragene Warenzeichen der
jeweiligen Inhaber. Die Wiedergabe von Marken, Produktnamen, Gebrauchsnamen,
Handelsnamen, Warenbezeichnungen u.s.w. in diesem Werk berechtigt auch ohne besondere
Kennzeichnung nicht zu der Annahme, dass solche Namen im Sinne der Warenzeichen- und
Markenschutzgesetzgebung als frei zu betrachten wären und daher von jedermann benutzt
werden dürften.

Coverbild: www.ingimage.com

Verlag: LAP LAMBERT Academic Publishing AG & Co. KG
Dudweiler Landstr. 99, 66123 Saarbrücken, Deutschland
Telefon +49 681 3720-310, Telefax +49 681 3720-3109
Email: info@lap-publishing.com

Herstellung in Deutschland:
Schaltungsdienst Lange o.H.G., Berlin
Books on Demand GmbH, Norderstedt
Reha GmbH, Saarbrücken
Amazon Distribution GmbH, Leipzig
ISBN: 978-3-8433-5291-8

Imprint (only for USA, GB)
Bibliographic information published by the Deutsche Nationalbibliothek: The Deutsche
Nationalbibliothek lists this publication in the Deutsche Nationalbibliografie; detailed
bibliographic data are available in the Internet at http://dnb.d-nb.de.
Any brand names and product names mentioned in this book are subject to trademark, brand
or patent protection and are trademarks or registered trademarks of their respective holders.
The use of brand names, product names, common names, trade names, product descriptions
etc. even without a particular marking in this works is in no way to be construed to mean that
such names may be regarded as unrestricted in respect of trademark and brand protection
legislation and could thus be used by anyone.

Cover image: www.ingimage.com

Publisher: LAP LAMBERT Academic Publishing AG & Co. KG
Dudweiler Landstr. 99, 66123 Saarbrücken, Germany
Phone +49 681 3720-310, Fax +49 681 3720-3109
Email: info@lap-publishing.com

Printed in the U.S.A.
Printed in the U.K. by (see last page)
ISBN: 978-3-8433-5291-8

This research is dedicated to

Diane, Andrew and Emma

It was a long journey. My thanks to you for your love, humour, support and patience, and for your faith that one day this work would be completed. XXXOOO

Contents   Page

Chapter 1 Introduction

Chapter 2 Significant Literature on Innovation and the Management of Change

Chapter 3 Method

Chapter 4 Wave Rider the Surfing Company
(Australia): 1969-2001

Chapter 5 Wave Rider the Surfing Company (Australia): 2001-2004

Chapter 6 Wave Rider the Surfing Company (Australia): Preliminary Analysis

Chapter 7 The Jiangsu Little Dragon Group Company (The People's Republic of China): 1958-2002

Chapter 8 The Jiangsu Little Dragon Group
(The People's Republic of China): November 2002-March 2004

Chapter 9 The Little Dragon Company
(The People's Republic of China): Preliminary Analysis

Chapter 10 Alpine Packs the Wilderness Company
(New Zealand): 1973-2002

Chapter 11 Alpine Packs the Wilderness Company
(New Zealand): 2002-2004

Chapter 12 Alpine Packs the Wilderness Company
(New Zealand) Preliminary Analysis

Chapter 13 Main Analysis

Chapter 14 Conclusions and Recommendations

Abstract

Innovation and Change Management:
A Case-study Approach

In the face of ever-increasing commercial complexity and competition, management practice has struggled to keep pace. Changing demands and technologies have produced a plethora of business fads with concomitant changes in management approaches, some successful, some not so. Neo-classical management orthodoxy – in practice for over a century – has been replaced by models of a more transient nature; and rational strategy has been replaced by strategic thinking, including emphases on innovation and core competencies, all with the aim of turning the corporate mix into a competitive advantage to exact leverage in the market. Being innovative in product and process is one way in which companies have survived and thrived.

To broaden the scope of scholarship in the field of innovation and change management, this research makes a contribution by using an abductive, case-study approach to investigate three companies, each from a different industry, and from three different geo-political environments. This investigation attempts to address the question of how three mature companies use processes of innovation and the subsequent management of change to generate sustainable leadership in their respective commercial fields, and how this may contribute to company longevity. This research is intended to provide an additional link between organizational research and managerial practice with the main focus on innovation as the catalyst.

The three businesses are: Wave Rider the Surfing Company, Victoria, Australia; Alpine Packs Wilderness Equipment Ltd, Christchurch, New Zealand; and the Little Dragon Group Company, Wuxi, Jiangsu Province, People's Republic of China. Wave Rider dates from 1967, and is an international leader in the manufacture of surf and snow products such as wetsuits, surf and snow-boards, as well as accessories such as surf and snow clothing, bags and tide-watches. Alpine Packs dates from 1973, and is a world leader in the design and manufacture of backpacks, outdoor attire, tents and sleeping bags. The Little Dragon Group dates from1958, and it is one of the PR China's foremost suppliers of white-ware products, especially automatic washing machines, air conditioners, refrigerators and dishwashers. Each of these companies expanded domestically, then globalized, and succeeded in capturing sizeable foreign markets within more or less three decades of their founding. Innovation has been the key to their success to date.

Innovative practices in the three companies comprised many permutations. This research examines their development, creating patterns of disruptive, incremental and discontinuous innovations to build resilience in their processes. The two main sensitising concepts that have been used are the congruence model, conceptualised by Michael Tushman and Charles O'Reilly in *Winning through innovation: A practical guide to leading organizational change and renewal,* published in 1997; and the disruptive innovation model first described in *The innovator's solution* by Clayton Christensen and Michael Raynor, published in 2003. These models, conceptualised only about five years apart, are reasonably compatible and show an evolutionary path in theory construction in the field of innovation research.

In much of the literature, examples of companies used to exemplify innovation and change, were typically from the domain of public ownership within market economies, particularly those of the United States and Great Britain. In contrast, this investigation analyses two privately owned companies: Wave Rider from Australia and Alpine Packs from New Zealand. Also standing apart from a large body of innovation research is the focus on Little Dragon, a company from a command economy, that of The People's Republic of China, ruled by a communist government. These three cases bring a fresh perspective to mainstream research on innovation and the management of change, by providing insights from a variety of industrial cultures, and from different forms of ownership. The investigation incorporates a focus on the comparative forms and levels of education that the industrialists underwent in these different environments, and the effects that these have had on their management.

Chapter 1

Introduction

1.1 Background

Competition within the field of commerce over the last thirty years has intensified dramatically, for many reasons, and with surprising outcomes. The lowering of trade tariffs and shifts in political hegemonies, the coalescing of markets into preferential trade blocks creating mass markets catered for by mass production, outsourcing production to third world labour markets, the improvement in communications and marketing, as well as the advent and creative applications of high technology, have all played their part in transforming commerce.

Globalisation and technology have turned the world into a jungle of competition. Globalisation and technology have been responsible for transforming production and management patterns. In a climate where consumers gauge the value of products by their own standards of what comprises the best, the cheapest, the fastest, or the smallest, the businesses competing to bring such products to market have either initiated change in order to remain competitive, or have had it forced on them, (Clarke & Clegg, 1998).

There are many definitions of both creativity and innovation. "Innovation is the conversion of new knowledge into new products and services." (Williams, 1999, p. 2). A number of epithetical definitions have arisen which clarify innovation, such as the one by Vadim Kotelnikov, "Science is the conversion of money into knowledge. Innovation is the conversion of knowledge into money." (Kotelnikov, www.1000ventures.com, retrieved February 25 2005).

11

Theodore Levitt is quoted in Shapiro as distilling the essence of creativity and innovation down to: "Creativity is thinking up new things. Innovation is doing new things." (Levitt quoted in Shapiro, 2002, p.7). Nicholas Negroponte and Stephen Shapiro echo de Geus' image of the business organization having organic qualities. They point to the need for creativity to be "nurtured like a living organism, permeating everything the company does, all the time, including the design and operation of its processes, [because] to be perpetually responsive to today's fast-changing markets requires a radically new approach to designing businesses." (Quoted in Levitt, 2002, p.9). Management must now moderate the tensions between a number of important industrial dynamics in which creativity is important. These include managing their production by means of fresh re-combinations of people, products, resources and strategies to "wow" the market. (Tushman and O'Reilly, 1997; Morgan, 2000; Christensen and Raynor, 2003). Management is responsible for the survival of their firms, and fighting for survival can take many forms, just one of which is satisfying shareholders who constantly knock on corporate doors for greater returns on their investments. (Christensen and Raynor, 2003).

Companies must fight for sustainability and growth. However, those facing life-threatening problems, such as declining markets and increasing competition, must look for their own solutions, and, they may survive if they find them. One of the most profitable solutions for a company is to be innovative, and to remain innovative and thereby have the competition follow in the wake of the market-leader. Companies therefore must respect the need for, and cultivate a depth of understanding of, innovation and change management. (Clarke & Clegg, 1998). To retain or increase their market share, companies must creatively deploy innovative strategies. (Hamel and Välikangas, 2003; Bean and Radford, 2002; the Australian Institute of Management, 2001; Leifer, McDermott, O'Connor, Peters, Rice, and Veryzer, 2000; and Williams, 1999). Each company seeks to distinguish its products and/or services from those of its competitors by increasing its competitive advantage, expanding its growth and refining its visionary drive on a continuing basis. Not only have successful businesses recognised the imperative of being innovative – so have governments, because innovation can underpin the success of an entire economy. This was demonstrated by *Growing an innovative New Zealand*, (2002), a policy document in which Prime Minister Helen Clark wrote, "[…] this work confirms the need to continue to transform the New Zealand economy. We need to become a more innovative, more confident, more flexible economy which is able to compete successfully on the international scene." (Clark, 2002, p.5).

To broaden the scope of scholarship in this field of knowledge, this research aims to make a contribution by using an abductive, case-study approach to investigate three companies, each from a different industry.

1.2 The research question

This investigation attempts to address the question of how three mature companies use processes of innovation and the subsequent management of change to generate sustainable leadership in their respective fields. These three businesses are: Wave Rider the Surfing Company, Victoria, Australia, from here on to be called "Wave Rider"; Alpine Packs Wilderness Equipment Ltd, Christchurch, New Zealand, to be shortened to "Alpine Packs"; and the Little Dragon Group Company, Wuxi, Jiangsu Province, People's Republic of China, to be referred to as "Little Dragon". The company names used here are pseudonyms to protect companies' right to anonymity; and similarly, the names of the employees who participated in this investigation have been given pseudonyms to protect their privacy, in accordance with RMIT University's ethical requirements.

Wave Rider dates from 1967, and is an international leader in the manufacture of surf and snow products such as wetsuits, surf and snow-boards, as well as accessories such as surf and snow clothing, bags and tide watches. Alpine Packs dates from 1973 and is a world leader in the design and manufacture of backpacks, outdoor attire, tents and sleeping bags. The Little Dragon Group dates from 1979 in its more contemporary form, (although it is correct to say that its earliest beginnings go back to 1958, when it manufactured ceramics and tools), and it is one of China's foremost suppliers of white-ware products, especially automatic washing machines, air conditioners, refrigerators and

13

dishwashers. Each of these companies has expanded domestically, has globalized and then succeeded in capturing sizeable foreign markets within more or less three decades of their founding.

1.3 Innovation and change management: Motives and goals

Innovation is a multi-faceted if not elusive concept, and as a result, its practice comprises many permutations. (Christensen and Raynor, 2003; Bean and Radford, 2002; Harvard Business Review, 2001; Taffinder, 1998). The implementation of change is elusive, and making the connection between innovation and change may differ from company to company. There are two main motives underpinning this research. Firstly, to discover the part that innovation has played in the success of the chosen businesses pertaining to three different industries in three geo-political environments. In much of the literature, examples of companies used to exemplify innovation and change, were typified from the domain of public ownership within market economies, particularly those of the United States and Great Britain. In contrast, this investigation analyses two privately owned companies: Wave Rider and Alpine Packs. Also standing apart from a large body of innovation research is the focus on Little Dragon, a company from a command economy, that of The Peoples' Republic of China, ruled by a communist government. These three cases are intended to bring a fresh perspective to mainstream research on innovation and the management of change, by providing insights from industrial cultures other than those from the United States or Great Britain, and from different forms of ownership. It is also relevant to enquire about the comparative forms and levels of education that the industrialists underwent in these different environments, and the effects that this has had on their management.

Furthermore, what part does strategy play in the success, or otherwise, of changes that follow in the wake of innovation? Christensen and Raynor quote Mintzberg and Waters when they advise, "Openness to emergent strategy enables management to act before everything is fully understood – to respond to an evolving reality rather than having to focus on a stable fantasy ... Emergent strategy itself implies learning what works – taking one action at a time in a search for that viable pattern or consistency." (Christensen and Raynor, 2003, p.221). The study will, in part, investigate whether managing the strategy for change in ways that are most appropriate to the contexts and circumstances, improve the odds that an innovative venture can succeed.

The literature provides a number of useful and relevant models for further exploration. Two such models include the "congruence model", conceptualised by Michael Tushman and Charles O'Reilly in *Winning through innovation: A practical guide to leading organizational change and renewal* published in 1997; and the "disruptive innovation model", devised by Clayton Christensen and Michael Raynor in *The Innovator's Solution*, published in 2003. These models, conceptualised only about five years apart, are reasonably compatible and show an evolutionary path in theory construction in the field of innovation research. The congruence model and the disruptive innovation model will serve as "sensitising" concepts (Blumer cited in Blaikie, 2000, p.85), as part of an abductive strategy, with which this investigation will be conducted.

The second motive in this research is to extend or otherwise modify pre-existing models, because the abductive approach lends itself to that. (Blaikie, 2000, p.126). Generating new theory derived from the data, has as its ultimate aim, the better informing of practitioners engaged in innovation and change management in the future. In keeping with the abductive investigative tradition, this investigation remains open to the concepts of theorists and practitioners other than Tushman and O'Reilly, and Christensen and Raynor, in order to assist in the generation of new theory. This research is intended to provide an additional link between organizational research and managerial practice with the main focus on innovation as the catalyst.

Chapter 2

Significant Literature on Innovation,
and the Management of Change

2.1 Introduction

The two elements of "innovation" and "management of change" are dynamically intertwined in industries where technological and management change is taking place, and the literature clarifies these inter-relationships in a wide range of circumstances, using industrial case-studies which cross many international borders. Innovation and change are universal phenomena, but successful transition may not be so universal. This is reflected in the plethora of models relating to innovation, but there is a comparative paucity of data and frameworks that focus on the implementation of change. This may be because a great idea and a great manager are inspirational. But for implementation to be great in producing results, its operations management must be uniquely destructive of an old order, yet every organization is different, and thereforethe processes concerned may be different from company to company. Implementation may also cause divisiveness, and can, by its very nature, cause chaos in an older order, and that may make it more difficult for an organization to feel comfortable in exposing itself to research and publication.

The quest is to find how creativity and its applied arm, innovation, may be better defined, appraised and implemented. A number of literary sources are examined and this progresses from the more populist but inspiring guides, such as those by Peters, (1997); and by Williams, (1999), to a number of significant academic works in the serious tradition of scholarly investigation into innovation and change management. These include Leifer et al's *Radical Innovation*, (2000);

Tushman and O'Reilly's *Winning through Innovation,* (1997); Christensen and Raynor's, *The innovator's solution: Creating and sustaining successful growth,* (2003); Hamel and Välikangas' "The Quest for Resilience" (*Harvard Business Review*, Sept. 2003), and Govindarajan and Trimble (2005). These are comprehensive studies which provide the industrial practitioner with a diversity of theoretical and practical frameworks, insights, processes and applications.

2.2 Volatility and turbulence: The world of business changes

The world of business at the outset of the twenty-first century is volatile and turbulent. Business has been undergoing transformation at an increasingly faster pace especially in the last two decades of the twentieth century, accelerated by an inter-related chain of economic realities such as the impact of knowledge economies, globalization, digitalization, systemic overhauls, quality management applications, human resource management trends, restructuring, re-engineering, and strategic management implementation. Each plays a part in increasing the pace of competition. However, this has also led to uncertainty. "The result is a bewildering profusion of management theories, concepts and fashions that often replace each other before they can become widely established." (Clarke & Clegg, 1998, p.1). The consumer's expectation is that product life cycles will shorten, design will be better, and follow up service will have to be of ever-higher quality.

Dr Ian Lin, Managing Director of the Quo Vadis Consulting Group, describes our world as "the Cyber Age" and comments that the industrial age is behind us and that we are,

> entering the new networked world of cyberspace – the global interactive multimedia information and communications network [characterised by a new type of consumption]. Gone are the old concepts of mass production and economies of scale, as we enter a new era of mass customisation and one-to-one personal relationships. Customers now want and can get better products, greater choice, shorter lead times, lower prices, more often, at

lower risk, supported by faster service – and from anywhere in the world.
(Lin quoted in Barker, Ed., 2000, p.1)

To remain competitive today, companies must do more than simply deliver products and services that are marginally better and cheaper than those already on the market. They must add features, improve functions and reduce costs more quickly – in addition to launching new lines and developing new markets.

2.3 Can the company survive?

In uncertain environments and intense competition from around the globe, what are the chances of a company surviving, let alone thriving? This question was posed by Lo van Wachem, the chairman of the Committee of Managing Directors at Royal Dutch Shell. He commissioned Arie de Geus, Head of Planning, to provide him with examples of companies which were Shell's equal in importance in their own industry, were older than Shell, and which had survived one or more major change in their environment yet had continued to trade with their "corporate identity intact." (De Geus, 1998, pp. 10-11). De Geus' line-up is disconcertingly thin: in North America he found DuPont, the Hudson's Bay Company, W.R. Grace and Kodak which were older than Shell. Amongst the Japanese companies, there were Mitsui, Sumitomo and Daimaru; Mitsubishi, and Suzuki dated from the Meiji Restoration in 1868. In Europe, de Geus found only forty corporations that met van Wachem's criteria. This is testimony to a high rate of corporate mortality over the last two hundred years, years in which competition was not even as vigorous as that in the twenty-first century.

2.4 The struggle for sustainability

Among the plethora of business practices intended to increase a company's competitive advantage in the market place, a cogent concentration on creativity and innovation is a key means by which the company may carve out ways of sustaining its commercial viability. Creativity is evanescent. How can a business think creatively, and challenge the status quo – whilst maintaining everyday operations and productivity for profit? In the case of creativity and innovation there are no rules, because every piece of creativity or innovation that is successful is unique. So how might creativity be achieved? Negroponte, co-founder and chairman of the MIT Media Laboratory, provides an enlightening opinion on the stimulation of creativity:

> Our biggest challenge in stimulating a creative culture is finding ways to encourage multiple points of views. Many engineering deadlocks have been broken by people who are not engineers at all. This is simply because perspective is more important than IQ. The irony is that perspective will not get kids into college, nor does it help them thrive there. Academia rewards depth. Expertise is bred by experts who work with their own kind. Departments and labs focus on fields and subfields, now and then adding or subtracting a domain. Graduate degrees, not to mention tenure, depend upon tunnelling into truths and illuminating ideas in narrow areas. The antidote to such cannibalization and compartmentalization is being interdisciplinary, a term that is at once utterly banal and, in advanced studies, describes an almost impossible goal. Interdisciplinary labs and projects emerged in the 1960s to address big problems spanning the frontiers of the physical and social sciences, engineering, and the arts. The idea was to unite complementary bodies of knowledge to address issues that transcended any one skill set. Fine. Only recently, however, have people realized that interdisciplinary environments also stimulate creativity. In maximizing the differences in backgrounds, cultures, ages and the like, we increase the likelihood that the results will not be what we had imagined. (Negroponte, 2003 February).

For Negroponte then, creativity must have an unpredictable quality that arises from people who can contribute to a re-combination or mix: the end result being greater – and different – than the sum of the parts. And he believes that standard ways of educating youngsters and standard ways of working in industries will not produce the required results.

19

Peter Drucker sees innovation as a key to growth: "Every organization – not just business – needs one core competence: innovation." (Drucker quoted in Kotelnikov, www.1000ventures.com, retrieved 25 February 2004.) Shapiro agrees with this bold assertion and adds, "The businesses that show the way in this century will be built not around a lot of heads and hands, but around a lot of hearts, around motivation, dedication, and commitment to creative thinking." (Shapiro, 2002, p.9). Alan Williams' definition of innovation is more prosaic: "Innovation usually refers to the commercialisation of new ideas and/or invention, products, designs, systems and resources." (Williams, 1999, p.14).

Growth, the capture of new markets and prosperity, increasingly depend on innovative strategies in product development, customer service improvements, marketing strategies and extracting efficiencies in supply chain management. Bean and Radford (2000), also emphasize the importance of innovation in meeting the needs of customers, and believe that in meeting those needs, the company has a future; clearly by inference they believe that the company which does not do so risks a perilous future:

> The capacity to innovate is the source of a company's enduring strength. Ultimately, innovation is a company's source of value. This aptitude for innovation and improvement is nothing less than a direct reflection of the organization's ability to change, to adapt to new and competent competitors, to skilfully fit its products and services to the ever-evolving needs of customers. The innovative organization, by its wits, frequently survives, continues, and succeeds. (Bean and Radford, 2002, p.ix).

Leifer and colleagues (2000) arrived at the following definition of a form of innovation they call "radical" innovation; it is one with the potential to produce one or more of:

- An entirely new set of performance features;
- Improvements in known performance features of five times or greater; or
- A significant (30 percent or greater) reduction in cost.

(Leifer et al., 2000, p.5).

20

Leifer et al. make an important contribution to the definition of innovation when they distinguish precisely between incremental and radical innovation and the different processes involved in bringing each to fruition. To them, radical innovation "concerns the development of new businesses or product line based on ideas or technologies or substantial cost reductions – that transform the economics of a business and therefore requires exploration competencies." (Leifer et al., 2000, p.5).

In Leifer et al. (2000), on p.19, in Table 2-1, the authors differentiate the incremental and the radical as follows.

Incremental versus Radical Innovation

Table 1

	Incremental	Radical
Project time line	Short term – six months to two years	Long term – usually ten years or more
Trajectory	There is a linear and continuous path from concept to commercialization following designated steps.	The path is marked by multiple discontinuities, or gaps, that must be bridged. The process is sporadic with many stops and starts, hibernations and revivals. Trajectory changes occur in response to unanticipated events, outcomes, and discoveries.
Idea generation and opportunity recognition	Idea generation and opportunity recognition occur at the front end; critical events are largely anticipated.	Idea generation and opportunity recognition occur sporadically throughout the life cycle, often in response to discontinuities (funding, personnel, technical,

21

		market) in the project trajectory.
Process	A formal, approved process moves from idea generation through development and commercialization.	There is a formal process for getting and keeping funding, which is treated by participants as a game, often with disdain. Uncertainty is too high to make the process relevant. The formal process has real value only when the project enters later stages of development.
Business case	A complete and detailed plan can be developed at the beginning of the process because of the relatively low level of uncertainty.	The business model evolves through discovery-based technical and market learning and likewise the business plan must evolve as uncertainty is reduced.
The players	Assigned to a cross-functional team, each member has a clearly specified responsibility within his or her area of expertise.	Key players come and go during the early life of the project. Many are part of the informal network that grows up around a radical innovation project. Key players tend to be "cross-functional" individuals.
Organizational structures	Typically, a cross-functional project team operates within a business unit.	The project often starts in R&D, migrates into some sort of incubating organization, and transitions into a goal-driven project organization.

22

Resources and competencies	The project team has all the competencies required to complete the process. The project is subject to the standard resource allocation process for incremental projects.	Creativity and skill in resource and competency acquisition – from a variety of internal and external sources – are critical to the survival and success of the project.
Operating unit involvement	Operating units are involved from the beginning.	Informal involvement with operating units is important, but the project must avoid becoming captive to an operating unit too early.

Leifer et al. also mention that they believe that the radical innovation life cycle has one other characteristic: it is context-dependent, meaning that history, experience, corporate culture, personalities and informal relations all matter, as they create a mixture of accelerating and decelerating factors. (Leifer et al., 2000, p.18).

2.5 The promising land of innovation

Apart from those already mentioned, the last decade has witnessed the publication of many thought-provoking studies concerning the significance of innovation for future prosperity, including Utterback, (1994); Frederick and Carswell, (2001); von Hippel, Thomke and Sonnack, (2001); Moss Kanter, (2001); Ellyard, (in Barker, Ed., 2000), and Williams, (1999).

A number of these regard innovation as the catalyst for change, either in the industry, or on a larger scale that includes widening markets, or benefiting society as a whole, not just favouring niche markets. Utterback, in *Mastering the dynamics of innovation* (1994), for example, defines the "dominant design" as relating to an innovation that embodies:

the requirements of many classes of users [...] even though it may not meet the needs of a particular class to quite the same extent as would a customized design. Nor is a dominant design necessarily the one that embodies the most extreme technical performance. It is a so-called satisficer of many in terms of the interplay of technical possibilities and market choices, instead of an optimizer for a few. (Utterback, 1994, p.25).

Utterback describes dominant designs which made profound changes to society, such as the typewriter, in the place of manual writing; the electric lightbulb, instead of the incandescent gas lamp; refrigeration, instead of transported cubic blocks of ice; and sheet glass cheap and strong enough to cover or enclose large areas transparently. Each of these changed the expectations of consumers in terms of convenience, economy and safety. But Utterback has a warning for those industries which relied in the long-term on optimization. He cautions,

Simply becoming better and better with current technology will not, in the long run, keep new firms with new technology from absorbing markets and relegating unresponsive established firms to the scrap heap of industrial technology. (Utterback, 1994, p.221).

Innovation is a driver for change. Change is a process that requires leadership. Change management is complex and requires courage and vision, strong internal and external networks and the ability to influence culture and modify industrial processes, frequently those of long standing which are obsolete by the standards of the day, but are difficult to remove because they have melted into corporate culture. (Australian Institute of Management, 2001; Bean and Radford, 2002; Kotter, 1996; Taffinder, 1998; Tushman and O'Reilly, 1997; and Pettigrew and Whipp, 2001).

Managing innovation and subsequent change is fertile ground for controversy and debate – there is no one formula where one size fits all. (*Harvard Business Review on Innovation*, 2001; *Harvard Business Review*, 2002 August). At one end of the spectrum are commentators, such as Hamel, 2000, who adopt a

24

strident tone: innovation is a means to a revolution in which there can only be winners and losers. He therefore provides a plethora of advice underpinned by an eclectic collection of global examples of the ways in which those who took the initiative and had the courage of their convictions, and so they benefited.

Like Hamel, Peters (1997), adopts an attitude that "you can't shrink your way to greatness." With these words as his subtitle, he asserts that effective innovation requires a radical, even an iconoclastic approach, which speedily and daringly discards long held public conventions, private beliefs, collective practices and corporate cultures. For example, Peters writes in chapter 1, "Think revolution, not evolution," (Peters, 1997, p.31), agreeing with Nicholas Negroponte that "Incrementalism is innovation's worst enemy," (Peters, 1997, p.26). His second chapter is entitled, "Destruction is Cool!" (Peters, 1997, p.35); and in chapter 26, he recommends that professionals should "Do whatever it takes," and "Challenge, challenge, challenge." (Peters, 1997, pp.216-217). "Why a white collar revolution? Think … Motivation […Think] New American Professional." (Peters, 1997, pp.180-182). While it may seem that Peters is indiscriminately destructive of long-held tenets of business and corporate behaviour, his tone is deliberately confrontational and at times excessively exuberant because he aims to shock his readers, involved in whatever sphere of business, out of their complacency before a competitor does it for them, and then it may be too late. This, of course, pre-dates an important tenet in Hamel and Välikangas (2003, Sept.) by about six years. Nothing is sacred, "Forget consensus […] three hearty cheers for the ones who disagree with you." (Peters, 1997, pp.114-115); and nothing can move too fast, "If things seem under control, you're just not going fast enough," (Mario Andretti quoted in Peters, 1997, p.493).

Before Peters may be accused for taking the need for change to a destructive extreme, he must be credited in the same publication with providing a great number of constructive insights, experiences, tips and advice. He advocates passion: "Passion demands p-e-o-p-l-e. People stuff is real stuff. People stuff is the only stuff," (Peters, 1997, pp.484-485); […] passion demands truth. Tell the truth! (Peters, 1997, p.487); passion demands obsession! (Peters, 1997, p.478);

25

Passion demands enthusiasm (Peters, 1997, p.480). He advocates that we pursue exemplars of design, such as the Body Shop, Nike, Gillette, and Chrysler, (Peters, 1997, p.431) and reinforces the role of training: "Train for diversity, train for whatever because good ideas come from differences."

Creativity comes from unlikely juxtapositions. The best way to maximize differences is to mix ages, cultures and disciplines." (Negroponte quoted in Peters, 1997, p.376). He also devotes a significant portion of his work to women as consumers and producers with talent and determination: "10.2 million women (20 percent of working wives) earn MORE than their husbands. Women purchase 51 percent of tires. Consumer spending by women: $3.3 trillion and purchasing agents for government and industry are greater than 50 percent of US Gross Domestic Product." (Peters, 1997, p.396). The significance of this observation is that innovation can play a vital part in helping to fulfil the needs and wants of women, as a new growth area for consumption.

2.6 Thriving on innovation

So how do they do it? According to Michael Porter, "there is an infinite number of possible strategies even within the same industry. No tool can remove the need for creativity in selecting the right strategy. Great companies don't imitate competitors, they act differently ... we do need to discover how the process of creativity takes place." (Quoted in Pettigrew and Whipp, 2001, p.111). And the survival, continuation and success which Bean and Radford (2002, p.ix) allude to as the reward of a company having a commitment to innovation has a number of practical implications. A company may have to create new markets in uncharted territories. The more common practice is for a company to match and beat a commercial rival, and if it succeeds, it is likely to have been through incremental improvements in cost or quality, or maybe both of those.

2.7 Managing change

In connection with change that innovation inevitably brings, theorists such as Morgan, 2000, assume a "How to ..." approach and have distilled change management to a formula which reduces everything to mechanical architectonics, so that change is conducted in enumerated steps. Whilst this is an earnest attempt to instruct the manager on an approach, it remains just that: one approach, and one size does not fit all. There are many contingencies which focus on one approach to the exclusion of others. This is because managing change is not necessarily a linear process in which everything goes according to plan, and this concept will be developed later. Obviously a plan is useful, but it must never be dogmatic and unresponsive to the employees whose working lives are being changed. (Porter, Dec 1996). Resistance can be strong even under a tolerant culture. A style in which change is mechanically thrust upon a workforce is deficient because it fails to incorporate the best of thoughts from the best of those who wish to do nothing more than cooperate and re-create stability: whatever "stability" may mean for them in the future.

Leifer et al. (2000) provides a design to effect organization and structures in order to nurture and grow radical innovation, but their ideas of incubation and the management hub are complex and require constant invigilation by management of their subordinates. Their model appears top-heavy with managerialism and decision-making, without the benefit of multiple employee inputs.

Christensen and Raynor quote both Mintzberg and Water: "Openness to emergent strategy enables management to act before everything is fully understood – to respond to an evolving reality rather than having to focus on a stable fantasy ... Emergent strategy itself implies learning what works – taking one action at a time in a search for the viable pattern or consistency." (Christensen and Raynor, 2003, p. 221). This is supported by Porter in his December 1996 article, "What is strategy?" published in the *Harvard Business Review.*

But strategy, like so many other aspects of implementation is still a cerebral undertaking albeit essential for successful change management in practice. For example, in the area of executive leverage on the strategy process, Christensen and Raynor (2003) advise that the management must retain careful control of the

27

initial cost structure of a new-growth business; actively accelerate the process by which a viable strategy emerges; and be prepared to intervene in adapting the strategy making process, so that choice about strategy to policy, habit, or culture because those can be the very anchors that impeded the development of the creative facility. (Christensen and Raynor, 2003, pp. 224-225).

Christensen and Raynor make one other comment at this point which is relevant to this investigation because two case-studies are founder-owner-operated: "We suspect that founders have an advantage in tackling disruption because they not only wield the requisite political clout but also have the self-confidence to over-ride established processes [...]" (Christensen and Raynor, 2003, pp. 276-277).

In their research of change management associated with innovation, W. Chan Kim and Renee Mauborgne (2001) focus on companies which have succeeded by circumventing traditional rivals by means of staking out new market space, in which there is no direct competition. They identify seven ways in which industries sought to create new markets and created new value curves. Companies can do this by looking across substitute industries, across strategic groups, across buyer groups, across complementary product and service offerings, across the functional-emotional orientation of an industry, and finally across time. (Chan Kim and Mauborgne, 2001, p.3). Larry Keeley, the president of Doblin in Chicago agrees with the virtue of lateral thinking:

> Companies miss out on all sorts of opportunities for innovation because they focus so closely on their competitors. If you map out the different types of innovation activity in a given industry, you'll almost always find that most organizations are concentrating on the same types – they're all investing in the same things, just to keep up. There may be a lot of activity in customer service innovation, for example, but nothing's happening in networking. [...] You can actually spend less time and make more money in innovation if you pay attention to the valleys, those places your competitors have overlooked. (Keeley, *Harvard Business Review*, 2002 August, p.42).

Home Depot is an example of a company that looked across substitutes by creating a market of do-it-yourselfers out of ordinary home owners; it did not create its $24 billion industry by capturing market share from other hardware companies. Lexus is a Toyota brand which looked across the strategic grouping of luxury cars like Mercedes and incorporated its automotive excellence at a much cheaper price. Philips is an example of a company which looked across a buyer group, and promoted the Alto environmentally friendly light bulb to CFOs and to public relations people because they tend to be influential employees and could drive sales within their own companies. The strategy of looking across complementary product and service offerings is exemplified by booksellers like Borders Books & Music and Barnes & Noble. These companies do not sell books alone, nor is their service extended merely to including sales of stationery. They include the sale of music CDs, food and beverages, opening for long hours, and providing huge choice of books both general and highly specialist. When Anita Roddick created the Body Shop, she was looking across functional and emotional appeal to buyers by the practicalities of refilling plastic bottles and minimising wrapping paper, as many consumers believe that wrapping is costly and wasteful. Looking at external trends can also create new opportunities for businesses. Netscape is an example of a company projecting trends considerably into the future and predicting that more, not less, internet software will be required. Finally, Kim and Mauborgne point to the Lexus again, this time as an example of a product which regenerated a large company. Within three years of its launch in 1989, sales from the Lexus represented almost one-third of Toyota's operating profit but it only represented 2 percent of its unit volume. (Kim and Mauborgne, 2001, p.29).

Considerable research has been performed on the subject of human resources and its development towards facilitating innovation. The Institute of Work Psychology at the ESRC Centre for Organization and Innovation at the University of Sheffield, has produced a set of managers' guidelines for developing an innovative culture, so that the problems, particularly those of employee resistance, are minimised by means of the careful recruitment, selection and education of employees from the outset. The two authors reporting on the research that the University has conducted in staffing for

29

innovative cultures, Kamal Birdi and Toby Walls, conclude that, "a holistic approach is needed to initiate and sustain innovation in organizations." (Birdi and Walls, 2003, p.1) By this they mean that employees must be "motivated and confident enough to continually try new things out [by being] equipped with the right types of knowledge, skills and abilities to both effectively generate and implement new ideas [and this would be facilitated if they were] given opportunities to explore, investigate and experiment." (Birdi and Walls, 2003, p.1). They believe that management should support [this] through active encouragement of these types of behaviours." At the macro level, the "organization itself should have structures and processes in place that allow for smooth transitions from the appearance of new ideas to their implementation." (Birdi and Walls, 2003, p.1). Their research shows that an innovative culture can be grown by management following these practices, a number of which have already been previously recognised as significant for the purposes of this study, and so it will suffice to elaborate on two or three of the features from the following list:

- Selecting innovative employees
- Training for creativity and innovation
- Developing a learning culture
- Empowering employees
- Setting up idea capture schemes
- Developing managers to support the innovation of others
- Making creativity a requirement of the job
- Improving employee participation in decision-making
- Having appropriate reward systems for innovation
- Allowing risk-taking as an acceptable mode of practice
- Encouraging investment in research and development
- Benchmarking (Birdi and Walls, 2003, p.1).

Firstly, what are the characteristics of an innovative employee? Birdi and Walls identify four key traits: openness to frequent change, active championing of change, unstructured approaches to work, and a preference to try doing things differently. It is acknowledged that every industry needs a variety and balance of personality types. Birdi and Walls recommend that selection for innovation using an instrument that they have developed through their research, should be deployed, particularly for positions in which the innovative spirit is a key component of the job. (Birdi and Walls, 2003, p.2).

How can employees be empowered? Empowerment is about the "devolution of responsibility for organising and managing work to individuals or teams," (Birdi and Walls, 2003, p.2). They suggest that empowerment can take the form of "delegation, job enrichment initiatives or setting up self-managing work groups." (Birdi and Walls, 2003, p.2). They postulate that "those who are empowered tend to develop better understanding of their work and are more innovative and open to new ideas. Empowerment facilitates innovation by not only giving employees the motivation, knowledge and confidence to generate new ideas, but has especial value with respect to implementation, by providing the opportunity to put ideas into practice." (Birdi and Walls, 2003, p.2). Coulson-Thomas cites two industries which exemplify empowerment and its corollary, decision-making: At MashreqBank, the whole management team, not only its upper echelon, participated in a review of vision, mission, goals and priorities. Secondly, the computer services group EDS involved staff at all levels in a basic reassessment of its functions and position in the market place. This resulted in a change of strategic direction by the staff rather than by the board of directors. This widened the empowerment concept to include thousands, not merely a few. (Coulson-Thomas, 1997, p.254). Coulson-Thomas agrees with Birdi and Walls on the subject of empowerment. He makes the observation that, "Managers fear that by giving some [power] away their own stock will be reduced. In reality, by releasing the latent energies and potential of others, and enabling and supporting their growth, the collective capability of the enterprise is enhanced. Empowerment can be a 'positive sum' game in which both 'giver' and 'receiver' benefit." (Coulson-Thomas, 1997, p.257)

What reward systems are appropriate for the inculcation of an innovative culture? Apart from the financial aspect, there are a number of other forms of recognition, such as recognition from immediate managers, public recognition in company newsletters or certificates of achievement. Birdi and Walls observe that "employees will perform more creatively if motivated by the work itself, rather than by rewards or punishments. This type of intrinsic motivation can be developed by encouraging employees to explore ideas they find personally exciting, reinforcing feelings of personal competence and creating an environment where people can freely exchange ideas and explore areas of mutual interest." (Birdi and Walls, 2003, pp.5-6). Hoechst have a guiding principle which is in agreement with Birdi and Walls' comments, when they state that, "Hoechst sees itself as a community of people working together in a lasting union, motivated by shared aims. We impose exacting standards on ourselves, our skills, our willingness to learn and our commitment to performance. Our financial rewards are commensurate with our own performance and the Company's success." (Quoted in Coulson-Thomas, 1997, p.262). Some companies have a reward system which is connected to customer satisfaction, however, it is clear that an industrial environment which fosters managerial support of innovative thinking, production and implementation, provides employees with a community in which their individual initiatives may have fertile soil to be cultivated.

It should not be taken for granted however, that all employees automatically feel comfortable in such an environment. As the research on Alpine Packs, one of the three prime case-studies, demonstrates, a proportion of employees do not wish to stand out as leaders, nor have their ideas be subjected to collegial scrutiny, least of all have them subject to managerial evaluation. They appreciated the liberality of an employee-focused community, but wished for nothing more than to leave the initiative to those who see themselves as leaders or innovators. This will be elaborated upon in the case-study itself.

2.8 Change management: Sustainability and learning

A significant practical implication is a company's ability to learn: if a company continues to transform itself to achieve survival, it will accomplish this in large measure by means of the continual acquisition of knowledge and skills of its employees. "Raising the fundamental intellect of your organization [...] is what makes organizations win" according to Jack Welch, former CEO of General Electric. (Welch, file://C:WDOCUME, retrieved 25 February 2005). The pervading view of organizations is that they are organic rather than mechanical entities, and that learning within it is not only possible but imperative. The company of the future is a "living company," (de Geus, 1999, p.236). The longevity and strength of a living company may be determined largely by its ability to grow, and that is largely dependent on its ability to learn. (Senge, 1990; de Geus, 1999). De Geus points to the partnership between the company and the employee:

> From a learning orientation, the nurturing of people and the nurturing of capital reinforce each other (p.28) ..... To manage a corporation effectively, we must learn how to treat institutions as living eco-systems – set up with the recognition that they will live or die according to the same natural laws that govern human growth and development. [...] It has to do with providing opportunities for managers to learn together. (de Geus, 1999, p.156).

And

> Shell has devoted enormous energy to discovering how their managers at all levels understand their environment, how that knowledge can be generalized and a common understanding generated as the foundation for action. (de Geus quoted in Pettigrew and Whipp, 2001, p.113.)

Learning is a cognitive as well as an experiential undertaking. Most of the publications cited have a strong theoretical base as well as a reasonably robust practical orientation, because each wishes to contribute to best practice in the field of innovation and change management. But in most of those cases, there is an imbalance. Theorists have been more frequently inspired by theory than by practice.

Leifer and colleagues (2000) make the point that if a radical innovation team contract with partners to compensate for missing capabilities or resources, they need to stay connected to the experience of their partners to be able to absorb and incorporate their partner's learning in future. (Leifer et al., 2000, p.63). Learning is of critical value because a radical innovation team's inability to replicate all the competencies contributes to the crisis-oriented management practices that often characterises radical innovation projects.

Furthermore, Leifer and colleagues assert that, "a learning plan – an alternative to a typical project management planning tool – is more appropriate and useful tool for radical innovation project management." (Leifer et al., 2000, p.64). Such a plan would consist of the following. It:

- Incorporates the results of uncertainty cataloguing;
- Spells out assumptions about each uncertainty;
- Presents approaches for testing each assumption and resolving each critical uncertainty through experimentation and learning;
- Prioritizes the assumption-testing tasks and defines a path for moving forward as quickly and as inexpensively as possible; and
- Serves as a log of the project's history – serving to guide not only the project but also the development of the database for the radical innovation hub.

  (Leifer et al., 2000, p.64)

A learning plan should be revised on a continual basis to reflect what has already been learned and what remains to be discovered. That makes a learning plan a guiding tool. Its flexible and fluid nature makes it an appropriate tool throughout the radical innovation life cycle.

2.9 Culture and employees: The human element

Culture refers to a pattern of behaviour subscribed to by people in groups, whether they are conscious of all its binding values or not. For example, those values may be remuneration, or technological innovation or employee well-being. Once an organization is past the initial start-up phase, the culture must decide whether to "pursue growth through further geographical expansion, develop new products, open new markets, or improve its cost and resource position", (Schein, 1992, p.314). Significantly, culture acted like a glue in the beginning but beyond that culture often manifests itself in the organization's structure and critical tasks. Culture, according to Schein, (1992, p.314) is "embedded in the company's credos, dominant espoused values, company slogans, written charters, and other public pronouncements of what the company wants to be." Schein points out however, that cultural elements again come to the fore when members consider mergers and acquisitions, when they appraise the introduction of new technologies, or when there is a crisis of some kind, as during all of those events, members are inclined to re-evaluate their collective values as they look for compatibility in their future careers with the company.

Employees' comfort within a particular occupational zone may lead them to revert to values which a company wishes to expand upon, or to change. This may lead to resistance to the change, which can subvert any manager's earnest attempts to effect change. For this reason, three groups of researchers, namely Leifer et al.; Tushman and O'Reilly, (1997); and Christensen and Raynor (2003), include guidelines for managers and industrial leaders to follow to smooth the path of resistance, and some of those guidelines will be mentioned below when those authors are examined in more detail.

Tushman and O'Reilly also point to the importance of aligning human resources with complementary aspects of an industry, as part of their congruence model. Before some aspects of human resources generally are examined, some key elements need to be detailed from their model. Tushman and O'Reilly begin by asking the following diagnostic questions: "Given the critical tasks, do people have the required competencies to perform them? Are there additional skills or incentives that are needed? Can employees be trained in these new skills or do we need to bring in new people?" (Tushman and O'Reilly, 1997, p.65). They cite the example of Grenzach, the Ciba-Geigy subsidiary, in which Hans Huber, the newly incumbent general manager in 1993, concluded that there were a number of HR deficiencies and incongruities: the engineering emphasis was too strong and working across boundaries and functions was inadequate for the new and congruent model. He also found that managers were entrenched in a top-down model and had no confidence in operating in a flatter model. Clearly, without those competencies, a congruent model could not develop, and a reward structure would have to be developed which rewarded new skills and competencies. These new competencies would eventually lead Huber to create a more congruent model for his chemical industry and its quest to become more innovative.

2.10 Innovation and change: Significant contributors based on dedicated research in the field

In 1986, Jack Utterback called for more research on innovation:

> A dynamic life cycle approach should be taken encompassing changes and interactions among variables and units over time as they are related to changing competitive, technical and other environments. In sum, a more holistic approach must be taken to the field through the study of large complex cases, through experimentation with practitioners, through the development of longitudinal databases, and sustained emphasis on well designed longitudinal studies. (Utterback quoted in Pettigrew and Whipp, 2001, p.286).

At that time, Utterback was aware that water-shed innovations, or discontinuities, could have a profound effect on the industrial landscape, but even though he was aware of the quest to harness that power, he was not sure how industries should go about it: "The central issue is not when or how this will happen, but that it will happen for sure. In the final analysis only that understanding will allow a firm to bridge a discontinuity, because only a total commitment will win the day." (Utterback, 1994, p.231). The following endorse Utterback's call for further research. Firstly, the studies published by the Harvard Business School Press in 2000 by Leifer, McDermott, O'Connor, Peters, Rice and Veryzer, which were based on research conducted between

36

1995 and 2000, using twelve radical innovation projects in ten established United States based companies. It is called *Radical innovation: How mature companies can outsmart upstarts.* Secondly, Pettigrew and Whipp published *Change management for competitive success* first appeared in 1991, and re-published in 2001 by Blackwell Business. They conducted their research between the end of 1985 and 1989 and their goal was to find why firms operating in the same industry and markets should produce such different performances across time, and to assess the contribution of they way those industries managed strategic change. As such, their research was significantly linked to the impact of innovation and change which resulted and how to manage change strategically effectively. They focused their research on the publishing, car, merchant banking, and life assurance industries in Great Britain. Thirdly, Tushman and O'Reilly published *Winning through Innovation: A practical guide to leading organizational change and renewal* in 1997. It is based upon 20 years' research on industries located throughout the United States, Great Britain, Germany and Japan. This was followed by Christensen and Raynor's *The innovator's solution: Creating and sustaining successful growth* (2003). Then, "The Quest for Resilience" (*Harvard Business Review*, 2003 Sept), by Gary Hamel and Liisa Välikangas makes a case for "resilience" as the key to future business success. Each of these publications built upon the key concepts of the previous one, creating an evolution of thought.

2.11 The main contribution of Pettigrew and Whipp (1991 and republished 2001)

Pettigrew and Whipp developed a strategic change model which appears to be a more basic forerunner to the models developed by Leifer et al., and by Tushman and O'Reilly. The three essential dimensions are process (change managers, models of change, implementation, pattern creation); content (assessment and choice of products and markets, objectives and assumptions, targets and evaluation); and context (resources, capabilities, culture and politics).

This model uses many of the same ingredients used by Tushman and O'Reilly, but the latter recommend a more prescriptive purpose. Pettigrew and Whipp highlight the interrelationships and dynamism between the elements within their model: "The point to appreciate is the richness of these contexts and their simultaneous shaping of strategic change. The hallmark of the processual dimension is that strategy does not move forward in a direct, linear way nor through easily identifiable sequential phases. Quite the reverse, the pattern is much more appropriately seen as continuous, iterative and uncertain." (Pettigrew and Whipp, 2001, p.27). It is this uncertainty that subsequent change models, such as the congruence model conceptualised by Tushman and O'Reilly (1997), attempt to eliminate in order to create more certainty and more control in chaotic markets which continue to buffet every industry "ship" at all times.

To provide leadership during today's turbulence, Pettigrew and Whipp recommend a transformational management style, (Pettigrew and Whipp, 2001, p.142). They also recommend managers who could "shape the change process in the long term rather than direct it through a single episode." (Pettigrew and Whipp, 2001, p.143). Being consistent, having an ability to motivate, and laying out a vision are recognised characteristics of industry leadership. Pettigrew and Whipp observe that the following appeared valid for viable industry development:

> Leading change in order to compete is not understood by reference to universal principles carried out by an exceptional individual. More effective in leading change appears to be: the use of varying leadership approaches over time; a combination of practices to address shifting competitive circumstances; the recognition that leader and context will affect each other reciprocally; and the use of operational leaders at all levels in the firm. (Pettigrew and Whipp, 2001, p.145).

It is interesting to note that Tushman and O'Reilly (1997) use the leadership of three CEOs in Apple Macintosh Computers to make the same point. The organizational evolution of incremental and revolutionary change at Apple, indicates that Steve Jobs was an effective leader during the innovation era, that

John Sculley was effective after him during the differentiation era, and finally during the maturity phase, sound leadership was provided by Michael Spindler. In each case, the CEO had different sets of skills to rebalance the essential elements of strategy, structure, people and culture – in short the key elements comprising the "congruence model". (Tushman and O'Reilly, 1997, pp.23-25).

Pettigrew and Whipp continue with an observation which foreshadowed an essential plank of the research of Tushman and O'Reilly. In relation to one of their case-studies, Longman Publishers, they comment on the leadership which had to combine multiple functions, and appears to allude to the management characteristics of an ambidextrous organization:

> Longman['s management] across the 1970s and 1980s had […] to: link continuity and change by preserving existing product strengths while moving into totally new markets; reconstituting its centre's role while preparing the case for the consequent restructuring of its divisions; adjusting the Longman culture by both surface interventions in the form of swiftly altering the role of financial reporting, but at the same time devoting seven years to the remoulding of the computing function. The problems of maintaining simultaneous action over a long-term process are at their sharpest in leading change. The need appears to be not boldness or decisiveness as much as a combination of planning, opportunism and timing of interventions. […] The result is that leading change necessitates a leadership which can operate with multiple levers and at multiple levels. (Pettigrew and Whipp, 2001, p.166).

To facilitate change, Pettigrew and Whipp (2001) point to three main sets of conditions on p. 165, which are later echoed in Tushman and O'Reilly, but in much more elaborate detail. The first condition relates to the climate within the firm which should be receptive to change with a clear justification for the changes to take place. Secondly, there should be the development of capabilities so the changes can be carried out. And thirdly, the change agenda must clearly set the direction of the business, and establishes the necessary visions and values. One of the considerable number of additions which Tushman and O'Reilly include in their chapter on strategic change was that the

CEO and his or her senior management team should create dissatisfaction with the status quo to provide employees with a bedrock for change, (Tushman and O'Reilly, 1997, p.199). They should then build in participation in order to overcome resistance, (Tushman and O'Reilly, 1997, p.200). Resistance, they believe, may also be overcome by recognizing and rewarding desired new behaviours, (Tushman and O'Reilly, 1997, p.202). Control may be further enhanced by using multiple levers to promote change, and while Pettigrew and Whipp recognise this as a managerial function, the example from Tushman and O'Reilly clarifies the significance of this approach. Tushman and O'Reilly refer to Philips the electronics giant headquartered in Eindhoven, in the Netherlands. In 1990, the company was ailing and the old management had only ever attempted single focus change, which proved ineffective. The new CEO, Jan Timmers, used multiple levers when he and his new management team insisted on employees acquiring new skills and they then concurrently implemented new structures, new operating processes, and new reward and promotion systems, (Tushman and O'Reilly, 1997, p.205). Management also made 100,000 employees redundant. The effect of this was that resistance in the culture of complacency dating back for decades, now did not have any undisturbed place to grow.

For Pettigrew and Whipp, there are five central factors in managing change for competitive success: environmental assessment, leading change, linking strategic and operational change, human resources as assets and liabilities, and coherence. (Pettigrew and Whipp, 2001, p.104). It is an integrated model which denigrates any notion that change may be practised as a unitary action. It also recognises the value of learning, as in this chaotic world, "the ability to learn faster than competitors may be the only sustainable advantage." (Arie de Geus quoted in Pettigrew and Whipp, 2001, p.294).

2.12   The main contribution of Leifer, McDermott, O'Connor, Peters, Rice and Veryzer (2000)

Joseph Schumpeter was originally credited in 1934 with the argument that small, entrepreneurial firms were most likely to be the source of most innovation. (Cited in Leifer et al, 2000, p.217). However, in 1950, Schumpeter reversed his earlier opinion because he believed that established firms were stronger in terms of technical progress due to their better access to resources.

Leifer and colleagues agree with Schumpeter's later opinion, as they answer the question of how large established firms could outsmart small entrepreneurial upstarts. They make a number of points but begin by pointing to the upstart's habit of only ever pursuing one opportunity to build a venture. They go on to state,

> Established firms have opportunities to form structures and systems capable of accumulating learning from an ongoing stream of radical innovation projects. They can create a discipline of radical innovation and a cadre of people who excel in it. They can provide attractive, continuing opportunities for innovation veterans, thereby retaining their resources, skills, and wisdom. Established firms can develop and embed in their structure a radical innovation capability that sustains a flow of radical innovations and the growth of the company.
> (Leifer et al., 2000, p.184).

Leifer, McDermott, O'Connor, Peters, Rice and Veryzer are strongly practical, and their work *Radical innovation: How mature companies can outsmart upstart upstarts* (2000) turns a commonly held view on its head: that only upstart firms can manage innovation and change, and mature companies cannot. They demonstrate that mature companies can and do, and that the source of this inspiration is radical innovation. They maintain that it may be orthodox, but incorrect, to believe that, "Small entrepreneurial firms are the source of most radical innovations. Large companies have a tough time getting it done." (Leifer et al., 2000, p.1).

41

Like Utterback, (1994), and Tushman and O'Reilly, (1997), Leifer and his colleagues share an interest in the reasons why successful companies seem unable to maintain their market lead for long. Radical innovation may be the key to long-term success in the market, but it can be an elusive goal. They point out first of all, that radical innovation has a transforming effect: "[It] transforms the relationship between customers and suppliers, restructures marketplace economics, displaces current products, and often creates entirely new product categories." The cite, for example, Kodak struggling to continue dominating the photography market based on film, when faced by strong competition from producers of digital imaging. (Leifer et al., 2000, p.3). As a market leader, Kodak was ironically one of the last to pursue digital imaging. One of the difficulties a company has, then, is recognising a radical innovation and then deciding how to develop and commercialize it.

Leifer and colleagues created the Rensselaer Radical Innovation Research Project and analysed a number of well-known companies including Kodak, DuPont, General Electric, General Motors and IBM, as these companies were in the process of developing radical innovations and then commercializing them. They describe in detail, the difficulties faced by employees at DuPont in the development of Biomax: "Ten years after start-up, the project's market success remained unclear". (Leifer et al., 2000, p.16). Leifer et al. arrive at the following general characteristics of the radical innovation life cycle:

- Long term – often a decade or longer
- Highly uncertain and unpredictable;
- Sporadic – stops and starts, deaths and revivals;
- Nonlinear – requiring a recycling back through activities in response to discontinuities and setbacks and a continuing application of all the key innovation project management competencies;
- Stochastic – key players come and go, priorities change, exogenous events are critical; and

- Context dependent – history, experiences, corporate culture, personalities, and informal relations all matter, creating a mix of accelerating and retarding factors.

Leifer et al., 2000, p.18).

Furthermore, Hewlett Packard maintain that, from the point of view of their overheads, a project cannot be launched unless it has a minimum of $250 million in market potential. Proctor and Gamble's minimum threshold is $100 million in the US market, but the company can leverage that revenue figure to $500 million through global sales. (Leifer et al., 2000, p.47).

Leifer and his team have recognised a number of the difficulties that firms face in committing themselves to radical innovation; they propose a constructive approach to neutralise those problems, in order to improve the chances of succeeding. To begin with, they recommend that the vagueness, or "fuzziness", which often surrounds a nascent project, needs to be crystallised through a three step process: idea generation, opportunity recognition, and initial opportunity evaluation, because doing so reduces the gap between a company's technical capabilities and the formation of a radical innovation undertaking. (Leifer et al., 2000, p.26). It must include present employees, or newly recruited staff, who have the ability to "think outside the box," even if only about three percent of researchers have the ability to make unusual connections. These employees must be supported and encouraged. (Leifer et al., 2000, p.31). Senior management had a responsibility to assist in this by providing resources for such employees or to the teams which they lead. Senior management also played an important function by articulating strategic intent.

The example of the confluence of these ideas used by Leifer et al. is Analog of the USA, in which a triumvirate of staff believed that it could play a major role in the electronic advancement of future automobiles, particularly through functions being controlled by chips that they could manufacture. Over a nine year period, the "fuzzy" front end was clarified, the technology and markets were evaluated, and a budget was awarded by the CEO Jerry Fishman, who had confidence in Steve Sherman as idea generator, and in Richie Payne as opportunity recognizer and champion. The triumvirate was finally successful.

Leifer and his colleagues' main thesis is that mature firms can outsmart upstarts; the example using Analog above is one such instance, even if the timeframe from conception to production was a nine-year one.

They acknowledge the challenges in managing radical innovation and recommend that managers of such projects have a number of competencies. (Leifer et al., 2000, Table 1.1, p.8). They include being able to manage radical innovation projects which may require the articulation of a vision, the capability of uncertainty-mapping, the development of and ability to follow a learning plan, the recruitment of champions and the effective management of organizational interfaces. Another challenge is being able to bridge resource and competency gaps which may require skills in resource acquisition and the establishment and management of internal and external partnerships. Finally, accelerating the transition from radical innovation projects to operating status may require skills such as the accurate assessment of the transition readiness of the project and the receiving unit, the development of people, practices, and structures for successful transitions as well as the ability to build bridges between organizational units.

To effect communication, transitions and coordination between people and ideas, Leifer et al. propose that a radical innovation project should develop a radical innovation "hub". (Leifer et al., 2000, p.51). The model's main constructs are listed below. The main functions which it should have, include:

- Taking responsibility for fuzzy front-end functions;
- Imposing continuity when staff retire or leave;
- Creating a network of idea generators and actively implement their ideas;
- Receiving, evaluating and relaying important information to key personnel;

44

- Acting as central information nodes and links between emerging technologies and commercial markets;
- Building project legitimacy;
- Overcoming resistance from inside the firm;
- Creating partnerships and generating funding;
- Creating a transition team from conceptual stage to production;
- Expanding or diminishing the number of staff working on the project, or changing members depending on whether their skills are required at a particular stage of development;
- Imposing "discipline" on a radical innovation project, which by nature is often chaotic;
- Assisting in, and rewarding those members actively involved in the ongoing cultivation of desirable aspects related to the firm's culture.

The hub is intended to be a complementary source of information and skills, but does not replace an effective manager. The right person to hold the position of manager has a challenging set of tasks. By building project legitimacy, such a manager has to communicate and sell the desirability of the project, and she or he would also drive towards demonstrable results to provide justification for funding, while attracting the support and critiques of lead users, creating links with a brand-name partner. Such a manager would then assemble and distil the best from a board of advisors, creating a support infrastructure, and then he or she must generate links with a business unit, and enthuse "superstars." In addition to all that, the manager of a radical project must also be able to handle course corrections in the style of leading and learning rather than managing and controlling in the traditional sense. Such a person must also be comfortable with uncertainty, yet be able to sell their vision. (Leifer et al., 2000, p.72). Leifer comments that many of the project managers they interviewed were unprepared for the stop/start nature of such work: "Many were surprised, frustrated, confused, and often overwhelmed by the morass they were charged with managing, and they struggled to learn as they moved forward." (Leifer et al., 2000, p.72). Clearly then, such managers require a greater degree of training and learning, possibly mentoring, to be able to overcome their inexperience in radical project developments as well as amending their own expectations and psychological obstacles.

Of the many individuals with whom a radical project manager must forge links, one of the most important is the individual with resource acquisition links to ensure that the project's main source of funding continues to supply, inspite of the stochastic nature of the project. The project manager and the fund manager should look to diversifying their sources of future funding to remove the excessive reliability that might be placed on one source.

Leifer et al. also point to the difficulties encountered in transition from prototype to production. A radical project manager should form a transition team through the project hub. Its responsibilities include dealing with technical specifications, assessing whether market expectations match reality, and overseeing market development.

Obviously, a radical project manager must have exemplary leadership skills, and the ability to impact on the firm's culture. Ray Stata had that impact as CEO of Analog Devices, and was renowned for breaking company rules when rules stood between an employee and an attractive business opportunity. His acquisition of a small engineering company to expand into a new technology was first decried and then applauded when it became integrated into Analog's operations. (Leifer et al., 2000, p.162). This nerve in radical innovation managers is often accompanied by the ability to ask questions, listen and probe, recognising problems, generating alternative development paths, obtaining resources and maintaining an open door within their project teams. (Leifer et al., 2000, p.168). Innovation can be better supported in an environment where managers and project champions personify the qualities it takes to be on the cutting edge of innovation. Undoubtedly, Stata helped establish an innovation-friendly culture in his firm. The 3M company also has a history of having management cultivate innovation.

Leifer et al. comment that the "ultimate challenge for senior management is to find the balance between focusing on the excellent performance of ongoing

46

mainstream operations in the short term and creating the future of the company by sustaining the search for new avenues of long-term growth through radical innovation." (Leifer et al., 2000, p.182). This complementarity forms the basis for the 1997 work of Tushman and O'Reilly's *Winning through Innovation*, and will be commented on below.

2.13 The main contribution of Tushman and O'Reilly (1997)

Why do leading firms so often lose their innovative edge, and how can they retain it? Tushman and O'Reilly's publication stands out because its theory and practice are based on long-term research, incorporating industries such as Ciba-Geigy (now Novartis), BOC Industrial Gases, Medtek, Hewlett-Packard, Ericsson, Southwest Airlines, Xerox, ABB, Philips, Sony, Oticon and others. These industries are, or have been, market leaders for a significant period, and have been through the fires of transformation traversing a period of twenty years or more. The results of their research, published in 1997, was entitled *Winning through innovation: A practical guide to leading organizational change and renewal*. It represents 20 years collaboration: "Over these two decades, our work on managing innovation, culture, leadership, and change has been shaped by two powerful forces: the evolution of our academic fields and our close interactions with thousands of managers." (Tushman and O'Reilly, 1997, p.ix).

Tushman and O'Reilly's starting point concerns the disturbing but everyday phenomenon of business and organizational failure. Indeed, failure so profound that over a series of years companies which may have been at the height of profitability, first showed signs of fading, then actually did fade to obscurity and finally ceased to exist. They use as examples, companies which produced semiconductors between 1955 and 1995 during which time eight companies ceased operations and never successfully converted to integrated circuits and later, to sub-microns. Why? Tushman and O'Reilly postulate that it was not a matter of not being able to keep up advancing technology. RCA was an example of a large company which failed to change because its sales in

47

semiconductors for years continued to be sound, and its management failed to make a decision whereby it would risk those sales while it was converting to a new technology which was yet unproven.   As such, RCA, like Sylvania, Rawland, Lansdale and the others, became a victim of its own success:

> But there is a dark side to this success.   As firms grow, they develop structures, processes, and systems to handle the increased complexity of their work.   These structures and systems are interlinked, making proposed changes difficult, costly, and time consuming to implement.   Structural inertia – a resistance to change rooted in the size, complexity, and interdependence in the organization's structures, systems and formal processes – sets in.
> (Tushman and O'Reilly, 1997, p.28).

The technology of today scoffs at semiconductors; the public of today may scoff at, or perhaps sympathise with the RCAs and Lansdales of yesteryear – if they remember them at all.   However, we should not be distanced by warps in technology and time and consider Tushman and O'Reilly's concept as having only historical applications related only to industries of yesteryear, or having relevance to organizations which were inexpertly managed and had Research and Development departments staffed by the inept.   The question needs to be asked: Are those management and R&D ineptitudes identifiable, and could they have been the reasons why failure or loss of competitive advantage occurred?

Tushman and O'Reilly's precept needs to be kept in mind when considering why it is that recently, serious questions have been asked about Boeing's state of competition with Airbus.   Up until 1990, Boeing sold 62 percent of the world's commercial jets.   Its closest rival was McDonnell Douglas which sold 23 percent, and Europe's Airbus was third and last with 15 percent of the market. In 2005, Airbus is expected to win more contracts for super-sized commercial jets because of its development of the A380, which can accommodate 840 passengers, in its double deck economy configuration, or it may carry 150 tonnes of cargo if configured for freight.   It threatens Boeing's 747, which seats four hundred fewer passengers.   At the June 2003 Paris Air Show, Airbus

48

announced 64 new orders for its planes; Boeing announced four. In early 2005, Boeing had no new orders for the 747, and Airbus had 149 orders for the A380. (*Borneo Bulletin*, 2005 Jan. 20, p.25). Robert Samuelson reported that, "Boeing became – like many industry leaders before it – overconfident. It fell behind in some areas. Airbus used CAD/CAM(computer aided design and manufacturing) to build planes before Boeing." (*Newsweek*, 2003, June 30/July 7, p.32). Airbus uses standard cockpits which saves in retraining pilots. And from 1995 to 2003, Boeing has not demonstrated any technological advances. Boeing's CEO, Phil Condit told the Financial Times: "We are going to in the commercial aircraft for a long, long, long time." (Quoted in *Newsweek*, June 30/July7, 2003, p.32). To go back to a key concept in Tushman and O'Reilly, no one is suggesting that Boeing runs entirely on the technology of yester-year. However, the question about its future strategy had to be asked. Just ten short years ago, no one would felt the need to ask it. It would appear from this that Tushman and O'Reilly's work has currency today as much as it did in relation to the time when RCA was thriving and then ended up disappearing.

2.13.1 The congruence model

Tushman and O'Reilly are also the originators of the "congruence model of organizational architecture." (Tushman and O'Reilly, 1997, p.59ff). Amongst others, they used Ciba-Geigy (now Novartis), BOC Industrial Gases, and Medtek in New York, to demonstrate the concept that success is driven by having strategy aligned with four organizational building blocks: critical tasks and work-flows, formal organizational arrangements, people and culture. "Critical tasks" include technical proficiency, functional orientation, and flows and processes; "culture" encompasses norms, values, communication networks, informal roles and informal power; the "formal organization" includes strategic grouping, formal linking, rewards and sanctions, information systems, human resource management systems and career systems; and "people" comprises human resource capabilities and competencies. Also broadly under "critical tasks" are strategy, objectives, vision, leadership, competencies, demography and group processes. (Tushman and O'Reilly, 1997, p.59).

Their argument is that when all these factors are aligned, or "congruous", the industry is in the best position to take advantage of opportunities and to function as an "ambidextrous organization". Such an organization "can sustain competitive advantage by operating in multiple modes simultaneously – managing for short term efficiency by emphasizing stability and control, as well as for long-term innovation by taking risks and learning by doing." (Tushman and O'Reilly, 1997, p.167). This means that the industry is able to sustain interlinking cycles of product manufacture as well as radical new product development in such a way that one, which may not yet be a revenue earner, is sustained by one that is, until it is ready to be mass produced and enter the market.

Tushman and O'Reilly promote the congruence model as a useful diagnostic instrument with which to measure "performance gap", (Tushman and O'Reilly, 1997, p.53), that gap being the distance between the desired organizational performance and actual performance. The recognition of a performance gap, measured in assessing the quality of extant strategy, objectives and vision, can then be related to the company's opportunity gap, which is a proactively created performance gap for future opportunities which the company must begin the cultivate today. An example of this is PepsiCo, which in 1990 had sales of $7 billion and earnings, which were up 10 percent on the previous year's sales. The president, Craig Weatherup, forecast a flattening of the soda market and therefore mandated a 15 per cent growth in earnings in the future. To achieve this, he changed strategy and objectives for his 30,000 employees, and by 1993 PepsiCo had met its 15 per cent earnings objective. (Tushman and O'Reilly, 1997, p.56).

Tushman and O'Reilly claim, p.165, that the "route to sustained competitive advantage [lies in] producing streams of innovation." As such, they are in disagreement with Peters and Negroponte cited earlier, because they have found a practical, indeed crucial, role for incremental innovation: it is this which sustains the industry while it is researching a breakthrough innovation. Tushman and O'Reilly cite Sony as an excellent example of an industry that nurtures innovation streams, and they maintain that the Walkman was a radical innovation a long time in the coming, but sustained as a development project through the munificence of routine product sales. Industries which are not aware of, or neglect to manage innovation streams of their own, they claim, are likely to become hostages to their past success, and will then become complacent, which is inevitably followed by them losing their competitive advantage.

> To the extent that the strategy or vision is wrong, no amount of diagnosis and root cause analysis will help. Organizations exist to accomplish strategic goals. If the strategy emphasizes the wrong product or service, to the wrong market, with the wrong technology and bad timing, no amount of organizational problem solving can help. Tight alignment with the wrong strategy ensures quick failure. (Tushman and O'Reilly, 1997, p.75).

Their remedy for dealing with a situation that demands efficiency and innovation, tactics and strategy, incremental and discontinuous change as well as other large and small changes is summarised as follows:

> We emphasize building executive teams and leaders throughout the organization who can simultaneously manage the strategies, structures, competencies, work processes, and cultures for short term efficiency as well as create the conditions for tomorrow's strategic innovation. We talk not about the organizational structure or culture for innovation, but about structures and cultures for strategic innovation and change. An organization with dual capabilities is able to maximise the probability that it will be more effective in the short term and make proactive and informed strategic bets. These dual organizational capabilities, anchored by a clear vision, enable managers to create both the expertise and luck to shape their firm's future. (Tushman and O'Reilly, 1997, p.178).

To demonstrate that it is a common phenomenon in industry, Tushman and O'Reilly describe a number of cases. Oticon, the Danish hearing-aid company is one of them. From 1958 to 1985, it dominated its market in the United States and Europe. Under the management of Bengt Simonsen and Torben Nielson, the company thrived on the technological excellence of its BTE (behind-the-ear)

51

hearing aid. According to Tushman and O'Reilly, it was to be predicted that the company would develop a technological arrogance and cultural insularity which was failing to note the innovation of another company, Starkey, in the United States. Starkey had reconfigured the BTE componentry to create a less obtrusive in-the-ear (ITE) product, and introduced it to the market in 1985. Oticon recognised it as a competitor, but considered the newcomer as technologically inferior to their own, and had difficulty adjusting to the concept of customising each ear piece to its intended wearer. Oticon considered it unnecessary to change, and its expertise and processes became obsolete at that point. Its processes, structure, and culture all prevented it from breaking free of its traditional view of the way a hearing aid should look and function. As a result, Oticon declined substantially in their United States market share in just one year: from 15 percent to 9 percent from 1985 to 1986. (Tushman and O'Reilly, 1997, pp.155-6).

To counter the slide into potential oblivion, Lars Kolind replaced Simonsen and his management team. His prime job was to drive Oticon's transition to the new dominant design in the hearing aid market. He oversaw a number of changes: He replaced the company's ingrained functional structure and culture with a robust cross-functional team; he substituted mobile work stations for offices, and he encouraged interacting and learning through face-to-face communications with other employees and with customers. The fruit of his labours was two-fold: Firstly, by 1995, Oticon's profits had increased ten-fold from their 1990 level; and secondly, the company successfully developed a breakthrough product, a digital hearing aid, with the potential for re-dominating the market and eliminating analogue-based hearing aids. (Tushman and O'Reilly, 1997, p.156).

2.13.2 The ambidextrous organization

The lesson from this example is clear. Tushman and O'Reilly point out that Simonsen should have recognised that long-term success depends on the ability to manage different kinds of innovation simultaneously within the company. "Given […] contrasting forces for change and stability, managers need to create ambidextrous organizations." (Tushman and O'Reilly, 1997, p.14). To remain successful, Oticon should have worked on developing incremental, architectural and discontinuous innovation at the same time. (Tushman and O'Reilly, 1997, p.157). Starkey's innovation had been of the architectural kind, meaning he had reconfigured an existing technology. At the core of Simonsen's problem lay an intransigence which refused to recognise the importance of superseding the original technology which Oticon had worked hard to achieve, coupled with a refusal to make the necessary organizational changes. Tushman and O'Reilly cite Lew Platt of Hewlett Packard, who also found it imperative, albeit difficult, to develop "a philosophy of killing off our own products with new technology." (Tushman and O'Reilly, 1997, p.157). Simonsen's failure to grasp the need to develop innovation streams in his company led to a financial crisis, to his removal and his replacement with a whole new management team, and other fundamental organizational transformation in order to shake off its own traditions – principally its view of what it considered its own technological superiority.

There can be no complacency concerning technological superiority, it is an ongoing quest for a company to become a technical market leader. Seiko, the Japanese watch maker, is an example of a company that has been able to manage innovation streams successfully. Seiko began by competing in the mechanical watch market in which it made a number of incremental innovations but it also experimented with quartz and tuning fork technology. In the mid-sixties, Seiko made the forward-looking decision to substitute quartz for their mechanical action. This discontinuous innovation increased the accuracy of the watch, dropped its price, and changed consumers' perception of the watch from a functional piece of jewellery to a fashion item. (Tushman and O'Reilly, 1997, p.160).

2.13.3 Managing the ambidextrous organization

In order for a company to make this leap of faith, Hewlett Packard's Platt points out, "We have to be willing to cannibalize what we're doing today in order to ensure our leadership in the future." (Tushman and O'Reilly, 1997, p.216). In the process of change, technological advancement drives innovation streams, but it is not technology which effects the transformation in an industry as much as management because management is charged with the responsibility for re-creating mind-sets, re-allocating and re-educating employees, who are frequently inertial.

Some industries have incorporated innovation streams as integral to their operations. Sony is one such example. Tushman and O'Reilly summarised Sony's practice as follows:

> Once Sony selected the WM-20 platform for its Walkman, it went on to generate more than 30 incremental versions within the WM-20 family. Indeed, in just 10 years, Sony was able to develop four Walkman product families and more than 160 incremental versions of those four families. Such sustained attention to initiating technological discontinuities at the subsystem level (eg flat motor and miniature battery), closing on a few standard platforms, and leading incremental product proliferation helped Sony control industry standards in its product class and outperform its Japanese, American, and European competitors. Through such proactive shaping of innovation streams, managers build on mature technologies that provide the base from which new technology can emerge. (Tushman and O'Reilly, 1997, p.167).

The managerial roles which Tushman and O'Reilly identified as necessary to move an industry forward in the way Sony did, are the architectural, the network builder and the juggler. (Tushman and O'Reilly, 1997, p.225). The manager as architect includes a number of functions, the most important of which is to build fit, consistent and congruent structures, comprising human resources and cultures designed to execute critical tasks in the service of strategy, objectives and vision. As a network builder, the manager must manage strategic change by shaping networks and coalitions down, across, up and outside his or her own unit. And as a juggler, the manager has to host contradictory strategies, structures, competencies, and cultures in service of incremental, architectural and discontinuous innovation, as well as integrating these contradictions with a clear vision. (Tushman and O'Reilly, 1997, p.225).

In summary, Tushman and O'Reilly offer the following as a "Lesson Learned", (Tushman and O'Reilly, 1997, p.218):

- Vision, strategy, and objectives are the bedrock for managing innovation and change
- Innovation is about execution, about getting it done
- Without a performance gap, innovation is unlikely
- Congruence is the key to diagnosis
- Inertia kills. Managing culture is the most neglected, and highest leverage, tool for promoting innovation and change
- Successful innovation requires skilled management of organizational politics
- Technology cycles drive innovation streams
- Ambidextrous organizations help compete for today and tomorrow
- Managing innovation streams means managing discontinuous change
- Innovation is a team sport.

In short, Tushman and O'Reilly maintain that those managers and their industries which together learn how to master innovation streaming are promoting their organizations from the present day's strength to be tomorrow's market leader.

2.14 The "disruptive" innovation, by Christensen and Raynor (2003)

Clayton Christensen and Michael Raynor considerably evolved the Tushman and O'Reilly congruence model which was underpinned by the efficacy of incremental and discontinuous innovation, when they published *The Innovator's Solution*, in 2003. Their focus is on the elaboration of a third innovation type, through the promulgation of a "disruptive" innovation, a dimension to innovation theory first introduced in a rudimentary form in Christensen's, *The*

Innovator's Dilemma, published in 1997. By "disruption", Christensen and Raynor refer to a product that is "simpler," "more convenient" and appeals to a "new [...] customer set" (Christensen and Raynor, 2003, p.32). The latter feature is particularly important for the efficacy of such a product because the "new customer set" they refer to now has immediate access to a product which either did not exist previously, or to which they previously did not have access, or one to which they did not aspire in the first place. This is possibly because it was too expensive, possibly because they could not engage with it in their life-style, or they lacked the skill, and they were therefore "non-consumers." For the innovative manufacturers, a disruptive product may open a sizeable new market of potential customers, who are content with a non-refined but functional and cheap product, which is attractive to them because the alternative is non-ownership and having to forego its use altogether.

The disruption concept is fundamental to cause and effect, predicting the outcomes of competitive battles in the market. Christensen and Raynor consider incremental and even discontinuous innovation as comprising "sustaining innovations" because they "target demanding, high-end customers with better performance than what was previously available [....] the established competitors almost always win the battles of sustaining technology." (Christensen and Raynor, 2003, p.34). This is because a better product may be sold for higher margins to their customers. But a disruptive product typically makes its entrance at the low end of the market and frequently competes against non-consumption, and therefore industrial leaders do not feel they are under threat "until the disruption is in its final stages." (Christensen and Raynor, 2003, p.46). They believe that, "when the disruptors begin pulling customers out of the low end of the original value network, it actually feels good to the leading firms, because as they move up-market in their own world, for a time they are replacing the low-margin revenues that disruptors steal, with higher-margin revenues from sustaining innovations." (Christensen and Raynor, 2003, p.46). In other words, a disruptive product could impact on the market in quite an insidious manner, eventually capturing increasing market share without the market leaders noticing the encroachment.

2.14.1 Examples of two early "disruptors"

Two examples of disruptive innovations demonstrate why they were so successful. Black and Decker introduced tools made with plastic casings and universal motors into a market in which electric tools were originally designed to be heavy and long-lasting. Realising that most do-it-yourselfers did not require professional tools, Black and Decker designed theirs to have an operating life of about 25-30 hours. Christensen and Raynor claim that "in today's dollars, B&D brought the cost of these tools down from $150 to $20, enabling a whole new population to own and use their tools." (Christensen and Raynor, 2003, p.56.)

Canon photocopiers had the same sort of impact on the market: The corporate photocopy centre, where a technician photocopied on the customer's behalf, lasted only until the early 'eighties. Then Canon introduced a countertop photocopier, and even though it had deficiencies such as the inability to reduce or enlarge, and had inferior resolution, its advantage was its low price, so that office employees had easy access in their own office hallways. Christensen and Raynor make the point that incremental improvement had a part to play; in Canon's case, that "little by little [the company] improved its machines to the point that immediate, convenient access to high-quality, full-featured copying is almost a constitutional right in most workplaces today." (Christensen and Raynor, 2003, p.57). In both instances, the disruptor moved up from the low-end of the market, with incrementalism eventually moving the product upwards to capture the larger share of the total market.

A vital ingredient in creating a disruptive product is to identify the need that the public need to have satisfied: "Only by staying connected with a given job as improvements are made, and by creating a purpose brand so that customers know what to hire, can a disruptive product stay on its growth trajectory." (Christensen and Raynor, 2003, p.95). The key to achieving success with a disruptive entrant to the market is to aim them at the low-end of the market, creating a business model "that can earn attractive returns to the discount prices required to win [the] business." (Christensen and Raynor, 2003, p.102).

2.14.2 The value of the non-consumption market

To Christensen and Raynor one of the greatest growth opportunities was in the nonconsumption market, because in this kind of market, people want satisfaction but before the advent of the disruptive product, "they put up with getting it done in an inconvenient, expensive or unsatisfying way." (Christensen and Raynor, 2003, p.102). Successful disruptors are invariably "simple, convenient, and foolproof," and "It is the 'foolproofness' that creates new growth by enabling people with less money and training to begin consuming." (Christensen and Raynor, 2003, p.111). Furthermore, they argue that, "The disruptive innovation creates a whole new value network. The new consumers typically purchase the product through new channels and use the product in new venues." (Christensen and Raynor, 2003, p.111). Examples of the latter include Intel's microprocessors and Microsoft's operating systems, which used IBM and Compaq as the channels to reach the end-user. Disruptive entrants become most prolific when sold through disruptive channels, because established products sell most profitably on a sustaining trajectory to customers who are already using a product to which they have become accustomed.

2.14.3 Disruptive production necessitates a split with the mainstream

In this context, managers and product developers need to "frame the disruption as a threat," (Christensen and Raynor, 2003, p.121) because they need to obtain access to company resources for the development of the product, and then work in collaboration with a team charged with building the business to search for opportunities of growth. To achieve this, Christensen and Raynor believe it is in the product's best interest to be split away from a company's mainstream production. They argue, "At the beginning of a wave of new-market disruption, the companies that initially will be the most successful will be integrated firms whose architectures are proprietary because the product isn't yet good enough." (Christensen and Raynor, 2003, p.142). Interdependent, proprietary architectures underpin differentiated products, and this combination leads to

58

strong profits. But when "dominant, profitable companies overshoot what their mainstream customers can use – then this game can no longer by placed, and the tables begin to turn. Customers will not pay still-higher prices for products they already deem too good. Before long, modularity rules, and commoditization sets in." (Christensen and Raynor, 2003, p.151). To take advantage of this, managers may find new opportunities for profitable growth through proprietary products, which require resource input on the improvement trajectory, so that an initial disruptor in crude form, may work its way up the market, developing ever wider consumer acceptance.

Of course, managing the growth of a disruptive product makes demands on the company, particularly its value. By "value" Christensen and Raynor refer to product profitability. At first, disruptors by definition, are slow to grow and generate profit. For this reason, they believe that it is easier to split off a production unit to function autonomously, than to attempt to effect pervasive change through the larger company.

2.14.4 The role of management in the disruptive model

Christensen and Raynor advise that in the process of change, managers should site a disruptor in an autonomous unit in which a "heavy-weight" team can give it the priority it needs. A heavy-weight team consists of employees whose functions and capabilities can re-combine with those of others and therefore in a creative re-mix they may be able to cross the normal boundaries of functional organizations. The effect of re-combining employees in such a way is that together they may create new processes and values to nurture and cultivate the new disruption in such a way that when it is ready to be released on the market, it may attract customers through one or more points of leverage, and thereby generate future growth. Christensen and Raynor are wary of placing manager(s) in charge of a new autonomous plant, if their managerial experience may be considered entrenched in processes of the mainstream, and if their problem-solving capacity is likewise too identified with mainstream problems. Managers must be receptive to new processes and new values. A part of the "new process" attitude is the need to formulate strategy that is different and that must

59

be pursued aggressively. This includes cost structures that customers find attractive: "Minimizing major cost commitments enables a venture to enthusiastically pursue the small orders that are the initial lifeblood of disruptive businesses in the emergent years." (Christensen and Raynor, 2003, p.227). Christensen and Raynor are insistent that, "CEOs must not leave the choice about strategy process to policy, habit, or culture." (Christensen and Raynor, 2003, p.225). There must not be a "one-size-fits-all" strategy, but in the emergent years, strategy must be appropriate to the circumstances in order to get a foothold into the market.

Timing and generating new growth can be difficult. This is particularly so if the core business growth in a company starts to decline, and new-growth ventures assume the responsibility for company health before it is ready. "The only way to keep investment capital from spoiling is to use it when it is still good – to invest it from a context that is still healthy enough that the money can be patient for growth." (Christensen and Raynor, 2003, p.243). The problem is that the company may then be placed under pressure to generate earnings. Christensen and Raynor advise under such circumstances that policies be put in place early, "to force the organization to start early, start small and demand early success." (Christensen and Raynor, 2003, p.246). The following comprise their main managerial approach to change:

* "Launch new-growth businesses regularly when the core is still healthy – when it can still be patient for growth – not when financial results signal the need.

* Keep dividing business units so that as the corporation becomes increasingly large, decisions to launch growth ventures continue to be made within organizational units that can be patient for growth because they are small enough to benefit from investing in small opportunities.

* Minimize the use of profit from established businesses to subsidize losses in new-growth businesses. Be impatient for profit: There is nothing like profitability to ensure that a high-potential business can continue to garner the

60

funding it needs, even when the corporation's core business turns sour." (Christensen and Raynor, 2003, p.246).

In this regard, Christensen and Raynor's model is reminiscent of Tushman and O'Reilly's "ambidextrous" organization. Both pairs of theorists recognize the need for product development to sustain the corporation's growth and corporate change, and that this should be an ongoing process before a market competitor forces such changes, in which case, it is likely to be too late. Christensen and Raynor identify the inertia concerning change through a company's own efficiency: "One reason that focused organizations perform so well is that their processes are always aligned to the task." (Christensen and Raynor, 2003, p.184). This means that a company's processes define its capabilities, but at the same time, they also define those tasks that a company cannot perform, or perhaps perform inefficiently and therefore uncompetitively. "Disruptive innovations typically take root at the low end of markets or in new planes of competition at a time when the core business still is performing at its peak – when it would [appear to] be crazy to revolutionize everything." (Christensen and Raynor, 2003, p.184).

Christensen and Raynor as well as Tushman and O'Reilly make the point emphatically that an organization can avoid the death spiral from inadequate growth, if it pursues growth before it becomes a life and death necessity to save the company. "The key to finding disruptive footholds is to connect with a job in what initially will be small, non-obvious market segments – ideally, market segments characterized by nonconsumption." (Christensen and Raynor, 2003, p.258). Again, Tushman and O'Reilly, and Christensen and Raynor are in agreement in the concept of ambidexterity, when the latter state that, "we believe that a predictable, repeatable process for identifying, shaping, and launching successful growth can coalesce. A company that embeds the ability to do this in a *process* would own a valuable growth engine." (Christensen and Raynor, 2003, p.278). This process would include operations running according to policy rather than financial pressures, leading from the top through support from the CEO or another senior executive who has his/her confidence. It would establish small corporate-level groups who can shape ideas into disruptive business plans; and it would include a system of training and re-training people throughout the organization to identify opportunities for disruptive product development which they would communicate to the corporate-level groups for action. (Christensen and Raynor, 2003, p.278).

Like Tushman and O'Reilly (1997), and Arie de Geus (1999), Christensen and Raynor consider training within the organization to be important:

> so that [employees] can instinctively identify potentially disruptive ideas and shape them into business plans that will lead to success. [...] Stand[ing] astride the boundary between disruptive and mainstream businesses, [managers must] actively monitor the appropriate flow of resources, processes, and values from the mainstream business into the new one and back again, [which] is the ongoing essence of managing a perpetually growing corporation.
> (Christensen and Raynor, 2003, p.283).

Christensen and Raynor make another interesting observation which may be relevant to two of the case-studies in question because they are owner-operated, (2003, pp.276-277): "We suspect that founders have an advantage in tackling disruption because they not only wield the requisite political clout, but also have the self-confidence to over-ride established processes in the interests of pursuing disruptive opportunities."

2.15 Porter's Contribution

The literature has so far focused mainly on the role of innovation and change management, but Porter's work (Porter, Dec 1996) opens a window to two closely related considerations, namely operational effectiveness and strategy. His perspective on the nature of strategy is useful for broadening the dimensions of analysis.

Porter states that while operational effectiveness and strategy are both essential, the two agendas are different, and their different purposes should be understood:

The operational agenda involves continual improvement everywhere there are no trade-offs. Failure to do this creates vulnerability even for companies with a good strategy. The operational agenda is the proper place for constant change, flexibility, and relentless efforts to achieve best practice. In contrast, the strategic agenda is the right place for defining a unique position, making clear trade-offs, and tightening fit. It involves the continual search for ways to reinforce and extend the company's position. The strategic agenda demands discipline and continuity; its enemies are distraction and compromise.

(Porter, Dec 1996, p.78).

In strategy, Porter believes that to be effective, a company should, "Think in terms of themes that pervade many activities, such as low cost, a particular notion of customer service, or a particular conception of the value delivered. These themes are embodied in nests of tightly linked activities." (Porter, Dec 1996, p.73). Porter's main concern is that companies are spending too much time and effort in getting operations to be effective, when it is possible those companies should first put a strategy in place so that operations can be more easily managed to produce a certain outcome.

2.16 "The Quest for Resilience" by Gary Hamel and Liisa Välikangas (2003)

In "The Quest for Resilience" (*Harvard Business Review*, Sept 2003), Gary Hamel and Liisa Välikangas make a case for "resilience" as the key to future success. Building on all of the methods for sustaining growth which have been mentioned above, Hamel and Välikangas believe that, "The ability to produce millions of gadgets, handle millions of transactions, or deliver a service to millions of customers is one of the most impressive achievements of humankind. But it is no longer enough." (Hamel and Välikangas, Sept 2003, p.11). They believe that, "for any [...] organization where more of the same is no longer enough, [...] optimization is a wholly inadequate ideal." (Hamel and Välikangas, Sept 2003, p.11). As an outcome, they concluded that this age is so turbulent and unpredictable, that "the only dependable advantage is a superior capacity for reinventing your business model before circumstances force you to." (Hamel and Välikangas, Sept 2003, p.1). It is a clarion call for embracing organizational change in the face of "creative destruction", (Hamel and Välikangas, Sept 2003, p.3), in the same way that a child is immunized against disease. In an organic environment, the living embrace to beat the pathogens in order to grow, and in so doing, they survive and thrive: "The goal is a company where revolutionary change happens in lightning-quick, evolutionary steps – with no calamitous surprises, no convulsive reorganizations, no colossal write-offs, and no indiscriminate, across-the-board layoffs. In truly resilient organizations, there is plenty of excitement, but there is no trauma." (Hamel and Välikangas, Sept 2003, p.2). Diane Coutu adds the following, "Resilience is neither ethnically good nor bad. It is merely the skill and the capacity to be robust under conditions of enormous stress and change." (Coutu, 2003, p.90).

Hamel and Välikangas identify four challenges that must be met before an organization can become resilient. The "cognitive challenge" refers to the need for a company to "become entirely free of denial, nostalgia and arrogance. It must be deeply conscious of what's changing and perpetually willing to consider how those changes are likely to affect its current success." (Hamel and Välikangas, Sept 2003,. p.3). The "strategic challenge" refers to resilience requiring "alternatives as well as awareness – the ability to create a plethora of new options as compelling alternatives to dying strategies." (Hamel and Välikangas, Sept 2003, p.3). The "political challenge" points to an organization being "able to divert resources from yesterday's products and programs to tomorrow's." (Hamel and Välikangas, Sept 2003, p.3). They add, "[…] it means building an ability to support a broad portfolio of breakout experiments with the necessary capital and talent." (Hamel and Välikangas, Sept 2003, p.3). Finally, the "ideological challenge" promulgates the view that "optimizing a business model that is slowly becoming irrelevant can't secure a company's future. If renewal is to become continuous and opportunity-driven, rather than episodic and crisis-driven, companies will need to embrace a creed that extends beyond operational excellence and flawless execution." (Hamel and Välikangas, Sept 2003, p.3).

For Hamel and Välikangas, the optimal solution is to build an organization that is "resilient" because that way, it has a "capacity for continuous reconstruction,"

64

since "It requires innovation with respect to those organizational values, processes, and behaviours that systematically favour perpetuation over innovation." (Hamel and Välikangas, Sept 2003, p.3). In the theories constructed by Tushman and O'Reilly (1997) and Christensen and Raynor (2003), the innovative product or service appears to come first. It may be either incremental, discontinuous or disruptive, and then they focus on adapting the manufacturing organization around it to facilitate the innovative process in the future that creates more of the same. In Hamel and Välikangas, (Hamel and Välikangas, Sept 2003), it is the other way around. They focus on the exact nature of the organization first, with the greater assurance that when this is suitably modelled for resilience, innovations will be easier to spawn, and may be spawned in greater numbers, and consist of a greater variety. Theirs is essentially a capacity-developing model.

2.17 The contribution of Govindarajan and Trimble (2005)

Govindarajan and Trimble's 2005 study, entitled *10 rules for strategic innovators – From idea to execution*, makes another significant contribution to the domain of innovation and change management. Their starting point is not the innovation itself but how to deliver an innovation's value through a series of processes that enable it to develop from its nascent stage into a market force. Because the "growth potential of any business model eventually decays [....] strategic innovation soon becomes the most attractive option [because] Companies that successfully execute strategic innovation can deliver breakthrough growth and generate entirely new life-cycle curves." (Govindarajan and Trimble, 2005, p.xxiii). They refer to the old business model as "CoreCo" and to the new order heralded by one or more innovations as "NewCo." (Govindarajan and Trimble, 2005, p.2).

The authors maintain that the most difficult challenge in the implementation of an innovation comprises the resistance that it has to face once it shows signs of success: when it has begun consuming more resources and then becomes the source of clashes between a company's old business model, and the new model in progress. Inspite of this inevitable conflict, CoreCo has to nurture its offspring, NewCo, because this is the old company's next source of profit. Yet it must do so without impinging on the success of its own immediate source of profit – decaying though it may be – as those funds are needed for the development of NewCo. It is difficult for managers to deal with a number of issues: the apparent conflict of interest, for example, that comes with devising new organizational norms and policies for NewCo, and relieving tensions when there is conflict between it and CoreCo. As well as that they have to create a new power and organizational structure for NewCo; and recruit and select talented and committed individuals to work for it. One great idea is not enough; nor is one great manager. And "creativity is only the dominant priority at the beginning of the innovation process." (Govindarajan and Trimble, 2005, p.5). Greatness lies in successful implementation, and that can best be achieved through "strategic innovation." This refers in the most basic sense to the ways in which a "great idea" is managed until it bears fruit. However, Govindarajan and Trimble admit "the *what* of strategy now focuses on innovation and change, [but] knowledge of the *how* is still nascent." (Govindarajan and Trimble, 2005, p.xxvi).

The authors identify three basic prerequisites to strategic innovation, that is, a strategy to get business innovation from plan to profits - from idea to execution. These are: Firstly, forgetting some key assumptions that made the current business successful; secondly, borrowing assets from the established organization to nurture the new one; and thirdly, learning how to succeed in an emerging but uncertain market. To achieve them, Newco has to succeed in three things: "It must forget CoreCo's business definition; secondly, NewCo must recognize that a different business model requires different competencies; and finally, Coreco must forget Coreco's focus on exploitation of a proven business model and shift to exploration of new possibilities." (Govindarajan and Trimble, 2005, p.7). This means that Newco has to consciously forget former assumptions, mind-sets, and biases because these belonged to a decaying model. And Newco must borrow assets from Coreco to gain access to resources with concrete value. Above all, Newco must learn because the company must

66

improve in its predictions of its business performance in order to generate greater profits.

Govindarajan and Trimble (2005) refer to a company's "DNA", meaning a company's essential features that give it its unique identity. These are staff, structure, system and culture. And the difference between CoreCo and NewCo's DNA is that CoreCo has operational experts as staff; a hierarchy as structure; focus on accountability as a system and is risk averse as a culture. But Newco employs creators and inspirers as staff; has a flat structure; focuses on learning as its driving system; and has a risk-tolerant culture. (Govindarajan and Trimble, 2005, p.13). This new DNA comprises the operational and philosophical forces that drive "forget, borrow and learn." Where Coreco has proven answers to what its business is and how it has to date succeeded, NewCo, its offspring, must alter the established organizational design, to give it a uniqueness. Coreco has resources that NewCo lacks, such as manufacturing capacity, expertise, sales networks and resourcing channels. NewCo requires access to these, but not in such a way as to make the relationship between it and its parent company too close, because then NewCo could not forge its own identity. And finally, Newco must develop its own success formula through its capacity to learn: it has to resolve critical unknowns in its business plan and arrive at a working model as quickly as it can. Govindarajan and Trimble conclude here with the maxim that "if NewCo cannot forget CoreCo's success formula, it will struggle to learn its own." (Govindarajan and Trimble, 2005, p.17).

The authors devote considerable time to learning, much of which may be summarized by focusing on their commentary on accountability in relation to learning. They believe that where CoreCo focuses its accountability to a plan, and on negotiation of targets, NewCo has an accountability to learning, through disciplined and rigorous execution of theory-focused planning, in which their ability to predict NewCo's performance is very important to the success of the enterprise. They must learn to face several critical unknowns, such as aspects of the market, its competition, the impact of new technologies, and whether the market can sustain profitability. Coreco, meanwhile continues to assume that its plan is correct, whilst NewCo tests the assumptions in its plan. Where Coreco

67

hides bad news when its assumptions are proven to be incorrect, it then redoubles its efforts to make its initial plan successful, and avoids risks to ensure its chances of achieving it. But Newco is purposefully vigilant about bad news and shares it transparently among its staff. If Newco should come up short of its plan, it re-examines its assumptions, scrutinizes the environment for unexpected change, and then revises its plan, if and only if, there are clear lessons to be learned from previous wrong turns. Instead of avoiding risks, it resolves critical unknowns through controlled experiments and carefully examined risks. (Govindarajan and Trimble, 2005, p.106). Therefore, planning and learning are underpinned by an appreciation of the unpredictable. The "theory focused plan" assists this, and the two authors itemize eight elements in such a practical plan: Describe how the business works, identify what can be measured, establish goals, create spending guidelines, predict performance, identify critical unknowns, analyze disparities between predictions and outcomes, and finally revise the plan in accordance with the findings. (Govindarajan and Trimble, 2005, pp.151-152).

In addition to advising the reader about planning, the authors also offer advice for overcoming the forgetting challenge. It may be facilitated through the deployment of every-day actions, for example, by hiring outsiders, reporting to someone on the board of Coreco who is more senior than the CEO of Coreco, taking care not to overstate the importance of the profitability metric, and developing a unique culture – beginning with a willingness to experiment and learn. (Govindarajan and Trimble, 2005, p.48).

Their recommendations for overcoming the borrowing challenge include choosing links that imbue NewCo with a crucial competitive advantage, changing incentives that strongly reward localized performance, and maintaining NewCo's nascent distinctiveness. (Govindarajan and Trimble, 2005, p.79).

In delineating a planning model, as central to strategic innovation, the authors comment that a proven business model can intensify the forgetting challenge, and Newco therefore must divert attention from the past.

The authors' ten rules for strategic innovation comprise a series of conclusions based on four years' research on a number of companies, of which the most commonly cited is ADI (Analogue Device, Inc). These ten "rules" are itemized and analysed in the discussion section of Chapter 14.2.11. It is in these ten rules that Govindarajan and Trimble are at their practical best in advising managers who engage in company change, what steps they should take, and what pitfalls to avoid.

2.18 Conclusion

This review examines a number of writings published by a range of authors: From populists and non-academic practitioners to highly academic empirical social scientists, all of whom have contributed to the elucidation of "innovation," and "change management."

All of them have observed that the company of today must increase its competitiveness in the face of global and chaotic markets which may leave that company vulnerable, and struggling for sustainability, let alone profitability. Creativity and innovation comprise a solution: That is, product and service re-conceptualisation to access potential markets and thereby increase market share. It requires an awareness that competitive advantage can be generated by creative thinking provided that it is accompanied by innovative, if difficult to implement, processes in manufacturing to bringing products to market.

Practitioners and theorists argue about whether incremental, radical or disruptive innovation is more effective. And they conjecture whether the propensity to innovate lies more with small entrepreneurial upstarts or established market brands. But most of all, the empirically-based publications focus on providing managers of today with a practical set of guidelines about what they should do, and how they should do it, if they want to continue being in business two or five years from now. They may use diagnostic tools that are to be discussed in this research, in order to assist the practitioners to evaluate themselves in the present, before they take steps to modify themselves for the future.

A line of evolutionary theory may be traced from Schumpeter and his early warning that only small and young companies incline towards innovation to Utterback (1994); Leifer et al.(2000); to Tushman and O'Reilly(1997); Christensen and Raynor (2003); Hamel and Välikangas (2003); and Govindarajan and Trimble (2005) - who all make a convincing case for established brands to succeed in the quest for innovation. They do so through the judicious application of diagnostic models, which help to reduce a highly complex organization to a simpler set of inter-connected constructs, ready for modification. They recommend that management re-conceptualises its company vision, manage change systematically, embed new structures and systems, promote organizational learning and cultivate simultaneous innovation streams, thereby modifying their culture to take advantage of dynamic, even turbulent market conditions to change constantly and seamlessly. However, the literature on the management of change remains somewhat vague through its very nature: it is not sound to be prescriptive with the minutiae of processes because all businesses are different. However, Govindarajan and Trimble (2005) stand out because of their ability to reduce complex processes of change down to a practical formula for strategic innovation: "borrow, forget, and learn." (Govindarajan and Trimble, 2005, p.7).

The main theories of Tushman and O'Reilly (1997), Christensen and Raynor (2003), and Hamel and Välikangas (Sept.2003), may merit further investigation in this study, using Wave Rider the Surfing Company; Alpine Packs, the Wilderness Company; and the Little Dragon Company. These may form some of the "sensitizing concepts" (Blaikie, 2000) in the work to come.

70

Chapter 3

Research Method

3.1 The research philosophy and strategy

It is clear from the literature that there is a large number of theories relating to innovation in all its many guises, and that there may likely be an equal number relating to the practices of change management. A theory, according to Blaikie, is an attempted answer to a "why" question, and the abductive strategy "is the origin of answers to 'why' questions." (Blaikie, 2000, p.143 and p.116).

To obtain answers to 'why' questions from the respondents in their own words and from within their own natural work environment, the case-study method and face to face interviewing were adopted as key components of the abductive strategy in this investigation. "It [the case study] allows, indeed endorses, a focus on just one example, or perhaps just two or three." (Blaxter, Hughes and Tight, 1996, p.66). Robert Yin defines the case study as "the method of choice when the phenomenon under study is not readily distinguishable from its context." (Yin, 1993, p.3). The strength of the case-study method is that it is "an empirical inquiry that investigates a contemporary phenomenon within its real-life context, [and it] addresses a situation in which the boundaries between phenomenon and context are not clearly evident," (Yin, 1993, p.59). Employees who participated in this investigation at Alpine Packs, Wave Rider and Little Dragon all had a definition in the broader contexts of their occupation, position in the company, committee membership and their general employment environment. These multiple roles provided a "richness of [...] context" which meant that the investigation should not rely on a single data collection method, and multiple sources of evidence were required. (Yin, 1993, p.3).

Yin states that one of the well-known uses of the case-study is its capacity "to develop new hypotheses [...] and assess outcomes" (Yin, 1993, p.59). Later, he went on to state that it also had a "distinctive ability to [...] Capture process and outcomes in a causal logic model [and] develop lessons generalizable to the

71

major substantive themes in a field." (Yin, 1993, p.75). Case studies may be progressed in a variety of ways. Yin (1993) identifies six case study permutations, along two dimensions: the number of cases: single or multiple; and the purpose of the study: exploratory, descriptive or explanatory. The cases in this investigation are both descriptive and explanatory.

Eckstein refers to "crucial-case studies", by which he means that a case may "provide[] a critical test of a theory, to corroborate, challenge or extend it." (Eckstein quoted in Blaikie, 2000, p.221). The generalizability of case studies has been questioned, particularly by those social scientists who have a preference for quantitative methods, but Mitchell makes the comment that, "The validity of the extrapolation depends not on the typicality or representativeness of the case, but upon the cogency of the theoretical reasoning." (Eckstein quoted in Blaikie, 2000, p.225). This researcher has used "holistic" case studies, each functioning as one consolidated unit, rather than a unit comprising individual, or split, cases embedded in the whole. (Blaikie, 2000, p.221).

To understand the behaviour of the individuals involved in each case study, the abductive research strategy was adopted, to generate theory from a "low stance" position, (Blaikie, 2000, p.241). Blaikie states that there are some underlying research concepts that must take their place in any social research. The first is "ontology" which he defines as pertaining to, "the claims or assumptions that are made about the nature of social reality, claims about what exists, what it looks like, what units make it up and how these units interact with each other." (Blaikie, 2000, p.8) Its partner, "epistemology", refers to "ideas about what can count as knowledge, what can be known, and what criteria such knowledge must satisfy in order to be called knowledge rather than beliefs." (Blaikie,2000, p.8). These are significant because together they refer to the validity of new social knowledge uncovered in the course of an investigation, and they are closely allied with the method(s) used to arrive at the outcomes of that investigation.

The interpretivist approach constructs theory that has its origins in employees' everyday activities, and in their own language and social realities. It comes therefore with the epistemological assumption that the social construction is the

72

participants' social reality, and from this reality, categories and concepts may be derived to form the basis of an enhanced understanding of the ways in which people engage with innovation, and innovation's connection with change management. "Interpretivism takes [...] the meanings and interpretations, the motives and intentions that people use in their everyday lives and that directs their behaviour – and it elevates them to the central place in social theory and research. [...] In short, in order to negotiate their way around their world and make sense of it, social actors have to interpret their activities together, and it is these meanings, embedded in language, that constitute their social reality." (Blaikie, 2000, p.115). The ontological assumption is that reality is "relativist" not "absolutist." The abductive research strategy was therefore a dynamic one because it evolved over the three years that this investigation took place, as a "developing" compilation, rather than a static assessment – a video rather than a photograph. This proved to be particularly valuable in cases where major change was occurring, as in the case of Alpine Packs, which underwent the transition from being a locally staffed company to becoming an outsourced company. This means that the theory produced as a result of this investigation will be relevant to the field, and will be time and space contingent, as are all theories in the social sciences.

The abductive strategy comprises two main aspects. Firstly, it describes the social actors' activities in their place of work; and secondly, it aims to extract categories and concepts that underpin an understanding of the issues involved on the 'stage' of work, where the 'actors' act out their roles. Because people are all different, the ontological assumptions are "relativist" rather than "absolutist", implying that there may be a number of social meaning and that these may be in a constant state of change. (Blaikie, 2000, p.116). In interviewing the employees concerned, questions need to be framed in an open-ended way to allow them maximum opportunity to answer in their own way. As in hermeneutics, it is a method of learning from the bottom up.

In selecting cases from three different countries, rooted in three different cultures, languages and forms of management, the researcher hoped that the research questions could be answered with the interpretive approach to the

73

enquiry. According to the principles of theoretical sampling, each case should serve specific purposes within the overall scope of the research. Yin identified three options, "choose a case to fill theoretical categories, to extend the emerging theory; and/or choose a case to replicate previous case(s) to test the emerging theory; or, choose a case that is the polar opposite to extend the emerging theory." (Yin, 1989, pp.53-54). Alpine Packs was selected because it was initially reminiscent of the Ciba-Geigy case in Tushman and O'Reilly (1997); Wave Rider was selected because it extended far into the unconventional, so it might assist in testing an emerging theory; and the Little Dragon Company was selected because it was an industrial product of a command economy driven by a Communist regime, therefore it might comprise a useful "opposite" to the conventions of a democratic government and a market economy.

3.2 Concepts and research questions

In attempting to make some determinations of the relationship between business success and innovation coupled with change, a number of core concepts were relevant to all three companies:

* Incremental , discontinuous and disruptive innovation
* Organizational change
* Change management
* Organizational culture
* Sustainable development
* Strategies for competitive advantage
* Globalization
* Competition
* Company resilience

Phrased as research questions, these concepts re-emerge as beacons to guide this investigation:

* What is the nature of, and the importance of, innovation to industry?

* How do industrialists from three diverse cultures interpret and implement "innovation"?

* Are there different forms of innovation towards which each business has a particular inclination?

* How do the three industries determine which innovations to pursue for commercialization?

* Is change management a complex strategic undertaking? Why?

* How has innovation assisted in the development of change so that these businesses could develop over a period of about three decades, thereby continuing to meet evolving market needs?

* In the opinions of senior staff, CEOs and other employees, which methods of innovation and management practices have been perceived as being most successful in achieving the sustainable prosperity of each of the three companies in question?

* Has private ownership provided advantages over public ownership in the implementation of innovation and change?

* Have their nations' general political and economic situations helped or hindered their business success?

To help answer these questions, Blaikie suggests using sensitising concepts because they help to frame the abductive strategy. He cites Blumer's precept of using a "sensitising" concept in preference to a "definitive" one because of the uncertainty that a paradigm relating to social phenomena could actually reflect the empirical world with complete accuracy. He believes that because there are different paradigms through which the social world may be interpreted, "we cannot set out with just a single view of the role of concepts in social research." (Blaikie, 2000, p.130). This is further substantiated by Yin who wrote that, "an investigator cannot maintain an objective distance from the phenomenon being studied. Inquiry is value-bound, not value-free." (Yin, 1993, p.61). The sensitising concepts that appeared of relevance were the "congruence model" devised by Tushman and O'Reilly (1997), the "disruptive innovation model" devised by Christensen and Raynor (2003) and later in 2003, Hamel and Välikangas published their research under the title, "The Quest for Resilience" thereby introducing yet another major concept: company resilience. These theories served as cogent and useful bases for further exploration, and they were conducive to the generation of further conceptualisation and theory. However, abduction allows for scrutiny of any theory that explains cause and effect in the field of innovation and change. Therefore, this research strategy has flexibility, yet also has "anchor points in interpretation of the findings." (Blumer cited in Blaikie, 2000, p.130). This strategy, then, appeared the most suitable for the purposes of this investigation. Blaikie casts the researcher into roles associated with this approach, whilst observing the roles played by the respondents: "These include the faithful reporter, the mediator of languages, the reflective partner, the conscientizer." (Blaikie, 2000, p.126).

In order to fully understand the social constructs under investigation, Blaikie recommends "immersion", or extensive contact, as the means by which the investigator may fully come to terms with the social actors and their stage. In reality this refers to the iterative process of in-depth interviewing and observing the 'stage', comprising activity on factory floors and in office complexes. The researcher was limited by time and expense, but extensively viewed all three business environments.

3.3 Language

Each industry uses specific vocabularies that are central to any discussion of innovation and change management, amongst its members. Because the abductive research strategy extracts social scientific accounts from employees of the three companies, their language and its meanings were included as part of the exploration process, as were equivalent terminologies that they used. It spanned the range from formal translations from Mandarin to English, in China; informal dialogue at Alpine Packs; and colloquial to slang usages at Wave Rider, particularly the language used in their website. The language aspect was problematic in China, especially in the case of the Deputy General Manager of Little Dragon, Mr Lei Yuan, because three translators were used during the course of two extensive interviews, with one sometimes deferring to another to produce the best possible translation of what Mr Lei had said. Dr Hing, on the other hand, was able to speak English, but it was a stylized formal register reminiscent of English textbooks from the 1960s. As has been made clear in the chapters relating to Little Dragon, the pace of development and the market aggressiveness of their industry are rooted in the competitiveness of the twenty-first century, even though their language was reminiscent of a former and slower era. Nonetheless, inspite of the difficulties associated with the translations, the researcher acted as "a mediator of languages," (Blaikie, 2000, p.126), as each respondent's language use was indicative of the role they played in the company.

3.4 The Process

3.4.1 Selection of Data Sources

Primary data was obtained from individuals in their day-to-day industrial settings. Most of the data were qualitative in nature, apart from factually based demographic data, and other factual data from such sources as company documentation and downloads from industry websites. The Chinese company under investigation offered readers of their website a choice of language, of which English was one, and it included considerable details about the aims and operations of the company in addition to descriptions of their products.

77

The sample that was used in this research followed the principles of theoretical sampling, as defined by Strauss and Corbin (1990). It was on the basis of concepts that have proven to be of theoretical relevance to the evolving theory. The population was intended to include individuals involved in a cross-section of management and other innovative activities in each company, but in practice this was not always possible. For example, at Little Dragon requests for an interview with particular role-holders, like the Head of Human Resources, always had to be organized through a third party. This was not always successful. At Little Dragon, management was insistent for the two years during which interviewing took place, that they alone should represent their company. Originally, Tushman and O'Reilly's congruence model identified four main groupings in an organization's architecture, so every effort was made that the population would be drawn from what they term Critical Tasks, Culture, Formal Organization and People (Tushman and O'Reilly, 1997, p.59). Christensen and Raynor's organizational model (2003) is not significantly different, but in practice the participation of an organizational cross-section was only possible in the Alpine Packs company. The researcher was able to interview employees as follows:

3.4.2 Alpine Packs

1. The Executive leadership   Stewart McBruce, Sandra Gupwell
2. Communications networks   Pearl Smith, Alice Jones
3. Human resources   Sandra Gupwell
4. Strategic groups   *Sales:* Joe Barnard
        Quality Management: Linda Maynard, Stuart Clook, Caroline van der Slee
        R&D: Rachel Burberry

3.4.3 Wave Rider

1. Executive leadership   Paul Sinclair, Will Waugh
2. Communication networks   *Publications and website*: Graham Herbert
3. Human Resources   Will Waugh (overseeing responsibility)

78

| 4. Strategic groups | *Competition coaching and sponsorship*: Graham Herbert |

3.4.4 Little Dragon

1. Executive leadership	Dr Hing, Mr Lei
2. Communication networks	Professor Pei-Yee (not an employee of the company, but communicated all arrangements, and translated dialogue)
3. Human Resources	Mr Lei (overseeing responsibility)
4. Strategic groups	None made available

The researcher contacted management staff first by e-mail, and asked if they could suggest other possible participants. It was expected that across these three cases, approximately ten individuals would be interviewed from each company, through cluster sampling, although it became apparent that this was a prohibitive goal in China because of the time it would take to harness the necessary resources for lengthy periods, particularly translators. The largest number of individuals who availed themselves was in Alpine Packs, where nine participants were interviewed in the first round; but then only four could be interviewed again in the second round, one year later, due to the business having been restructured to outsource its production in Asia, resulting in the redundancies of some former interviewees. Nonetheless, in each case, the employees who were interviewed were the ones who, arguably, had the most to contribute to this investigation. For example, in the Wave Rider case, there were only three participants, but they were the two founders/directors with almost forty years' standing, and their publications manager who had been with the company a decade. These three men were therefore in the best position to provide in-depth answers.

Since the abductive method uses an iterative approach, it was anticipated that each respondent would be interviewed more than once, and some respondents up to a number of times, depending on the outcomes of the earlier interview, but only the following could be interviewed twice:

3.4.5 Alpine Packs

Stewart McBruce

Sandra Gupwell

Joe Barnard

Alice Jones

3.4.6 Wave Rider

Graham Herbert

3.4.7 Little Dragon

Mr Lei

The second iteration added considerably to the meaningfulness of the original data from the first interview, and to the researcher's understanding of innovation and its connection to change as they evolved. Each industry was contacted a year after the initial interviews, and each one had evolved rapidly to meet market demands. Blaikie wrote, "[...] these re-descriptions can be developed into theories that go beyond everyday knowledge to include conditions of which social actors may be unaware." (Blaikie, 2000, p.116). However, it was clear to the researcher that each business was under so much pressure, that the leadership of each company understood the changing demands of its business well, particularly the connection between innovation and change, and each was attempting to either maintain, or regain, a sustainable position within the market, by whatever means necessary. This applied particularly to Alpine Packs.

The criterion for judging when to stop theoretical sampling is the category's or theory's "theoretical saturation." By this term Glaser and Strauss referred to the situation in which the researcher "sees similar instances over and over again, [and he or she] becomes empirically confident that a category is saturated ... when one category is saturated, nothing remains but to go on to new groups for data on other categories, and attempt to saturate these categories also." (Glaser and Strauss, 1967, p.65). Theoretical saturation occurs at the point where respondents have nothing further to add that could lead to further discovery. (Blaikie, 2000, p.206.) This researcher felt that "saturation point" was not entirely reached, but because of his family's move from New Zealand to Brunei in late April 2003, the researcher was considerably curtailed in the ability to conduct face to face interviews, due mainly to cost of travel and accommodation. However, in March 2004, the researcher did travel back to China to interview the management of Little Dragon, partially funded by RMIT's research fund. Participants from the other two companies were contacted and interviewed by telephone.

The researcher found that the telephone was at best only a satisfactory instrument for interviewing purposes, and at worst it led at times to a degree of lack of clarity. This necessitated questions requesting clarification. The telephone was used in dialogue with Alpine Packs and Wave Rider employees, only. It would not have been satisfactory at all for conducting an interview with Little Dragon, because of the need for translations, necessitating a three-way line. Conducting an interview face to face, where expression, volume, tone and body language also communicate part of the interviewee's message was beneficial to the research outcome in the first round of interviews. For example, in the case of Alpine Packs, it was not only what employees said about Stewart McBruce as Managing Director, it was the way they said it: their deep respect for him in that capacity, was made instantly clear through facial expressions indicating complete sincerity. Therefore, the decision to terminate the data collection was made once the researcher considered that sufficient data had been generated to meet the stated objectives.

3.5 Data Generation and Timing

Data was generated by semi-structured interviews over the period from August 2001-May 2004. This type of interview proved flexible and adaptable within a variety of contexts, companies and individual styles of discourse, and it was also useful in pursuing unexpected paths and cues suggested by theoretical sensitivity, as explained by Glaser and Strauss in 1967. Each interview was expected to take about one hour, and Alpine Packs' management thought that was an acceptable length of time for employees to be away from their work. The exceptions were the Chinese participants, each of whom allowed the interview to proceed to three hours; and Will Waugh of Wave Rider also proceeded to discuss his industry for about three hours. Warren states that "Interview subjects are [...] to be viewed as meaning makers, not passive conduits for retrieving information from an existing vessel of answers," and therefore, the questions should be framed "interactionally, aiming to understand the meaning of respondents' experiences and life worlds [...] because meaning making is centre stage in the interpretive process." (Warren, 2002, pp.83-84). The researcher found that in all cases, without exception, the respondents spoke unhesitatingly and positively of their work place.

With the prior agreement of the participant, the interviews were recorded and later transcribed for analysis. The Wave Rider interviews were professionally transcribed by secretarial staff at the Christchurch Polytechnic School of Business; all the rest were transcribed by the researcher. The researcher also made notes at the time of the interview, so that these could be compared later with recordings and the transcripts to sharpen the focus and accuracy of what had been said. Note-making was also a safeguard against recorder failure. In the case of two out of the three interviews with the Chinese, the batteries failed, and the higher pitched voices of the Chinese women translators were not well recorded during the first interview with the Deputy General Manager, Mr Lei. The configuration of the furniture also proved less than conducive to robust interviewing. In Chinese style, the boardroom was large and was dominated by a huge central table; with only five people seated around it, there were large empty spaces between each of the speakers – leading to muffled recording, and making rapport-building comparatively difficult and time-consuming. It was therefore as well that physical notes were made at the time. As a result of these difficulties, the first interview with Mr Lei, lasting about three hours, took three complete work-days to piece together afterwards, and the transcript was sent back to Professor Pei-Yee at the University of Southern Yangtze, who had performed the instantaneous translations, for her verification and correction.

Furthermore, the researcher was aware of Warren's reminder cautioning "researchers against importing one set of linguistic and cultural assumptions into another when interviewing between cultures." (Warren, 2002, p.97). The host in the first round of interviews at Little Dragon, assumed the role of company story-teller, and the researcher had to be patient and had to listen. After that, the prepared questions had to be re-formulated in easier-to-translate terms to elicit a clear answer.

In China, the approach of informing the researcher about the company prior to responding to questions, was also the way the General Manager, Dr Hing, approached his interview. Because the Chinese experience was markedly different in emphasis from those of Alpine Packs and Wave Rider, it appeared to the researcher almost as if the research strategy in China might be better called "grounded" because of the interviewees' penchant for telling their own stories. Nonetheless, in due course, they also answered specific questions in considerable details, and their replies substantiated one another. Their responses elicited some interesting, and unanticipated data.

After the completion of each round of the three companies, the transcripts were analysed in readiness for the next round to refine the focus on the research objectives. Warren quotes Kvale in comparing interviewing to Shakespeare's "man" in that there are seven stages to completion: "thematizing, designing, interviewing, transcribing, analyzing, verifying, and reporting. By thematizing, he means thinking about the topic of interest to the researcher and its fit with the interview method; qualitative interviewing is designed with the aim of thematizing the respondent's experience as well." (Kvale quoted in Warren, 2002, p.86). Warren makes the comment that to maintain integrity with the abductive approach, "the design of qualitative interview research necessarily places limits on standardization and the working relevance of existing literature." (Warren, 2002, p. 86). As results will indicate, each employee in each of the three companies recounted elements of experiences in the work-place, a considerable number of which the researcher could not have anticipated.

3.6 Interview dates

3.6.1 Alpine Packs Interview Series 1

Table 2

Name	Position	Medium	Date
Stewart McBruce	Company Founder and Managing Director	Face to face	April 11 2003
Pearl Smith	Production Manager	Face to face	March 28 2003
Sandra Gupwell	Co-Founder Co-Director, and Manager HR	Face to face	April 4 2003
Alice Jones	Group leader and supervisor	Face to face	April 2 2003
Caroline van der Slee, Stuart Clook and Linda Maynard	Quality management	Face to face	April 2 2003
Rachel Burberry	Head of R&D	Face to face	April 4 2003
Joe Barnard	Head of Sales	Face to face	April 4 2003

3.6.2 Alpine Packs Interview Series 2
Table 3

Stewart McBruce	Managing Director	Telephone	May 21 2004
Sandra Gupwell	Co-Director and Manager HR	Telephone	May 28 2004
Alice Jones	Group leader and supervisor	Telephone	June 14 2004
Joe Barnard	Head of Sales	Telephone	June 14 2004.

3.6.3 Wave Rider Interview Series 1
Table 4

Name	Position	Medium	Date
Paul Sinclair	Co-founder and Co-director	Face to face	August 24 2001
Will Waugh	Co-founder and Co-director	Face to face	August 24 2001
Graham Herbert	Head of publicity and communications	Face to face	August 24 2001

3.6.4 Wave Rider Interview Series 2

Table 5

Graham Herbert	Head of publicity and communications	Telephone	January 20 2004.

3.6.5 Little Dragon Interview Series 1
Table 6

Name	Position	Medium	Date
Lei, Yuan	Deputy General Manager	Face to face	November 18 2002

3.6.6 Little Dragon Interview Series 2
Table 7

Lei, Yuan	Deputy General Manager	Face to face	March 22 2004
Dr Hing, Wenxiang	General Manager	Face to face	March 24 2004

3.7 Data Reduction and Analysis

The original intention was that the Christchurch Polytechnic Institute of Technology (CPIT) was to purchase the latest version of NUD*IST software mainly at the instigation of the Nursing Faculty, and also at the researcher's request, so that qualitative researcher might create categories and index the data more easily and accurately. The researcher's enquiries revealed that this purchase had not eventuated, and was unlikely to. In connection with computer analysis, Thomas Richards and Lyn Richards (1994) made a study of computer-based qualitative data analysis (QDA). They concluded that computers were of assistance in a number of minor ways, but that, "The problem and the excitement is that QDA is probably the most subtle and intuitive of human epistemological enterprises, and therefore likely to be the last to achieve satisfactory computerization." (Richards and Richards, 1994, p.18). Even allowing for the software technology to have improved since 1994, its unavailability in Christchurch, was frustrating. Eventually, the pursuit for a computer-based analytic package was abandoned, and instead, Dr Judy Miller,

Senior Lecturer in the Education Faculty of the University of Canterbury in New Zealand, demonstrated useful analytic techniques and practice for the researcher and for other members of the CPIT School of Business Research Committee in 2002, particularly with regard to QDA. Acting as a consultant to the School for about eight months, she demonstrated practical methods that were drawn from the writings of Strauss and Corbin, Blaikie and Yin. Coding, particularly colour coding, became a prominent focus in weekly practice sessions. Colour coding "represent[ing] the operations by which data are broken down, conceptualised, and put back together in new ways", (Strauss and Corbin, 1990, p.57) was therefore used as standard practice in analysing all data in this investigation.

Open coding and axial coding were both used. "It is the central process by which theories are built from data." (Strauss and Corbin, 1990, p.57). This is consistent with Blaikie, who describes the process of analysis (Blaikie, 2000, p.240) as a "spiral" one, in which the researcher describes, then classifies and finally connects. This reiterates therefore that classification is not a neutral process. Theoretical frameworks were used in order to generate more theory. Therefore, the researcher allowed each participant to contribute and each one built further upon the original "high stance" position (Blaikie, 2000, p.241), enabling the industrial stage to be more the domain of the actor than the researcher. For this reason, the interview with Wave Rider's Paul Sinclair lasted one hour and ten minutes – but with his business partner, Will Waugh, it lasted over three hours because of Mr Waugh's obvious inclination to answer questions very fully, but he also went considerably over the question boundaries, so the researcher acquired raw data beyond his original expectations.

Blaikie cites Bryman about the abductive approach being conducive to uncovering surprise elements in the data generated by a flexible approach such as semi-structured interviews. In other words, there is value in the stimulation of the unexpected with regard to theory formation. "[…] qualitative researchers tend to the view that the predominantly open approach which they adopt in the examination of social phenomena allows them access to unexpectedly important topics which may not have been visible to them had they foreclosed the domain of study by a structured, and hence potentially rigid, strategy." (Bryman quoted

86

in Blaikie, 2000, p.253). This was verified by a number of such instances. In China, it was the unexpected way in which Dr Hing explained that he allied himself with Toshiba, potentially his greatest opponent in the market. In the case of Allied Packs, it was the way in which the two directors explained the reversal from their business strategy after thirty years' undeviating consistency. And in the case of Wave Rider, Waugh and Sinclair evinced surprise that their passion for a sport enabled a business partnership to prosper and change the public attitude towards surfing, from society once dismissing it as a fringe activity to respecting it as a sport. These data, or "unexpected anomalies" (Blaikie, 2000, p.149), have played a role in the theory generation in this investigation, as the flexibility of the interview method to extra information that would not have come forward with a less flexible technique.

The data were finally reduced to "statements of relationships between concepts." (Blaikie, 2000, p.163). In the words of Schofield, the aim has been "to produce a coherent and illuminating description of and perspective on a situation that is based on and consisted with detailed study of that situation [three primary case studies] ..." (Schofield quoted in Blaikie, 2000, p.252).

Chapter 4

Wave Rider the Surfing Company:
Overview 1969-2004
and first set of in-depth perspectives covering 1969-
2001

4.1 Overview 1969-2004

Australian teenagers Paul Sinclair and Will Waugh created Wave Rider the Surfing
Company in 1969, trading originally in wooden, and later, fibreglass surfboards.
Within two years, however, their company had created a profitable niche in sales of
what was to be their greatest "breakthrough" innovation, the dual-density wetsuit.
And within a decade from there they expanded operations in France, Spain, Portugal
and England. Manufacturing, distribution and sales in California followed soon after
that. But company growth did not progress in a linear way. As the two following
chapters demonstrate, its growth was marked by parallel developments, the occasional
backward step, and lurches forward.

The successful development of the two initial core products was followed by the
development of the tide-watch, a time-piece that enabled surfers to 'catch' the best
waves, which were largely tide-generated. The popularity of the sport and its lifestyle
was fuelled by Wave Rider's sponsorship of professional competitions, first confined
to the ocean, and later these expanded to encompass the challenges of snow-based
competitions in the mountains. The interest of its youthful target audience was
consistently stimulated by cable and later, satellite television coverage, particularly of
the annual Wave Rider Pro. With this exposure, surfing gradually changed from
being perceived by the public as being rooted in a "fringe", or even "counter" culture,
to a universally acclaimed sport of skill and pleasure. Operations expanded into

Canada, Mexico, Argentina, Chile and Brazil, and Wave Rider's following increased in South Africa and New Zealand.

As active participants in the sports of surfing and skiing, and as 'test-pilots' of their products, Paul Sinclair and Will Waugh placed faith in their own judgment of what comprised product quality, as well as in the judgments of their fellow surfers, skiers and snowboarders.

By the turn of the twenty-first century, Wave Rider had expanded its product range to include footwear, eyewear, backpacks, wallets, and fashion youth wear for both surf and snow. Boards could be customised by a customer's choice of "shaper", a skilled board craftsman, employed by Wave Rider at its head office and factory in Torquay, Victoria, and the next generation of "breakthrough" innovations had arrived. These included "Code STL" board-shorts which had their seams electro-welded rather than stitched; a web-site that informed as well as entertained, paying particular attention to using youth slang and colloquialisms to effect an ever expanding culture of fun and irreverence; creating products for the female market; and Wave Rider 's controversial move to outsource its clothing production in Asia.

Wave Rider's development may be seen as an evolution marked most of all by developments in the technology of wetsuits and watches. As these two products became market leaders, consumers placed their high expectations in their continued quality.

With the retirement of the founding partnership in 2003, some believed that the company was breaking with its past, and that it would continue to grow the brand through some form of product discontinuity. However, it appears to the researcher that Wave Rider is unlikely to deviate from those products and practices which have enabled it to play a leading role in the surfing world from the 'seventies onwards. Its culture has consistently been proud, strong, and irreverent towards 'establishment' values of the aged and sedate. Its stated vision is to be "the ultimate surfing company" in the world and under the new leadership of David Vaughn, the company appeared at the time of writing to be continuing towards that very goal.

4.2 First set of perspectives, covering 1969-2001: Products and practices that built the brand

In 1969, two young Australian surfers wanted to finance their lifestyle in leisure, and within months of proceeding to combine pleasure with business, they created a surfing cottage industry that was to become a multinational industry within ten years. They achieved this mainly by impressing the surfing fraternity with their passion for the sport, and the sport, the industry and the related technologies matured and expanded together.

Bells Beach near Torquay, one hour's drive south-west of Melbourne, was the place where the Wave Rider business began. This is the company's manufacturing and administrative headquarters. According to Paul Sinclair, they were just "young blokes stumbling around." (Sinclair, Aug 24, 2001). And even though the partnership began by manufacturing surfboards, including boards made from wood, Wave Rider's recognised core product today is wetsuits which insulate the serious year-round surfer from the frigid winter waters and biting wind. O'Neill, the American wetsuit producer, had exported some of its products to Australia in the 1960s, but supply could not meet demand. Wave Rider attempted to capture a large market share through three innovative strategies: first, to distribute their wetsuits to retailers on the strong reputation of the boards which they had been supplying in Australia for about two years; second, to design their wetsuits to the performance demands of the surfers (rather than divers); and finally, they exchanged international surfers' wetsuits at competitions at Bells Beach, with their home-crafted product to take back to their own countries. This was to create an international awareness that wetsuits with surfer-specific qualities were now available from a fledgling company in little-known Torquay, Australia. One of the earliest batches of commercially produced wetsuits ended up in Hawaii, the United States, and South Africa.

Today surfing is much more widely accepted as a wholesome recreation, indeed, it has become a professional sport featuring some of the world's most skilled and practised athletes. The devotees' passion for the sport was captured by Waugh, "The thing that most impresses about surfing is the pleasure of riding nature's energy, being swept along by the waves, the thrill. It's irresistible really." (Waugh quoted in Herbert, 1999).

That passion was translated into the vision that drove the company into the twenty-first century. That vision was, and remains, "to be the ultimate surfing company." Waugh explained, "When we say [we want to be] regarded as the ultimate surfing company in all that we do it is certainly in innovation and product. We are very much product and innovation driven, but marketing, services, business practices [should] be very good as well." (Waugh, Aug 24, 2001). Sinclair maintained that, "Just because you are the biggest doesn't mean you are the best." According to John Stensholt, writing in 2001, Wave Rider was estimated to be the second largest surfing equipment manufacturer in the world after Billabong, which had floated shares on the American market. (Stenholt, July 2001). Wave Rider is a private company, and appears to continue that way.

According to Sinclair, achieving that vision must start with, "[consumer] recognition and being proud of our products. If we are surfing or snowboarding, we want to make sure that the products suit the environment [....] if you have to waterproof a wetsuit, let's waterproof it properly for technique; snow-wet, [let's waterproof it properly] so we know it's waterproof freezable."(Sinclair, Aug 24, 2001). Sinclair's view of innovation was that, "it is really recognising what comfort the customer needs and making something that will provide that need. The recognition of the innovation comes in the commercialisation." (Sinclair, Aug 24, 2001).

With the commercialization of a number of innovations came company expansion each time to meet increasing demand for the new product. At the time of the launch of the dual density wetsuit in 1975, the company had to shift their operations from private homes in Torquay and Paul Sinclair's garage, to new premises. These were custom-designed to meet their manufacturing needs, such as space, room for storage, more and larger shaping bays for boards, tables for cutting neoprene and the need to accommodate staff of about forty in total. In the 'nineties, a parallel expansion occurred when the RD4 titanium neoprene and the Xpandx neoprene wetsuits were launched in 1994 and 1995 respectively. These led to further expansion of operations in Torquay, with similar further growth in USA, France, Japan, South Africa, Brazil and Argentina.

4.3 Building competitive advantage: Innovation, management and culture

Both Waugh and Sinclair were surfers themselves, and their community at Bells Beach was "just a bunch of mates". (Sinclair, Aug 24, 2001) So they understood the needs of surfers not only through their own direct experience, but also through the needs, ideas, and suggestions communicated within their tight-knit community. "Obviously wetsuits keep you warm, but beyond being warm we needed flexibility for the type of movements that the surfer wanted, particularly the paddling. We made the wetsuits to very clear specific surfer needs," (Waugh, Aug 24, 2001), while at the same time, developing an eye for "a touch of look and style of how surfers wanted it to look." (Waugh, Aug 24, 2001). He went on to place the wetsuit in the business domain: Wave Rider 's recognised core product is wetsuits and we began with surfboards and they are just as core [...] but surfboards are made by thousands of people all over the world, but wetsuits is the thing that really clicked for Wave Rider ." (Waugh, Aug 24, 2001). Both partners stated earnestly that, "The people who ran the company were – and still are – the test pilots." (Hynd, Jarratt and Carroll, 1994, p.8).

Being "the test pilots" as active participants in the sport, was part of their success formula in the achievement of competitive advantage. The other part was their insistence on asking the customers what they wanted – and listening to their replies. One of the earliest and most significant innovations in wetsuits was the combination of two thicknesses of neoprene rubber in different parts of the suit. This was the outcome of the learning inherent in their own experience as well as that in the experience of others. Sinclair remembered, "Really it is all very simple: you just go and ask the customers what they want. I remember we made a big song and dance [when] we were the first wetsuit company to produce what we called at the time, the 'dual density' wetsuit. [This meant that] instead of making a wet suit all [of] 3 mm thickness, we put 3 mm in the body to keep warm and 2 mm thickness in the arms, so they had more mobility. I can still recall some kid in a surf shop on the east coast of America saying, 'Why don't you put 2 mm arms on it?' And I thought 'That's not stupid, let's do it'." (Sinclair, Aug 24, 2001). For Sinclair and Waugh then, one of the most reliable sources of innovation to which their industry readily responded was "the customer, over and over and over." (Sinclair, Aug 24, 2001). Their management of the issues always related to the demands of the consumer. Tom Curren wrote that above all, the company wanted to "maintain the bottom line of great surfing and quality equipment." (Curren, 1994, p.2).

The brand was created through the intuition that enhancing surfing pleasure could be exploited. Sinclair's entrepreneurial astuteness shows in his comment that, "without the personal motivation and perseverance it [successful business] just doesn't happen. You might have an understanding of the market but unless you have a personal motivation and a commitment that perseveres to doing something about it nothing will be achieved." (Sinclair, Aug 24, 2001).

In his personal management style, he admitted that, "it is difficult to avoid having to step on a few toes." (Sinclair, Aug 24, 2001). His lack of awareness may also account for his regret that they failed to penetrate the North American market to the extent he wished: "In the last ten years [...] we have failed to do in America what we have done anywhere in Europe and Australia and other countries." He attributed that to lack of management skills on his part, and a lack of insight into candidates' competence for the senior management position. (Sinclair, Aug 24, 2001). Sinclair and Waugh maintained that all employees should be surfers because it assisted them to understand their customers and enhance rapport: "We employ people of certain ages, who are the customer, and talk to the customer, because if you are the customer you can talk to them a bit easier." (Sinclair, Aug 24, 2001). Communication to him was important and his view of how it should be conducted was clear: "Certainly we try to be blunt which is another word for 'don't beat around the bush', be honest and communicate openly. There should no hindrance to that here. For example, if a subordinate is having trouble with the boss, it's stated policy that that subordinate can leap frog the boss and go to the next one, or to me indeed. We have had one or two problems there where the boss doesn't like that, but I don't care." (Sinclair, Aug 24,

2001). But there is considerable caring about Wave Rider's involvement in its community, "In our companies we talk about our responsibility not just to our customers but to our crew here, furthermore to our local community and the environment." (Sinclair, Aug 24, 2001). The company in Torquay continues to support a number of sports clubs aside from surfing itself.

Will Waugh expressed his management philosophy in a different way. With neither he nor his business partner having had education beyond secondary level, the number one criterion common to the whole workforce was that they be surfers. Only a few females, wetsuit sewers, were exempted from this. From that base Waugh and Sinclair built much from very little. "Some of the component parts are successfully identifying and appointing, going through a successful search and appointment process of the right people getting the right raw material, the right tools to work with, the right procedures, the right systems, right resources, management systems and procedures. So over time, we've developed all sorts – any number of procedures and systems that cover wide ranges of the business, not just simple manufacturing stuff but things with respect to say market research and identifying customer need at all kinds of levels. We have procedures for them to follow, so it works, but you get it wrong. It's a trial and error thing – you get it wrong more often than not; you get somewhere near right but you want it to be better you want it to be best or excellent." (Waugh, Aug 24, 2001). Since Wave Rider employed surfers, it appeared that their more formal education began with the commencement of their employment with the company: "We've got any number of self taught hands on, we've got people here that are tradesmen and are running really big divisions and are really good at it. They might lack some of the educational areas and that might be their biggest weaknesses, but jeez, they learn those areas fast and they overcome it. But just hands-on real knowledge, of market knowledge, of the product, practical problem solving, making the right decisions. We've got a lot of those, and we keep growing those, and they keep being attracted." (Waugh, Aug 24, 2001). But he conceded that "We need some that are specifically educated in the mix [as well]." (Waugh, Aug 24, 2001) The tertiary educated employees they have contracted from time to time, have been marketers, to assist with particular campaigns. They have not employed management consultants at any time during the history of the company.

94

Sinclair and Waugh had a singular focus on the consumer. For them, the service that Wave Rider provided to the customer was borne out of the passion for the sport, and from the passion for maintaining the company reputation. Waugh explained that for 25 years, Wave Rider provided a faulty product return service. "People returned their [damaged] wetsuit and we wanted to minimise the time it would remain in the factory to no more than 24 hours, to keep the customer happy. So we would either repair that wetsuit, or, if we couldn't repair it we would make a decision to replace [it] and then send it back to the customer. We have had this quick turn-around policy for a very long time, and for the most part we've been able to meet that standard. When I say 24 hours, I mean [that] we give ourselves the flexibility for it to be 48 hours but certainly no more." (Waugh, Aug 24, 2001). But the practice also extended to replacing the occasional fatally flawed product, "[the] expectation would be to give the [customer] a new one so we gave them a new one. You just met all expectations." (Waugh, Aug 24, 2001). For years, one might say that they have been pre-empting consumer protection legislation. For Waugh and Sinclair, excellence in everything that was associated with the Wave Rider brand meant they "want to stay very true to [their] surfing roots." (Waugh, Aug 24, 2001).

Likewise they shared the complaints mail and telephone calls. Even though the company expanded rapidly through the 'seventies and 'eighties, both Sinclair and Waugh found time to deal with complaints. While this is now a function of their service centre, they still participate in the processes that turn customer complaints into compliments – although given their many present responsibilities they do so somewhat more irregularly now. They prided themselves on receiving e-mails and letters extolling the excellence of their products and services. This refers particularly to instances where these exceeded customer expectations such as the longevity of one of their wetsuits. However, Waugh continued, "Then you get the others that have our name on it, and people have reminded us that the service was less than their expectation and you know they're a good wake-up call, and you go 'woah' – we follow up on those." (Waugh, Aug 24, 2001).

While individual consumers received individual care and attention, Waugh and Sinclair were aware of the need to scan the horizon to maintain the company's advantage, that is, never to lose sight of the bigger picture. Waugh admitted to a "love affair" with the market as a whole. He described it as "a fascination and curiosity and some interaction and relationship with the market where primarily we're fulfilling those regular day to day market needs, consumer needs, but more than that, we're scanning to see those unfulfilled consumer needs and niches." (Waugh, Aug 24, 2001). Not that simple awareness of such needs and niches was enough. Sinclair added, "without the personal motivation and commitment and perseverance, it just doesn't happen. You might have an understanding of the market but unless you have a personal motivation and a commitment that perseveres, nothing will happen." (Sinclair, Aug 24, 2001) Therefore, in the late 'seventies, Wave Rider began producing what came to be called 'surf-wear', casual clothing, a product the company had not previously manufactured. And before the 'eighties ended, Wave Rider ventured into two other product lines, applying their innovative spirit to the design and production of tide-watches, followed by mountain-wear, which was protective outer wear for skiers and snowboarders. Its culture of youth, energy, and freedom was expanding into the market as a product of fun and energy, possibly a precursor to 'extreme sports' today.

The tide-watch was bought and developed in the early 'eighties. Its wetsuits were selling in continually greater quantities. Success bred success. The tide-watch was a companion product to the surfboard and the wetsuit, designed to be used both in and out of the surf. Waugh and Sinclair knew that the blue-print for the watch which they had purchased in Mississippi, USA, needed to be developed and manufactured with precision. With watches they were meticulous. The watches were manufactured to be genuinely waterproof in conditions which tested ordinary watches, even those which claimed to be waterproof. And they were light-weights, rather than the heavy-weights which had been manufactured for divers. But the most innovative feature of the Wave Rider watch was the tide-tracking function. Wave Rider wanted surfers to be able to catch the best waves as much as possible, and the quality of the surf was often dictated by the tide. A watch that could keep track of and indicate tidal movement was not something that Wave Rider invented, but one which it instantly recognised as having value to its niche market. This technology had been invented by a recreational fisherman in the USA, but he was unaware how to bring it on to the market, when Wave Rider entered into an agreement with him. It was a bought technology, no less so than Little Dragon's two purchases from Matsushita. Seizing the opportunity,

96

Wave Rider entered a market in which it had no experience, no manufacturing facilities and only a multitude of watch manufacturing competitors with robust reputations, particularly from Switzerland and Japan. Yet the waterproof standard and the tide-predicting functions were the two features that gave Wave Rider a competitive advantage in its niche market. As Waugh commented, "Nobody else had done that in watches before. There are all kinds of watch technologies from Europe, particularly emanating from Switzerland and Japan, but no one had made this combination of function and technology." (Waugh, Aug 24, 2001). In fact, today's watches come in one of three categories: "Ultimate", "Core" and "Classic". The first is waterproofed to 300 metres, the other two are waterproofed to 200 metres and 100 metres respectively. (*Wave Rider ATS Guide Manual*, 2001, pp 8-10). According to Waugh, the tide-watches are a "very big" seller, further enhancing the company's competitive advantage in its target market of youthful consumers.

Waugh and Sinclair stayed as true to their roots in the manufacture of watches as they did with their wetsuits. Their watch-manufacturer was 'by trade' a surfer, rather than an exacting watch specialist. "Our supplier is an Aussie guy, a surfer, [and] we have a very close relationship with him. He has a factory in Hong Kong. It's an environment [created] to Swiss manufacturing standards, which is the highest level: it's absolutely dust-free. It's temperature controlled, and humidified to a very strictly-maintained standard," explained Waugh, (Waugh, Aug 24, 2001). Wave Rider extended its appeal when it added a look to their watches that created demand in the youth fashion market. Waterproofing and tide predicting functions were of lesser interest to non-surfing teenage consumers, admitted Waugh, "but they bought them all the same." (Waugh, Aug 24, 2001).

At the same time as the tide-watch was positioning itself as a newcomer that wanted to be regarded as serious competition in an established market, Wave Rider began to expand its product base into mountain-wear, which was another already-established market dominated by other companies. However, Wave Rider succeeded because they perceived a specialist need that was not already being met. It occurred as Sinclair and Waugh enjoyed the exhilaration of skiing, which they had discovered in the early 'seventies, and they found it to closely parallel the sensation of surfing. In the same way in which they had met the needs of surfers, they understood and met the needs of skiers. Their aim was to make their mountain-wear functional, comfortable and reliable. During the decades of the 'eighties and 'nineties, Sinclair and Waugh spent much of each winter at Victoria's Mt Buller: Sinclair on the Ski Patrol, and Waugh becoming a ski instructor there. Once again, they were the test-pilots, albeit in a new environment, and it provided excellent opportunities for innovative product development in specialised mountain-wear design and performance. Functionality was as important in unforgiving mountains as it was in unforgiving oceans. Innovation in this context, for example, referred to the development of "molecular pores" in mountain-wear apparel, combining much needed warmth with equally needed ventilation for complete comfort. (Hynd, Jarratt and Carroll, 1994, p.52). The first range of Wave Rider of mountain-wear came onto the market in 1987.

The Wave Rider culture, the power-house of their plant in Torquay, is of particular interest when focusing on the company's success. First, it is enlightening to look back to the 'sixties. Like a number of innovators of their generation, Sinclair and Waugh changed the perceptions of the society in which they grew up, and this became part of the practice that publicized their brand. Generally speaking, surfing in the 'sixties and early 'seventies used to be regarded as a "fringe" even "counter" culture, often consisting of various forms of disaffection in the young. These were mainly youths who had a loathing for the politics of the times, particularly the Vietnam War, and they had contempt for the rigid authority exercised by parents, schools, factories, universities, the police and other governmental agencies. It was a time of youthful rebellion often manifested through the growth of long hair, experimentation with drugs and the participation in other anti-authoritarian activities, like public protests. Surfing tended to be identified with that anti-authoritarian image, and it existed in the category of 'fringe' or 'alternate' lifestyles. Sinclair recalled, "In those days [surfing] was new, and different and 'cool', and there was a bit of anti-establishment about it, which appealed to me. And once you catch your first green wave on a board, your life changes really, it's such a fantastic buzz. Once I'd done it, I just wanted to do it all the time. The power and the allure of the ocean are just so strong." (Sinclair quoted in Herbert, 1999). The initial logo which Waugh and Sinclair used on their products incorporated a lotus flower as a symbol of youth's quest for peace and freedom. This has since changed to a stylized wave crashing onto the shore.

The culture that developed inside the industry maintained its legacy of irreverence and fun, and it is one of the company's enduring strengths. It is redolent with its own jargon, as well as disdain for formalities and social niceties, as captured in the language they use. That language is a mixture of colloquialism and slang. An aspect of this is that people are given nick-names, like Will Waugh's is "Claw", and Paul Sinclair's is "Ding-Sing." In the *Wave Rider 25th Anniversary Catalogue* (1994) there are descriptions of some famous surfers, cultured by Wave Rider, including: "'Rabbit' Wayne Bartholomew, grommet – A flamboyant, guts-up original who taught the world how to surf Pipe backhand. […] Rab was one of the pioneers of pro-surfing, who probably suffered financially by doing too much too soon. But the buzz was always more important than the bucks to Bugs. He was a man after Wave Rider's heart." (Hynd, Jarratt, and Carroll, 1994, p.22). Not surprisingly, the Rider's employees' "uniform" is a "T-shirt and shorts", and staff in Torquay "still chase waves during work hours, and work harder when [they] can't surf." (Herbert, Jan 20, 04). Paul Sinclair commented, "Money is not why we did it […] it's not why we do it today, and it's not why we want it done in the future either, because if it's done for money and profit, it won't be Wave Rider ." (Sinclair, 24 Aug 2001).

In keeping with their culture of close communication with their consumers, Wave Rider's website has comments from the champion surfers whom they have sponsored in the past. Their comments relate to wave conditions at various beaches, as well as the shapes of boards to take advantage of those conditions. Mick Fanning, Wave Rider's current champion, explained his working relationship with his "shaper", "I speak to Darren pretty much everyday when I'm at home, because I've always got a bunch of new boards to try and give feedback on. I can ride just a few waves if I like a board and whether I want to keep using it. I've been riding Darren's boards for so long now, we only need to talk about minor tweaks when it comes to looking at board measurements." (www.waverider.com/content/anmviewer).

4.4 Continuing the industrial evolution: the imperative of change

Innovation continued as one of the principal drivers for Wave Rider as it continued to develop and expand. By 1990, Wave Rider had evolved considerably, and had found ready markets overseas where their products were well received. By that year, they had developed licensees in Japan, South Africa, Brazil and Argentina, and equal-partner franchises in the USA and France.

Competition acted as a powerful catalyst for industrial evolution a number of times in the 'eighties and 'nineties. In the following comments focusing on an innovation which Wave Rider's competition brought onto the market in 1995, Waugh imparted his frustration about the opposition's innovation beating Wave Rider in its own core business. He explained, "A few years ago, one of our competitors [O'Neill] came out with a wetsuit innovation which was perceived to be quite significant. I guess in the long haul, maybe it wasn't that significant, but at that point in time, it was perceived to be an innovation, a strong innovation. New, different, better, by way of performance and function." Next he emphasised, "And that's the thing that Wave Rider prides itself in doing. So these other people developed the product, marketed and distributed [it] with this innovation." (Waugh, Aug 24, 2001) This innovation was a wetsuit without a zipper.

Waugh's frustration was not aimed at Billabong as much as his own company's failure to have arrived there first. He recalled that Billabong, "made this wetsuit without the zip. They did the whole package so that's not good for us because it should be us making that innovation. So it's good for their company and their brand and they've got a score on the board as an innovator. [But] that was a failure on our behalf because we had the materials! [...] Certain technologies had improved, we even had made some wetsuits along this line, just some specialised wetsuits for other purposes, but we didn't recognise the need, or recognise the possibility, and put the thing together." (Waugh, Aug 24, 2001). For someone with such a deep understanding of what it meant to think outside the square, Waugh had been caught out by complacently thinking inside the square. However, "innovation" did not just cover Billabong's newly designed product; equally, it covered Wave Rider's response to that challenge.

The response was swift. "We were able to respond and put a similar but better wetsuit into the market within a month, within a matter of weeks. [We] advertised the wetsuit and blunted the impact of our competitor. As it turned out, our wetsuit was a little better than the other one [...] In the medium term we were recognised as being a co-inventor, and in the longer term, as it turned out, the new generation of back zip wetsuits turned out be better in the long run. So once again, now two or three years down the track, we had completely better wetsuits, but [O'Neill's innovation] had quite an impact at the time, and it should have been ours." (Waugh, Aug 24, 2001). Despite Wave Rider eventually improving on O'Neill's innovation, Waugh still passed harsh judgement, "We were slack." (Waugh, Aug 24, 2001). Sinclair recalled that when the Torquay plant was forced to make this sort of instantaneous change in response to a competitor's innovation, it was "like turning around a bloody aircraft carrier." (Sinclair, Aug 24, 2001). It necessitated implementing new design and machine specifications after considerable consultation and coordination between executive and operations management, design staff and employees, all conducted in the atmosphere of an international crisis.

Not to be caught off-guard again, Sinclair and Waugh were adamant that they, "sharpened up [their] whole act," and they "have taken back the leadership position with respect to innovation." They have just "driven harder." (Waugh, Aug 24, 2001). As a result, Wave Rider launched the Ultimo Elasto Wetsuit in 1998, and in 2001, the company launched the Elastomax with colour mesh, leaving O'Neill and other surfing wetsuit makers without products of comparable qualities and consumer appeal.

However, whilst the company was diversifying into related accessories such as clothing, Sinclair made it clear that he was wary of change for the sake of change; all the expansionary moves made by Wave Rider were very carefully calculated to produce the intended effect. And Waugh cited an instance where financial difficulties occurred due to over-borrowing because they lacked effective strategy: "The banks that've been your mates for years and giving you all the money you want, and saying take all the money you want [...] all of a sudden they're not so friendly [...] Things start falling through the cracks cause you haven't built the procedures and systems to handle that level of growth, and [you] don't cope so well." (Waugh, Aug 24, 2001).

It appeared that both Sinclair and Waugh were more comfortable discussing the fundamental philosophies of the company than its financial fundamentals. To them, the challenge between man and nature was, and continues to be, central to the passion shared between Wave Rider's founders, the oceans and the mountains – and therefore the business. With the company having helped in the transformation of the public perception about the sport there were consequences. One effective and innovative way in which they legitimised surfing was by sponsoring surfing competitions so they became keenly contested annual events. These competitions over the years attracted increasingly large numbers of young devotees, and they drew media attention to exotic beach locations, including Sunset Beach in Hawaii.

Sponsorship of competitions was initially a means to obtain exposure in the market for their products. To understand their commitment to sponsorship, it is necessary to go back to the time when they commenced this. In 1970, the World Amateur Surfing Titles were staged in Torquay, which put the company on the international map. Three years later, Wave Rider sponsored the first Australian professional surfing contest at Bells Beach. Michael Peterson claimed the $1,000 first prize. In 1974, Coca Cola took its queue from Wave Rider and sponsored the first Surfabout Competition in Sydney. Between 1973 and 1980, there were many more competitions staged in Australia, and Wave Rider gained more international recognition as surfers entered them and then returned home to their own country with Wave Rider wetsuits, especially to the USA by way of Hawaii, where surfing had originated and had traditionally been a strong sport. By 1980, the world professional surfing circuit grew to ten events in five countries with more than $US200,000 in prize money, which was almost three times the amount offered in 1976. In 1981, Wave Rider broadened its horizons by sponsoring the first Wave Sailing Classic at Point Danger, assisting the spread of the brand in Europe where board-sailing was stronger than surfing. Six years later, one of Wave Rider's sponsored surfers, 16-year-old Nicky Wood, became the youngest winner of a pro-World Championship in front of a home crowd of 20,000 spectators at Bells Beach. Then one year later, in 1987, the first Wave Rider Pro took place at Hossegor in France, as part of the ASP World Tour. This event was highly successful and was voted by the world's elite pro surfers as the "contest of the year". Like the Wave Rider Pro at Bells, Hossegor has run every year since its inception, and it is now a permanent fixture on the international circuit. This further cemented Wave Rider's worldwide reputation.

In recent years, Wave Rider again broadened its sponsorship and now encompasses the passion of mountaineers. In 1997, Wave Rider took over the sponsorship of the Heli Challenge in Wanaka, in New Zealand. This was a new loose form of competition involving the world's best free-skiers and snowboarders. Although this was a departure from Wave Rider's usual maritime sponsorships, it was consistent with ultimate sporting challenges, and the media provided more global exposure for the company. To raise its profile still further in the USA, Wave Rider took over the sponsorship of the World Cup of Surfing at Hawaii's Sunset Beach in 1997. A year later the Pro-Surfing's International Circuit comprised 21 events in eight countries, offering a total of $US 1.89 million in prize money. Most recently, in 1999, the company branched into organising two more international events: the Wave Rider Mountain Challenge in France, and the Wave Rider Cup at Reunion Island's St Lieu.

4.5 Future aims

At the same time as they increased their competition sponsorships, Waugh and Sinclair commenced, "The Search", their long-running marketing campaign. This spin renewed the company's focus on manufacturing and delivering the best possible products and services in the future.

> "If you're going to roam around the world getting into travel and adventure, if you're going to be right out on the edge, you need products that are functional. Stuff that really works for a surfer, or works for a snowboarder, or works for a free-skier, or works for a wind-surfer. That's part of our quest – the Search for the best materials and technology to make products that really work when you're on the edge. The Search is the glue that connects people to Wave Rider and it provides Wave Rider with its inspiration and future direction." (Waugh quoted in Herbert, 1999).

In attempting to meet demand from surfers around the world, the company grew from two founders in 1969, to three hundred employees in Australia, and a further 1,000 worldwide by 2001. Will Waugh commented, "Wave Rider has always been driven by certain fundamental values, among those are making functional, quality and innovative products for surfers and people of like mind."

Waugh saw his own and Sinclair's achievement as a legacy to pass on to the next generation. The legacy was their experiential learning: "It's the stewardship on the principles and values, the brand values, stewardship on a lot of the knowledge [that] we have of the market and the principles on how our industry works." (Waugh, Aug 24, 2001).

During the last three and a half decades, Will Waugh and Paul Sinclair sourced their "functional, quality and innovative products" from a passion for their sport and lifestyle. Not from schematic visions or fully articulated business plans - least of all when they were young. Plans were to follow, and indeed they played key roles in the development of Wave Rider as a business as the years went by. But for Waugh and Sinclair, innovation began most of all with their passion for a sport.

Chapter 5

Wave Rider the Surfing Company

Second in-depth perspectives,
covering mainly 2001-2004

5.1 Strategic change and innovation

"If we don't innovate, somebody else will. We want to retain the perception in the market that we are innovative and functional." (Graham Herbert, 20 Jan. 2004).

A significant change came with the retirement of the two founder-owners of the company in 2003, paving the way for new management after more than thirty years of consolidation under one business partnership. Paul Sinclair and Will Waugh confined themselves from that point to company decision-making at board level. They were still the two majority shareholders. This therefore still effectively gave them directive, if not, operational power. At the time of writing, Sinclair still resided in Victoria, but Waugh had retired to the Gold Coast.

The CEO for the company was now David Vaughn, and second tier management was represented by two other senior executives who were appointed to head operations in Europe and the USA. Australia/New Zealand was managed by a general manager who reported directly to David Vaughn. Under the level of general manager was a tier of senior managers who were responsible for the development of a particular product, and in turn reporting to them was another tier consisting of marketing and sales staff, as well as team sponsorship in connection with national and international surfing competitions. In January 2004, Wave Rider employed approximately 170 staff in Australia, with a world-wide work-force of about 1400 staff, as products were manufactured in Victoria as well as being outsourced to Vietnam and PR China. Graham Herbert, Wave Rider's publicity manager, considered that the leadership The change was "a break with tradition, because up until the creation of the board, and overseas CEOs, Doug and Brian effectively ran the company, so this structure is a break, but it is also a recognition that needed to occur for the business to continue to grow." (Herbert, Jan 20, 2004).

Growth at the time of writing was effected through product diversification that was set in progress during the last few years of the original management, and included footwear, eyewear, videos and DVDs of surf action, and ever-enlarging ranges of existing products such as surfboards, watches, surf-wear, wetsuits, and carry bags as well as wallets. The range of mountain-wear was also expanded, and included outer clothing made of 'sport-wool' that allowed perspiration to escape through miniscule pores.

However, with the recognition that continued growth was desirable for the future of the company, there was an equal recognition that some things would be better left unchanged because they underpinned the fundamental philosophies and operations of the company. While Paul Robinson of *The Age*, May 25, 2002, wrote that Wave Rider was "considering a float on the stock exchange," as a likely future change resulting from Sinclair and Waugh's retirement, this was speculative on his part, and the Wave Rider board did not entertain the notion seriously because its members did not believe it to be in the interests of the company, nor of its customers. The main reason was that having public company status frequently meant having to compromise on the quality of product and service, in order to focus on delivering maximum returns to shareholders, as did Wave Rider's competitors, Quiksilver and Billabong. Compromise was never Wave Rider's driving philosophy, as Herbert commented, "Wave Rider continues to drive its employees to design and make the best products and deliver them on time. We plough much of the profit back into the business, so we're not driven to increase profits in the same way." (Herbert, Jan 20, 2004). It was therefore a strategic decision to remain a private company to secure more sustainability in the market of the future, meeting the market's well-recognised demand for quality.

106

Wave Rider was aware of companies like the one that produced the "Bodyglove" brand, which imitated Wave Rider's original designs without any design input of their own. The imitators' means was then to create the cheapest possible price range, and own, using large outlets such as department stores to stock their products, rather than selling them through dedicated stores like Wave Rider, which focused on providing personalised service. Herbert believed that Wave Rider's market knew quality, and demanded it in every product they purchased. Herbert believed that "The emergence of imitators is an inevitable fact, people will always take market share off established companies. [But] The authenticity and integrity of a brand like Wave Rider is a significant factor to take into consideration in the design and manufacture of our next product." (Herbert, Jan 20, 2004). He admitted that some of his customers were being wooed away by the advertising and appealing prices of another company, but he believed that when they bought a competitor's product, they "find that it is not of the same quality, and they come back to us." (Herbert, Jan 20, 2004). An aspect of the quality of Wave Rider's wetsuits was their ten-year warranty, "if they send it to us within ten years we will repair [stitching and other faults] at no charge." (Herbert, Jan 20, 2004).

In recent years, Wave Rider made a number of innovations although arguably none ranked with the success of their "breakthrough" dual-density wetsuits of the 'seventies. The most recent innovation is the board-short called 'Code STL', and this has now become a core-product. The International CEO was given the responsibility for designing a new board-short so that it would become a market-leading innovation. Herbert judged, "We believe he's done that. There's two years' work gone into that. He had to identify the technology and implement that technology." (Herbert, Jan 20, 2004). The company claimed that the board-shorts were, "the best fitting because mould assembly allows the fabrics to be contoured to fit and move with the body [...] they are the most comfortable because of the absence of stitches [which] means discomfort from sewn seams is now an irritation of the past." (www.waverider.com retrieved Aug 17, 2004). The seams were electro-welded and they were guaranteed for the lifetime of the product. "They've done very well for us in their first season. This is an innovation." (Herbert, Jan 20, 2004).

The second recent innovation is the way in which the company has expanded contact with its target market through the use of a website – designed to be a teenage favourite. It proved to be an efficient way of showing their product range to a target market that is so large, and is sited in very culturally-diverse international locations. The site is coordinated and maintained by one full-time employee, with one person who is a specialist in inserting photos and video clips, and a number of employees who write the script. In matrix fashion, the designer of the site is also a designer of T-shirt graphics for the company. The web-site has a magazine-style format, is regularly updated, and reflects Wave Rider's culture of irreverence and fun, particularly with regard to its predominantly-teenaged readership. Its language and its graphics, many of which are dynamic and interactive, are also good examples of the irreverence associated with its brand. For example, this item on the menu page, "If you have to pick your nose, or scratch an annoying itch, which finger would you use?" (www.waverider.com retrieved Dec 14, 2003). It gives the reader five choices to click on with the mouse. This registers as a vote, the result of which will then be revealed at a later date. In a similar vein, one of the models in the shoe range for males is called "bastard." (www.waverider.com retrieved Aug 17, 2004). According to Herbert, the company's need to inform, as well as to entertain its market in these ways, "has been identified for us by a number of brand experts." (Herbert, Jan 20, 2004).

Newsprint, specialist magazines (of which there are about two dozen world-wide), and point-of-purchase sale-material have also been successful. In the area of major surfing events, Wave Rider has enjoyed coverage around the world in syndicated news segments, particularly the Wave Rider Pro and Bells Beach, year after year.

Not all publicity has been good for them, however. Responsiveness to bad publicity may not be in the same league as it was in the Johnson & Johnson Tylenol scare, but it was an example of best practice in the interests of consumers, nonetheless. This example was that Wave Rider's irreverence and saturation in youth culture was considered to have gone too far when a T-shirt graphic became an object of parental ire. It showed, in a stylized way, a couple engaged in a sexual act, and when a group of parents objected, Wave Rider withdrew this clothing item from all outlets throughout the world. Herbert maintained that the company held "an iconic place", particularly in Australia, and so the company wanted to protect its reputation "jealously." (Herbert, Jan 20, 2004).

The company also wanted to grow that reputation with female surfers. More typically perceived as a male sport, the company has been attempting to expand that perception with many products catering specifically for girls and women, such as wetsuits, footwear, sunglasses, bags, wallets, backpacks, surf and beachwear. (www.waverider.com retrieved Dec 14, 2003). In 2003, Wave Rider introduced more women to the sport. It held an event called 'Wave Rider Girls Go Surfing Day'. It was a coaching clinic specifically organized for women under the instruction of coaches accredited by Wave Rider. In the northern hemisphere winter 2004, the Wave Rider-sponsored surf team comprised thirteen members of whom three were women: Jacqueline Silva, Julia Christian and Elise Garrique, (www.waverider.com retrieved Aug 17, 2004).

Further innovations occurred in the two products in which the Wave Rider brand was most famous: the wetsuit and the tide-watch. This was the areas where customers' expectations were the highest, according to Graham Herbert, (Jan 20, 2004). The latest product in the wetsuit range was the "SlickSkin", still made of dual density, but it had a "SlickSkin coating on the neoprene. This helped to shed water off the suit very quickly, even though it was not water repellent. This ensured that the neoprene did not hold the water for as long as more conventional models, and the wind did not chill the surfer to the same extent, making it a warmer suit. (www.waverider.com retrieved Aug 17, 2004).

Herbert stated, "We [Wave Rider staff] are directed to seek out innovative new materials and technology to keep to the forefront. We don't want gimmicks, we want things that are highly functional." (Herbert, Jan 20, 2004). This was clear in the watch line, where a significant innovation was the "SSS Cruise." This watch took the mechanical energy created by movement and turned it into electrical energy, storing it in the capacitor. This eliminated the need for springs and batteries. A fully charged capacitor could drive the watch for about six months. (www.waverider.com, retrieved Aug 17, 2004). The 'wave energy system' technology possessed considerable sophistication: "Every movement of the oscillating rotor in the SSS Cruise is turned into a magnetic charge. The rotors in kinetic watches can spin 100,000 rpms faster than a Formula 1 race car [engine]." (www.waverider.com retrieved Aug 17, 2004). Even a less sophisticated Wave Rider watch than the SSS Cruise had more features than conventional watches by other manufacturers. A good example was the 'Atlantis ATS Super Tidemaster', which had eight functions: normal mode (actual time); tide; tide range; dual time (time in second location); timer; EOL, (end of battery life); alarm; and a stop-watch. (www.waverider.com, retrieved Aug 17, 2004). As Herbert maintained, "Our competitors would agree that our wetsuits and watches are market leaders because of their quality. And we now want to generate a similar perception about our board-shorts, backpacks, sunglasses, and so on." (Herbert, Jan 20, 2004).

The last Wave Rider innovation was dedicated to company staff who wanted to expand their education. Education used to mean that staff initially were moved around the organization to learn of its various functions and inter-relationships. But that proved insufficient for the kind of professionalism the company required for the future. Since 2002, therefore, the management has taken notice of employees' ambitions for the future, and met those by putting staff into courses to enhance their professionalism.

It can be seen therefore, that Wave Rider continued to evolve early into the twenty-first century, but from a strategic point of view, slow and steady outmatched fast and furious. This was a strategic decision made by the board, confident that sustainability could be better obtained through persistence with the philosophies and practice with which it had originally grown up since 1969.

5.2 Globalization: Exploiting opportunities in new environments

Globalization occurred early in the '80s for Wave Rider, at a time when the concept was not yet industrial common currency around the globe. In 1983, Sinclair and Waugh gained a French ally named Francois Perot who became Wave Rider Europe's manager and the third shareholder in the company. In 1985, Wave Rider USA under the management of Leigh Tonay, saw a large growth spurt, and the company joined the USA Surf Industry League to further cement its place in the American market.

Rapid expansion on the back of significant advances in board, wetsuit and watch technologies meant that successful operations also began in Japan, South Africa, Brazil and Argentina. That meant the company was led by four primary directors by 1995, with principal direction emanating from Sinclair and Waugh as majority shareholders, based in Victoria, Australia.

Waugh recalled that exploiting opportunities outside of Australia was important to grow the brand, as surfing was still a minority sport. In order to achieve a reputation for their company, he and Sinclair decided only a decade into their careers to expand overseas to reach more of their fraternity, scattered in far-flung beach locations. The south of France was their first overseas foray due to customer demand being strong from the very first introduction of Wave Rider products there. Waugh stated, "Again it's customer stuff [...] we had a consumer pool from them, consumers want[ing] our products, and in the first place they were surfers." (Waugh, Aug 24, 2001). But he was quick to point out that, "it's a different world, and there is challenge, and it's exciting [because] we're very strong brand in France, [and subsequently], in Spain and Portugal, and there's a lot of surfing there now." (Waugh, Aug 24, 2001). He had realized early in this initial exploit that the French were different as a culture: "the French appear to have different ways of doing things and appear to have different tastes [...] When it gets to business procedures, nine times out of ten, if you've got it right in one country, it doesn't have to be Australia." (Waugh, Aug 24, 2001). He made the point that management and communication processes, and manufacturing procedures and systems had to be shared between countries so that no one had to "re-invent the wheel every time." (Waugh, Aug 24, 2001). He attributed part of Wave Rider's success not only to transplanting the technology from its home base in Torquay, but on sharing knowledge: "Someone's come before, and they know how to achieve this, and I follow the process and to some degree it still allows them some scope for creativity and innovation." (Waugh, Aug 24, 2001).

This "scope" enabled Francois Perot a measure of creative licence to cater to local tastes. Significantly, French taste derived from a Romance culture of which Spain and Portugal also partook. This franchise gave Wave Rider an excellent base from which to manufacture most of its products, apart from its tide-watches, for three Mediterranean countries with ideal surfers' coastlines, according to each their own preferences for colour and style – something that would have been difficult to achieve from Torquay. Waugh was clearly delighted with the sales of Wave Rider products in the Mediterranean, without being fully able to articulate why there appeared to be a natural affinity between an essentially Australian product and a 'Romance' consumer. "If you can understand their behaviour, you can learn how you have that romance with them. You know, what steps or what buttons you need to press to resonate, to get a response from them, to have your brand resonate with them." (Waugh, Aug 24, 2001). For that reason, it made good business sense to have appointed a Frenchman to the job, and then to promote him to the position of co-director – his cultural input alone was an invaluable asset to the company.

The North American market was a different story. Wave Rider had been selling there since the early '80s but without that "resonating" relationship. "Certainly, USA, Canada, Mexico, but we've been more successful in Europe." (Waugh, Aug 24, 2001). He explained that the American market was very "fundamental" because Wave Rider's main products in the USA "are our wetsuits and watches – our real technical solid core." (Waugh, Aug 24, 2001). He distinguished between the American and European markets: "In Europe, they take all the peripheral products with the Wave Rider brand [...] a wider range of products. It seems to have more impact, more appeal impact. In America, it's hard for us to grow strongly outside of the core market. [...] We don't have anywhere near the penetration or the success with the consumers in the USA as what we do in Australia, New Zealand, and what we do even in France, Spain and Portugal." (Waugh, Aug 24, 2001).

However, by 2002, aspects of globalization had become a contentious issue. Paul Robinson, Workplace Editor of *The Age*, wrote on May 25 2002, in an article entitled "Wave Rider's winning wave may extend to Asia", that the company was "pondering an offshore move for its clothing business [...] looking to China or Vietnam as their T-shirt and board short base." (Robinson, May 24 2002, p.16). Anger was directed at this prospect because the Textile, Clothing and Footwear Union estimated that 30 Wave Rider employees could lose their jobs, which would be a significant loss in a community as small as Torquay. Robinson reported that the anger was driven by those individuals who felt that this was the community that took "a couple of surfies from rags to riches", and they should honour their obligation to their employees. For good

112

measure, Robinson reiterated that *BRW*'s richlist estimation of Sinclair and Waugh's fortunes stood at $A241 Million. (Quoted in Robinson, May 24 2002, p.16).

Herbert expressed the situation at the beginning of 2004, when outsourcing for clothing had become a reality: "These are the choices we have to make. We investigate these companies thoroughly. We demand a trial to make sure that they can manufacture what we want. Company reps go to Asia to check on quality and maintain it. They must be good if they are to keep the contract. Wave Rider would not have been able to keep going if it had not outsourced to Asia in order to save on wages. Our major competitors have also gone that way. Wherever possible, we've attempted to obtain exclusive arrangements, because it maintains our standards and builds stronger relationships. This way they're not distracted by the demands of others." (Herbert, Jan 20, 2004).

5.3 Sustainability: Surviving and thriving

The company continued to thrive. World Search Co. Ltd. took over the licensed manufacture and distribution of Wave Rider products in Japan and Taiwan. They opened their first Wave Rider store in Tokyo's top of the range youth fashion district, Harajyuku, in August, 2004. "Both companies are predicting strong but stable growth, and a mutually beneficial working relationship." (www.waverider.com retrieved August 17, 2004). This was just one more example of Wave Rider's continued globalization, and its ability to contract viable joint ventures.

Clearly, Wave Rider survived beyond the retirement of its founders. They left a legacy that consisted of almost four decades' learning: specialist knowledge in their field, best practice, discerning markets and a strong culture. These were passed on to those who followed in their wake. By Waugh and Sinclair's retirement, their product range was greater than it had ever been, consisting of products that encapsulate the life-style with an end to achieve 'The Search'.

One of the driving forces in the company which is most likely to sustain its essential character is its culture. Most employees were, and continue to be, active participants in surf or snow sports. Herbert added, "We don't have a uniform, apart from shorts and T-shirts; there's a casual air, and that goes back to our brand-value of irreverence, or not taking ourselves too seriously. This is the way it's been since the late 'sixties." (Herbert, Jan 20, 2004). Its present level of sustainability would indicate that this may be the way it will likely endure for some time yet.

Chapter 6

Wave Rider the Surfing Company

Preliminary Analysis

6.1 Congruence, ambidexterity and disruption

In *The Innovator's Dilemma*, Clayton Christensen identified two categories of innovation that he called "sustaining" or "disruptive'. (Christensen, 2003, p.258). He categorized incremental and discontinuous innovation, much as they were defined in Tushman and O'Reilly (1997). A disruptive innovation described a product that was less than perfect, yet inexpensive and convenient, that might be purchased by consumers at the low-end of the market who were presently nonconsumers, or who were consumers looking for a better product than they could presently purchase with limited funds. (Christensen and Raynor, 2003, pp.38-39). According to this definition, Wave Rider the Surfing Company innovated two disruptive products. The rest of their innovations comprised mainly quality improvements, and therefore would be better referred to as sustaining innovations. The two disruptions were the dual-density wetsuit and the tide-watch. This particular type of wetsuit entered at the low-end of the market because it was convenient as it allowed manoeuvrability for the rider, and it was a low-cost investment for them, particularly in comparison to the suits available on the market made by O'Neill of the USA, which were heavy and were targeted at deep-sea divers.

The second disruptive product was the tide-watch. Like Seiko, (Christensen and Raynor, 2003, p.63), it disrupted the established order of watches because it was also aimed at the low-end of the market and specifically targeted the less-well funded market of surfing youth. Because it allowed the wearer to predict high tides in his or her vicinity, it brought a truly innovative dimension to a time-piece. Because of its

115

quality precision and water-proof features, it appealed to its market, and it eventually made its way to the higher end of the market when it incorporated still more features, but they tended to be of a sustaining kind, such as the incorporation of a stop-watch mechanism. Waugh commented that the watch had been a "very big seller for the company." (Waugh, Aug 24 2001). In appealing to a market of "new or less demanding customers", (Christensen and Raynor, 2003, p.34) it opened up new opportunities for growth. Wave Rider would only sell the watches through their dedicated stores, and wearers were advised that the company would only guarantee their waterproof quality, provided that the batteries were changed by the company to re-seal the watch-case. The guarantee would lapse if the batteries were changed by a regular jeweller. This had the added benefit of increasing the foot-traffic through Wave Rider stores.

In *Winning through innovation* (1997), Tushman and O'Reilly observed with concern that even the best managed companies could fail for various reasons: they "missed strategic opportunities or [there might be] a failure to implement strategic change." (Tushman and O'Reilly, 1997, p.216). Indeed they could become trapped by their own success, (Tushman and O'Reilly, 1997, p.215). Their solution to the dilemma of obsolescence, and ultimately failure, was the creation of ambidextrous organizations. This would entail "taking advantage of technology cycles and driving streams of innovation," to sustain market leadership (Tushman and O'Reilly, 1997, p.215). In the thirty-five year history of Wave Rider, did the company achieve congruence and ambidexterity to maintain sustainable competitive advantage? And if Sears, Philips of Holland, Oticon and IBM suffered one or more periods of difficulty, was Wave Rider subject to the same forces, and did it suffer the same way? If it did not, why not? The model which Tushman and O'Reilly implemented to diagnose a number of companies may be equally applied to Wave Rider, although it is a smaller company than those mentioned, and the other difference was that it was privately owned.

The fundamental building blocks of congruence, and therefore business success, are tasks and work flows, human resources, organizational structure and systems, and organizational culture. Waugh showed insight into business success in a very similar way, although he expressed it differently: "Some of the component parts are successfully identifying and appointing, going through a successful search and

116

appointment process of the right people, getting the right raw material and then giving the right raw material the right tools to work with, the right procedures, the right systems, right resources, management systems and procedures so over time we've developed all sorts." (Waugh, Aug 24, 2001). All of these were sufficiently robust for their founders to implement them in all their international plants and outlets with some minor regional variations, to create one of the world's best known sporting brands. Not all of these building blocks above can be itemised, but inferences of congruence may be made using a number of related factors. One significant factor in determining Wave Rider's success was the growth of the company. In 1969, when it was incorporated as a company, it employed Paul Sinclair and Will Waugh who were based only in the country of their origin; by their retirement in 2003, the company was employing approximately 1,400 staff in almost a dozen countries, including 170 employees in Australia. There was only one period in which growth declined and that was in the late-eighties. It was a short interval when they "lost [their] way," (Sinclair, Aug 24, 2001). He was referring, amongst other things, to a period when they injected too much capital into research, without having the expertise necessary to obtain beneficial results. This included trying to fly a small-engined plane through a hurricane to simulate the force exerted on a human being caught in a broken barrel wave. They sold the plane when it was clear that they could not obtain useful measurements from the experience – all the more so since they had risked their lives in the process. Hurricanes, like broken barrel waves, were generally unforgiving. Whilst the company was a privately owned one, profitability in precise dollar terms would not be discussed by Herbert, Sinclair or Waugh, in spite of being requested to answer questions relating to company finances. However, Waugh faxed a page with financial data taken from *BRW* magazine to the researcher about a month after the interview, which is discussed below. It gave indications of Wave Rider's financial health in comparison to its competitors.

One other revealing indicator of company health then, lay in the way in which its track record of innovation may be correlated to its expansion, which is in turn indicative of its productivity and profitability. In 1969, Wave Rider barely met high demand for short-boards, and production of boards took place in Paul Sinclair's garage. One year later, the company was receiving up to 100 wetsuit orders per week, and production of wetsuits was spread through a number of private homes in Torquay for cutting and sewing. Following the launch of the highly successful dual density wetsuit in 1975, Wave Rider moved to new premises in Torquay. Between 1980 and 1984, the Aggrolite and Super Xpandex Neoprene with super-flexible K-tron kneepads were launched, which correlated with expansion into the USA and France. By the time the Automatic Tide System (ATS) Tidemaster watch was launched, Wave Rider enjoyed growth in the USA, and was commencing operations in Japan, South Africa, Brazil, Argentina and New Zealand. An important part of this success was the 'winter' element: by 1986, Sinclair and Waugh had discovered the exhilaration of snow and ice, and began manufacturing mountain wear for skiers and snowboarders, and this led to increased profits in those countries where consumers could spend winters in the snow and summers in the surf. By 1996, the scale of Torquay operations required another expansion, and the custom-built manufacturing plant and adjoining office complex were constructed, serving as the company's headquarters till the present time.

Further to consistent expansion, both the founders as well as the company itself have come under financial scrutiny to ascertain the worth of each, inspite of the owners' reticence in this regard. In "Wave Rider's winning wave may extend to Asia" in *The Age*, May 25, 2002, Paul Robinson wrote that in the *BRW* Rich List, "its board-riding entrepreneurs amass[ed] a $241 Million fortune." This is in Australian dollars. In *BRW*, July 6, 2001, John Stensholt in an article entitled, "Strategy: Sportswear goes sky-high", reported that the estimated Wave Rider sales for the year to June 30, 2000, totalled approximately $300 Million, and that the estimated market capitalization of the company amounted to $800 Million. In comparison, Stensholt valued Billabong's sales to June 30, 2000, at $225 Million, Globe's at $131 Million, Mambo's at $55 Million and the only major surf company to exceed Wave Rider's sales was Quiksilver, which had sales of $515 Million. In terms of capitalization value, only Billabong's exceeded Wave Rider's, with a value of $1,070 Million. Globe's value stood at $538 Million; Mambo's stood at $125 Million and Quiksilver's stood at $578 Million. In these instances, the dollar refers to US dollars. Only Wave Rider was still a private company – all the others had been floated on the American stock market. Billabong started shortly after Wave Rider did in 1969; the operators were "mates" who resided in the flat above Paul Sinclair and Will Waugh. (Stensholt, July 6, 2001).

Stensholt's article focused specifically on casual wear, in which Wave Rider sales clearly competed well. He referred to casual wear, as "street-wear", and explained why this form of clothing sold so well. "Sue Dixon, [....] from fashion-forecast company Purple Bull, says the sector offers a combination of high profit margins (averaging 17-20 %) compared to about 6% in the overall retail sector, rapid sales growth and a product that would unlikely to go out of fashion soon. Young kids want to wear the brands and so do people over 30. People grow up with a brand and stick with it." (Stensholt, July 6, 2001, p.1). Therefore, Wave Rider's expansion into casual wear was a well-calculated move in the early 'eighties, and added to their overall profitability and capitalization value.

Sinclair and Waugh calculated the value of the tide-watch to the company as astutely as their casual wear. By the time the first watches came onto the market, Wave Rider was no longer a nascent brand in youth culture. The right "look" that Sinclair first ascribed to the wetsuit was also later ascribed to the watch, and whether consumers bought them for tide measurements or not, Waugh commented, "They ['re buying] them just the same," (Waugh, Aug 24, 2001), demonstrating the product's marketability.

These factors indicate that Wave Rider was most likely a congruous organization in the way it functioned in its routine operations: its systems and employees around the globe were designing, manufacturing and successfully selling products which the aquatic sports and fashion youth markets wanted to purchase, and this led to considerable expansion in a relatively short time. Was it also an ambidextrous organization?

Ambidexterity refers to concurrent streams of innovation: "the need to create incremental, architectural, and discontinuous innovation requiring managers to balance contradictory pressures [such as] the organizational competencies to simultaneously host the multiple strategies, structures, processes and cultures needed to be successful today and to create the conditions for discontinuous innovation in the future." (Tushman and O'Reilly, 1997, p.222). Waugh provided a revealing insight: "We've had probably reasonable growth profit margin. It's never been extravagant but we've always maintained a reasonably healthy gross profit margin, we've in most

119

cases been able to control our expenses therefore we have had some profit. *In most cases that has financed our growth and that, to some degree, controls our future.* [But] what we have found is that you have to be careful about extreme growth." (Waugh, Aug 24, 2001). The emphasis is the author's: the italicized line indicates that profits from one generation of products were used to finance the development and expansion of the next generation. Therefore, Wave Rider demonstrates ambidexterity.

An example of how Sinclair and Waugh deployed this strategy was their investment of profits to purchase the watch from its American inventor, to develop constantly new wet-suit technologies and eventually to evolve production into lucrative brand clothing, sunglasses, footwear and carry-bags.

There appears to have been only one time when financial prudence escaped the founders, and this is worth exemplifying because it shows what can occur when insufficient care is taken with finances, and the company clearly lost its capacity to be profitable, let alone ambidextrous. The relief in Waugh's expression when he and Sinclair returned to their core business eventually, should be noted. "In the 'eighties, we had a couple of outside advisers who'd been helping us and we allowed ourselves to be focussing on the numbers, making decisions for short term profits, rather than focussing on the product and the long term good for the brand. We definitely lost our way there for a couple of years and we really got into problems – interest rates were really high at the time, we owed the banks a lot of money, a lot of other businesses were going down the gurgler, and we were very concerned that the banks would call in the loans." (Waugh, Aug 24, 2001). [...] "So we decided to sell the business in America, keep it as a licensee, but sell it to a company called Raisins. They paid half the money upfront and that helped us get over our problems in Australia, but the real thing that helped us get over our problems here was to focus on the product, on reality and [to] get rid of those two outside advisers, and again we took off with another period of solid growth." (Waugh, Aug 24, 2001). At the point where the company's congruence allowed itself to become unbalanced, the company ceased to function in the way it was intended. It lost alignment, and then deviated from its vision to its own detriment. However, such a mistake never occurred again: in the words of Esther Dyson, "My motto is, 'Always make new mistakes.' There's no shame in making a mistake. But then learn from it and don't make the same one again. Everything I've learned, I've learned by making mistakes." (Dyson, Aug 2002). This also worked for Sinclair and Waugh.

6.2 Culture

Congruence was critical over the years to achieve success. But of all its component parts, culture played a more important role in the evolution of congruence within Wave Rider than it did at the Little Swan Group Company, or at Alpine Packs. Systems must still be contingent upon a human 'glue' which keeps them functioning effectively, and helps management to evolve them to meet new exigencies over the years. Waugh summed it up well when he stated, "we're passionate about what we are doing , we believed in it. We were just sort of part of this surfing culture – we didn't want to go outside of this surfing culture [everything] week to week seemed to be working sufficiently well that we didn't have to look outside." (Waugh, Aug 24, 2001). Tushman and O'Reilly also identified culture as having the power to make or break a company, and they exemplified the problems with British Airways, (Tushman and O'Reilly, 1997, pp.31-32) and IBM, (Tushman and O'Reilly, 1997, pp.33-34). These problems included employee complacency, an obsession with internal procedures, and a lack of focus on the changing demands of the market. The cultural perspectives at BA were subsequently diagnosed and then changed using seminars that succeeded in orienting employees' focus towards the customers and their needs. However, at Wave Rider the culture was more than a superficial veneer layered upon company functions – it was the lubricant which made its machinery run. The role it played, and continues to play, is critical when considering the success of this company. Even Graham Herbert, Media Manager of the company since October 1994, under-rated its true significance, although he described some of its characteristics vividly and succinctly: "We don't have a uniform, apart from shorts and T-shirts; there's a casual air, and goes back to our brand-value of irreverence, or not taking ourselves too seriously. We have to meet deadlines, but we're encouraged to surf and enjoy ourselves. This is the way it's been since the late 'sixties. The purpose was to provide an environment where Wave Rider crew can live their Search. The search is to do with your perception of freedom." (Herbert, Jan 20, 2004).

Herbert also stated an essential truism about its culture in the same interview by observing, "Vast proportions of our employees are active participants, or have an interesting the sport and lifestyle." (Herbert, Jan 20, 2004). Waugh stated this in a more philosophical manner, but both drove towards one essential truth about why this company succeeded, particularly since some would say it did so against the odds: no management training, manufacturing or marketing experience on the part of anyone at executive level. The core of the answer lay in the active surfing participation of its following.

> "If you're going to roam around the world getting into travel and adventure, if you're going to be right out on the edge, you need products that are functional. Stuff that really works for a surfer, or works for a snowboarder, or works for a free-skier, or works for a windsurfer. That's part of our quest – the search for the best materials and technology to make products that really work when you're on the edge. The Search is the glue that connects people to Wave Rider, and it provides Wave Rider with its inspiration and its future direction." (Waugh quoted in Herbert, unpublished papers.)

Later Herbert took Waugh's original position a little further still:

> "Really living the thrill of discovery – of self and more. Waiting for the next storm to generate epic waves or dump fresh deep snow. Their lives centred around the Search. These people will always need functional and durable products. Products that will enhance their own experiences of seeking to find something that can never be held – moments of pure exhilaration and fun where nothing else matters." (Herbert, unpublished papers).

The key is that the staff at Wave Rider are the original 'Searchers', and while there are other organizational elements whose significance should not be discounted, it was these Searchers who provided the 'glue' that nurtured and propagated the company for 35 years. Therefore, since employees were also consumers and the company's "test-pilots" (Sinclair, Aug 24, 2001) they committed themselves to the business with the same passion that was characteristic of their founders.

This can be further demonstrated with particular poignancy when a small sample of surfing personalities who led the company's expansion, are identified: Paul Sinclair and Will Waugh were surfers, and they competed for Victoria during the late 'sixties when surfing in Australia was in its infancy; Butch Barr, surfer, was the company's first accountant; Will Spong, surfer, became the first designer in surf clothing; Pat Morgan, surfer, introduced Sinclair and Waugh to windsurfing; Francois Payot and Alan Tiegen, surfers, set up the franchise in France; Ray Thomas, surfer, set up Wave Rider operations in the USA; Peter Hodgart, surfer, set up the licence in Japan; the same man created the operations relating to the development of the tide-watch; Randall Hawkins, surfer, introduced Sinclair and Waugh to skiing at Mt Buller; Gary Crothall, surfer, is Wave Rider's longest serving employee as warehouse manager in Torquay; and more recently, Graham Herbert, surfer, was appointed Media Manager and Team Coach. From this short line-up alone, it is clear that Waugh was accurate in his portrayal of his workforce as being composed of "likeminded" individuals.

However, the world typically expects innovation to come from a laboratory, not from a miscellaneous assortment of surfers. Wave Rider has played to this expectation with the creation of "Professor Q", a virtual character who appears in many pages of the company's web site, (www.waverider.com), complete with white lab coat, heavy spectacles, moustache, beret and a mixture of archaic as well as slang phrases. An example is, "Shove that thread in your needle and stitch it," when he's referring to the SLT Code board-shorts, (www.waverider.com/rd, p.1). It is ironic that no actual professors or laboratories were ever consulted on any of Wave Rider's innovations, because they would probably not have been "likeminded" individuals. No doubt as a non-surfing 'geek' in his misspent youth, Professor Q must remain a virtual entity for the entertainment of a generation of teenagers, who might find it hard to believe that the **virtual** in today's media was inspired by the **mundane** of yester-year: two self-taught men driven merely by the passion for a sport.

6.3 Change

Wave Rider's culture is idiosyncratic and unique, and it was perpetuated for almost four decades by its original founders, because as their personalities and practices evolved, they kept reinforcing it. It was from within this culture, not just from the two founders, that every innovation and subsequent changes emanated. The creative and industrial processes which gave birth to the boards, then the wetsuits, the watches, the clothing, the snow products, the prize monies for the many competitions, and the Code STL board-shorts, were bound by bonds much stronger than those that could be manifested through the ordinariness of the world of work alone. When Sinclair commented: "the power and the allure of the ocean is just so strong," (Sinclair, Aug 24, 2001), he was pointing at the heart of his company, a heart that beat rhythmically with the tides. And as founders they persuaded others that this was the life-style to emulate. Echoing the sentiments of Paul Sinclair, for example, Graham Herbert wrote, "In the beginning [...] we made products for ourselves. Products that would enhance our own enjoyment and experience of surfing and travelling. Searching. Living to surf. Surfing to live. A better performing surfboard. A better wetsuit. Mountain-wear that worked." (Herbert, unpublished papers).

Therefore, it is clear that Wave Rider did not suffer the same problems faced by some other industries cited by Tushman and O'Reilly. They point to Jan Timmer of Philips, (Tushman and O'Reilly, 1997, p.217), as an extreme example of an industrialist who had to make drastic changes to save his company. But to be fair, neither did Sinclair and Waugh walk into the same minefield that Timmer did. The two were their own original architects for innovation, culture and change. Changing from sales to their immediate circle, publicizing their products and creating a reputation for quality, required Sinclair to travel considerable distances with wetsuits in the boot of his car. It explains why they were so eager to exchange wetsuits with foreign surfers who occasioned Bells Beach – it meant that these products were going to be transported to surfers in South Africa, the USA and Hawaii, and hopefully make a name in those locations even before they could develop full recognition with small surfing numbers in Australia. It also explains why change in the form of internationalization took place so early in the life of the company, because it was the only way of creating an unbroken period of sustained growth. (Tushman and O'Reilly, 1997, p.215). The market for Wave Rider became a world market in order for the company to remain viable in the early years, because the Australian market was still so small, and as a sport, surfing was marginal. It was more than just the development of export markets - it led to propagation of the company itself. As Waugh explained, the increasing value of the Franc in relation to the Australian Dollar in the early 'eighties was the final deciding factor in Wave Rider engaging Francois Payot to head French production and sales. (Waugh, Aug 24, 2001). Wave Rider's actions were also aligned with Christensen and Raynor's recommendation that change be effected through the setting up of autonomous units to generate new growth markets. (Christensen and Raynor, 2003, pp.198-199).

The other major changes included the creation of a mountain product line of equipment and clothing in the mid-eighties, and this added to the company's profitability. Then in 2002, the company began outsourcing much of its production to South East Asia, and while there were issues and complexities involved, they vetted their outsourced firms with care, and unlike Alpine Packs, insisted on exclusive contracts in order to enhance brand loyalty in a work environment that had to be a controlled from Torquay. (Herbert, Jan 20, 2004). Exclusive production may have been possible because of Wave Rider's considerably greater production quantities than Alpine Packs'. Their means of maintaining quality control and means of communication are however, much the same as Alpine Packs'. Herbert detailed the following in an e-mail communication to the researcher, written 20 Aug 2004, "We only work with factories that comply [with] recognised global standards for manufacturing processes/procedures, which involves producing sample garments to our specifications at various stages of development for review/approval, pre-production checks of all components, in-line inspections, end-of-line inspections and constant compliance checking. Finally, various Wave Rider staff conduct regular factory visits, covering everything from broad strategic planning issues through to addressing development and production issues." As Tushman and O'Reilly remark, "[....] how [should a company] proactively lead innovation and change; how to move from today's to tomorrow's strength." (Tushman and O'Reilly, 1997, p.216). Both Wave Rider and Alpine Packs have outsourced within the last two years, yet each was determined that the quality on which each built its reputation, should maintain it through rigorous systems to ensure continuity, in case a deterioration effected a loss in brand loyalty. At Torquay itself, the company continues to produce custom-designed wetsuits and custom-built surfboards. It also remains the home of the surfers, both men and women, whom it sponsors in international competitions.

6.4 Approach to innovation

The company took the pursuit of innovation seriously ever since it achieved its greatest discontinuous innovation in wetsuits, and began manufacturing their entire production with dual density neoprene from 1975 onwards. This was followed by a succession of incremental innovations in wetsuit design and materials such as the Aggrolite range launched in 1980; the Super Xpandx Neoprene in 1984; the RD4 Titanium Neoprene in 1994, which reflected body heat back to the body; the Elastomax, with colour mesh in 2001; and finally the SlickSkin released in 2002. Technology improved each wetsuit series, attempting at first to create manoeuverability and warmth in the mid-seventies to maximising warmth with a minimum of neoprene in 2004. As Sinclair said, "As the customer became familiar with and comfortable with our brand and its quality so they were ready then to take on another group of products. They expected it actually, [they were] not just ready for it, and we recognised that expectation." (Sinclair, Aug 24, 2001). For that reason, the company was open to other innovations: the tide-watch, custom-designed and built surfboards, mountain products and mountain wear, backpacks, casual wear, and eventually sunglasses, footwear and wallets/purses designed for both male and female. In other words, the company generated products designed for two principal environments with the target market being the young, or those who were "like minded," (Sinclair, 24 Aug 2001), because this was part of the vision of being "the ultimate surfing company." (Sinclair, 24 Aug 2001).

An aspect of developing innovation at Wave Rider was to keep everything in-house and never to allow scientists to dominate, although the benefit of their scientific expertise could obviously not be ignored. This was demonstrated by Herbert's comments that the STL board-shorts were developed by the International CEO, who was given the specific responsibility for designing a new board-shorts, which Wave Rider hoped would become a market-leading innovation. It took two years to bring to market. "He had to identify the technology and implement that technology." (Herbert, Jan 20, 2004). The overall responsibility for the development of the product from conception to production remained with a surfer. However, it is not yet clear whether the board-shorts comprise a radical innovation or merely an incremental one. The criteria to apply here come from Leifer et al. who pointed out that a radical innovation had to comply with one or more of three criteria: "An entirely new set of performance features; improvements in known features of five times or greater; or, a significant (30 percent or greater) reduction in costs." (Leifer et al. 2000, p.5). It may be some time yet before Wave Rider can evaluate market response, but the company believes that the shorts provide an entirely new performance features, (Herbert, Jan 20, 2004), but this is singular rather than the plural of Leifer's definition, which might compromise it as a radical innovation, technically speaking.

There did not appear to be any situation or episode in Wave Rider's history when it became vulnerable to the menace of its own success, as in the case of Oticon and IBM. Apart from a temporary problematic financial situation in the 'eighties previously mentioned, the company appears to have continued to expand in products and internationalization processes, in order to remain true to its vision as well as to its own marketing strategy, the Search.

6.5 Strategy

For Will Waugh, the strategy was to command, "A leadership position in innovation, and product, and marketing, and in business practice." (Waugh, Aug 24, 2001). He explained that product development was the result of both following and leading the market: "You just met all expectations." (Waugh, Aug 24, 2001). Their commitment to excellence was clear, "You know we would never be satisfied that we have excellence on all standpoints, but we certainly are very committed to it." (Waugh, Aug 24, 2001). Waugh was referring here to a situation which Tushman and O'Reilly called a "performance gap" (1997, p.218), without which innovation rarely takes place. "It is the ability to create problems or opportunities while a firm is doing well that allows the most successful managers to capitalize on incremental and discontinuous innovation and change." (Tushman and O'Reilly, 1997, p.220). There have been incremental innovations where the trajectory was continuous path from concept to commercialization following a planned pathway. And yet Wave Rider's trajectory throughout the existence of the company also showed signs of the radical because it was characterized by discontinuities, or gaps. There were stops and starts. And trajectory changes occurred in response to unanticipated events and outcomes.

The attempt to achieve excellence encompassed production as well as service. For example, Wave Rider watches maintain their warranty only when their batteries are renewed in a dedicated outlet. The big surfwear companies distribute stock only through surf shops and youth-oriented clothing chains, avoiding department stores and discounters. When questioned by John Stensholt in the *BRW* (2001, July), about Wave Rider's sales strategy, Graham Herbert was reported as saying, "The company has no plans to change its distribution strategy. We exclusively distribute through specialist shops, and we will never be sold in any other places. Our market has no problem at all in going to the specialist shops to buy our product." Dedicated outlets are a means of communicating with the public because this way they generate an ambience, for example, through promotional campaigns and large still photos of successful surfers and skiers in action, reminiscent of the head office decorations in Torquay. Wave Rider, like Billabong and Quiksilver, restricts its marketing efforts to the surf industry, avoiding mass market campaigns. Wave Rider places much of its advertising in surfing magazines such as *Australian Surfing Life* and *Riptide*. It is also a heavy sponsor of world surfing events and individual surfers and skiers. Stensholt also observed that surf brands were keen to stress their small and humble beginnings, and avoided a "corporate image." (Stensholt, 2001, July). The "corporation", redolent with old men in dark suits, is the very antithesis of the pursuit of pleasure on the part of today's youth, and the company would never want to be associated with it.

6.6 Learning

Learning for Sinclair and Waugh meant adapting to the conditions of the time. It could be argued that each of their products is but a physical manifestation of a customer need, and therefore the two needed to identify it, design it and manufacture it. Flexibility was also an aspect of learning: Waugh observed that when he and Sinclair first granted a licence to colleagues in the south of France, French tastes were different, and "creative licence" was required to meet that market. The two also learned to produce, market and distribute, as well as learning about management and human resource management. Sinclair stated, "So I guess learning interaction with people, just learning what makes people tick, and [about their] motivations, has probably been the most interesting." (Sinclair, Aug 24, 2001).

Learning as a means to assist achieving the goals of the company has become more apparent in recent years. Waugh commented that staff learned on the job; then the company moved staff who showed potential, around from division to division to increase their knowledge of the business; and finally, Herbert observed that staff who had potential and ambition were now given the opportunity to enrol in courses to extend their professional input into the company. Even the learning process had to be learned.

6.7 Leadership

Tushman and O'Reilly state that, "Successful innovation requires skilled management of organizational politics." (Tushman and O'Reilly, 1997, p.218). Inspite of its global structures, effective power at Wave Rider up to the time of Sinclair and Waugh's retirement was consolidated in the hands of only four board members: Sinclair, Waugh, Payot, and Tonay, representing the interests of Australasia, France and the USA. No other players were even close to that power, since it was an unelected power that was directly connected to share ownership of the company itself. There was no evidence produced at any time during the research on the company that power-play by other employees had ever been an issue, or that indeed it had ever taken place.

Comment has already been made about the density, loyalty and cohesion of Wave Rider's culture. It helps to explain why "inertia", so prevalent in most situations of change in Western manufacturing, was again no problem for Wave Rider. "Inertia kills. Managing culture is the most neglected, and highest leverage, tool for promoting innovation and change." (Tushman and O'Reilly, 1997, p.218). In this instance, the situation does not apply. Wave Rider moved from a cottage industry to a multi-national enterprise in thirty years largely on the strength of its bedrock culture. The only time when this was almost derailed was in the late 'eighties, when two "outside" (Sinclair, Aug 24, 2001) consultants drove him and Waugh towards short-term profits and away from the product. And they were never surfers. They were fired.

Sinclair and Waugh's leadership may have lacked formal technical or business education, but it was rich in instinct, astute observation and strategy. Their main strategy was to maintain innovation to the forefront in its three main forms of the incremental, the architectural and the discontinuous, particularly in their two lead products: wetsuits and tide-watches. Their second main strategy was to effect quality by remaining a private company in order to keep control of cash-flows; to control, inspire and finance their own version of R&D; and to remain loyal to the consumer's expectation of those standards which they believed comprised excellence in product and service. Andrall Pearson substantiates that stance:

> Superior service can be an illusory and impractical goal for many large retailers. It simply takes more management and discipline than they can muster to bring so many outlets up to a higher-than-average level of service and keep them there.

> The moral here is that your strategic vision has to be grounded in a deep understanding of the competitive dynamics of your business. You have to know the industry and your competitors cold. (Pearson, Aug 2002, p.121).

6.8 Conclusion

"Vision, strategy and objectives are the bedrock for managing innovation and change." (Tushman and O'Reilly, 1997, p.218). Sinclair and Waugh founded a business based on a vision that theirs would be the "ultimate surfing company", and in almost a forty-year period they continued to nurture it successfully with streams of innovations, lively marketing strategies and a loyal culture of employees who in turn created brand loyalty in an ever-widening circle of "like-minded" consumers. The two are now retired but they have still retained their majority shareholding and therefore have retained effective power. It is not clear what that means in terms of future directions. Judging by the success of the past, which can be a dangerous thing according to Tushman and O'Reilly (1997), and Leifer et al.(2000), it would appear

130

that continuity of past strategies by the company in this case would serve it well, because of its emphasis on consumer-inspired streams of innovation. This strategy has been the source of Wave Rider's competitive advantage for four decades, and that's how it cultivated its own brand of resilience. (Hamel and Välikangas, 2003, September).

Finally, spark@cnn.com, retrieved on March 6, 2005, revealed that Paul Lunn of Seachange Technology, had launched a wearable shark-repellent electronic field, after years of ocean trials in South Australia. It is aimed at deep-sea divers and surfers, adding about a one pound weight to a surfboard. It can be typified as a disruptive technology because it is proven to be effective, inexpensive, in demand, and it increases water safety in the South Australian bight by driving out sharks from five to eight metres' proximity, when nothing else can accomplish that. It remains to be seen whether Wave Rider will utilize this invention to maintain surfer safety for its clientele. With all manner of sharks ever-present in Wave Rider's very foreshore, particularly the notorious great white shark, this electronic repellent would arguably have been a more lucrative innovation for Wave Rider to incorporate within its product range, than electro-welded boardshorts. While shark-repellent technology is not within its expertise, Wave Rider could possibly create a joint venture with Seachange Technology, and this innovation would keep Wave Rider to the forefront of surfer technology, even if it was not their own innovation. But neither was the tide-watch. Likewise, the management of Seachange Technology may see that Wave Rider has a ready-established market for such a product, and both companies would benefit from the other. The management of both companies may consider the benefits and then act accordingly, as the management of Little Dragon did – the necessary technology was simply purchased to achieve the desired results. As will be seen in the Main Analysis Chapter (Chapter 13), companies can support each other for mutual benefit, and thrive on each other's strengths. There are times when they rely as much on other businesses as they do on their own retail customers.

Chapter 7

The Jiangsu Little Dragon Group Company in the People's Republic of China

Overview 1958-2004
First perspective 1958-2002

"First-class enterprises form standards and benchmarks; second-class enterprises form brands; and third class enterprises form products." Lei Yuan, Deputy General Manager, the Jiangsu Little Dragon Group Company, 18 November 2002.

7.1 Overview of the business and change: 1958-2004

Having a population of four and a half million, Wuxi is a city situated approximately 120 kilometres north-west of the great commercial centre of Shanghai, on the shores of Lake Taihu. To the Chinese, it is best known for its production of light to medium sized household appliances and its prolific textile industry.

The People's Republic of China (China) has been in the process of tumultuous change particularly with its provisional entry to the World Trade Organization in November 2000, a preliminary agreement that will be finalised in 2005. It has been slowly moving away from a command economy to a mixed economy and with these changes, demand for new products has grown rapidly. Such growth was anticipated with great international optimism in the 1990s and attracted large international investments in an attempt to tap the supposedly larger market opportunities that this growing economy could present to the world. Due to problems with infrastructure, regional government requirements, and market resistance, many of the foreign firms withdrew after suffering large losses (Singh, Pangarkar, & Heracleous, 2004). However, there are positive changes happening within Chinese industry that will continue to increase capital flows in the future. Transfer technology figures alone are sizeable: Dougherty (2003) points out technology transfer contracts amounted to several billion US dollars per year in the 1980s, climaxing to over ten billion dollars in 1995 and this represented about one-sixth of total machinery and transport imports. Actual foreign direct investment ranged from one-half to nearly the same amount as machinery and transport imports, flooding in at the rate of about ten billion dollars in 1995. Little Dragon's technology acquisition was one aspect of China's economic change. The country is in the process of significant economic expansion.

One and a half years after first investigating Little Dragon, the company may be characterized by confidently determining its own globalization strategies, and it is particularly active in collaborating with German, Japanese and American companies in process and product innovation. With rapidly evolving markets, Little Dragon also found itself subject to competition from Toshiba in the washing machine line, within the Chinese domestic market. However, Little Dragon adopted an innovative strategy to safeguard its own lead product. The company dealt with this threat by forging an alliance with Toshiba, and produced the Japanese high-technology giant's washing machines for them in Wuxi, thereby creating a commercial symbiosis to the advantage of both companies.

7.2 The first perspective 1958-2002: Products and practices that built the brand

While a considerable amount has been written concerning the failures and successes of foreign firms operating in China, little has been revealed about the Chinese firms that have had to make the shift from a planned economy to an economy that is beginning to respond to market forces. Little has been told about the Chinese firms that have had to compete with large and experienced multinational corporations. It could easily be surmised that Chinese manufacturers have survived and prospered because of the protected environment in which they operate, particularly in relation to their favourable exchange rate. As the following case demonstrates, there are inventive anomalies. The example of the Jiangsu Little Dragon Group Company (Little Dragon) highlights how success is being achieved through the application of innovation and pragmatism, but the really revelatory detail about this company concerns its early methods for acquiring such innovations.

Little Dragon is one of China's one hundred largest companies, with a domestic labour force of approximately 10,000. Its core business is manufacturing household appliances, some of which, such as dryers and washing machines are also constructed to commercial specifications. The washing machine is their largest seller, but the company also manufactures air conditioners, refrigerators, freezers, dishwashers, dryers, and dry-cleaning appliances. Little Dragon had total assets of 10.6 billion Renminbi in 2003. In 2003 it achieved sales of over ten billion Renminbi. In 2002, its exports totalled $US 180 million (Littledragon.com, retrieved 16 Nov 2004).

The Little Dragon washing machine, consisting of three action variations, has been the top selling brand in China since 1994, the year they sold 640,000 units, which put the company in first place. The company began washing machine sales in twenty-fourth place in 1989. But only five years later, it made a profit of 70 million Renminbi from washing machine sales alone. How did a former ceramics, pottery and tool producer achieve this, and in such a short timeframe? And did the re-combination of foreign technology and domestic innovative activity lead to productivity improvements?

The company has achieved innovation in both product and process, more particularly in later years as it changed direction and underwent major changes in management. To put this innovation into context requires an outline of the company's main developmental phases. Innovation has been integral to that development, but surprisingly it did not consist of the normal in-house discontinuous variety.

The company's history can be divided into four periods: from 1958 until 1978, it produced mainly pottery, ceramics and a variety of tools. From 1979 until 1989, the company relinquished ceramics and explored the market for domestic appliance demand, and began producing washing machines in 1979. From 1989 until 1999, a major strategic plan witnessed rapid development in home appliance production, with

134

particular emphasis on the washing machine. And in the fourth phase, from 2000 to the present, the development has been in high technology expansion into a variety of appliances, with the washing machine as the lead product. An important aspect of the fourth phase has been the improvement of the lead product to make it a globally competitive product. The hi-tech device which now distinguishes later models from their previous siblings is "fuzzy logic", which is a sensor that automatically adjusts water levels and the power that is used to drive the turbine depending on washing weight and condition. The company is now not only China's main washing machine supplier but it also exports to South East Asia, North America and the Middle East. From 1989 to the present, the company expanded at a rate of about 18 percent per year.

There are American, European and Australian white-ware manufacturers who also produce the washing machine as a basic "must have" domestic appliance in the contemporary family, each with its own style of technological development. From where, or how, did Little Dragon obtain its technology when it did not have a history of technological advancement prior to 1979? It is a considerable shift to go from producing ceramics like exterior wall-cladding tiles, to producing electrically powered white-ware.

In a study completed by Wu, Ni and Cao from Zhejian University in 2002, which focused on productivity increases in businesses in Zhejiang Province, they found that the acquisition of technology was far from successful. It was found that 21 percent of businesses could only imitate foreign products and technology; 30 percent of small businesses and 12 percent of medium size businesses could innovate independently; 20 percent of businesses could create new products independently and 22 percent of businesses could make their own technological innovations. Wu, Ni and Cao concluded that the greater the sophistication of the technology acquired, the lesser the chance of successful improvement in Chinese productivity. They also concluded that "cooperation and coordination with the foreign enterprise is one of the channels to improve Chinese enterprises' ability to gain a late-comer's advantage." How then did Little Dragon succeed?

7.3 Building competitive advantage: Innovation, management and culture

In the mid-seventies, the company strategy focused on the production of the washing machine, and in order to commence this, they bought washing machine components from Matsushita in Japan. However, the components were difficult to clone, and this resulted in a product that only had the "appearance" of the original. In 1987, the company took the step which propelled it into serious production. They imported critical technology from Matsushita at a cost of US$4.1 million. Ten years of relatively unsuccessful imitation was capped by a technology transfer fee, and the external sourcing of Matsushita's high technology product and some of their engineers. This propulsion into high technology expertise acted as an instant catalyst, which enabled the company to design further proprietary technology of their own. By 2002, it had 150 technology patents, one of which was held in the United States. The expertise consisting of purchased knowledge as well as incremental innovations in washing machine technology from their own R&D gave the company its competitive advantage. In the year the company paid Matsushita its transfer fee, its newly acquired technological accelerant led to speedy market acceptance of its washing machines, and its sales were split 75 percent in the Chinese market, and 25 percent in markets abroad, mainly Thailand.

The external sourcing of technology from Matsushita was so successful for Little Dragon that between 1999 and 2000, it repeated this means of kick-starting another line of white-ware development. The company paid US$2.9 million for air-conditioning technology, and in so doing it is attempting to repeat the process previously so successful in washing machine manufacture.

The company was not satisfied to only possess a new technology. It determined that it also needed to innovate in a number of other areas, as manufacturing of new products for new and shifting markets required improved skills in management, as well as employee relations, remuneration and R&D.

Management made the decision to purchase technology. At the same time, it engaged in improved marketing and planning, in order to predict market demand. It correctly predicted that the Asian demand for hygiene and cleanliness was underpinned by the need for machinery of high quality and durability. Management believed that if technology could be purchased as a commodity, and make an instant change for the better, then perhaps management skills could be purchased in the same way, and the changes it would effect might produce similarly desirable outcomes. In 1994, the company applied to the Beijing government to create a board that would represent the interest of capital, consisting of nine Chinese members and three from abroad. Such a composition was highly innovative, even radically countercultural, at the time, because China still functioned as a command, and largely isolated, economy. The company invited the United States Educational Foundation to be one of the three foreign members, and the Foundation accepted this invitation, and continues to hold a seat at the time of writing.

As a result of board diversity, the company has achieved what was planned, as explained by the Deputy General Manager, Lei Yuan: "We have an innovative plan that has three main planks: To have a lead product, the washer that is first in the market; to have higher return from less investment; and higher return with less risk. This is what I mean: our strategy in focusing on washers is to go in for larger scale production, to absorb technology and to pay attention to patenting our expertise. By a higher return with less investment I mean that we put 2 to 4 percent of sales into Research and Development, but we know we are still backward in expertise and capital management. By higher return with less risk I mean that we have to make up for our disadvantages. It is hard to find good friends, harder to find good competitors. So we keep on good terms with everyone." (Lei, Nov 18, 2002). In the same year, the company included reforms in its ownership by a process of "social shareholding" which enabled eleven percent of shares to be held by foreign companies, although the company itself owned the largest percentage of shares. The company was listed on the Sheng Zheng Stock Exchange.

Under the new management, the company also diversified its employee skill and ethnicity bases. The culture is now no longer exclusively Chinese, and uniform in behaviour patterns. Technical expertise, especially, was recruited from the United

137

States, Japan, New Zealand and Canada, with skilled talent lending its name to the particular process which the engineer devised. For example, the washing machine metal folding line was created by a New Zealand engineer, and it is called the "Scott" line, even in Mandarin, as a tribute to his ingenuity and contribution to the company. The Deputy General Manager conceded that only one senior engineer came from within China, having completed his PhD in mechanical engineering in France; the rest were, and continue to be, sourced from abroad. The technology which the company developed, as well as its comparatively cheap labour costs, became the bedrock of its competitive advantage. As a result, the most senior engineers were paid in the region of US$100,000 per year, although some salaries rose above that amount because the top figures were negotiable, with no pre-determined ceilings. This compared to assemblers, sourced locally from the city of Wuxi, who earned between US$2,500 and US$3,000 per year. The top engineering incomes should also be seen as highly favourable in comparison to various strata of management: supervisory management earned about US$4,000 per year, management with a Master's degree earned about US$8,000, and higher echelons of management, but not top management, earned in the vicinity of US$12,000 per year. The company remunerated on educational qualifications, experience and performance. Those employees with a PhD, regardless of whether they were employed in management or engineering, were accorded a free apartment and the service of a car as a standard remuneration package. The company considered the pay relativities an essential reflection of the primacy of top engineering as the means to create continuous upgrading of their products. "The quality of the product reflects the quality of the employees." (Lei, Nov 18, 2002). This philosophy straddles the findings of Montemayor (1996), which claim that high performance companies with innovative strategies often have innovative pay policies and that companies that emphasise cost leadership reward differently.

To evaluate employee performance, the company devised an achievement assessment system in which performance was assessed on various criteria, and by a number of co-workers. Working attitude is important to the company. The employee writes a self-assessment, one is written by the manager to whom the employee reports, and anyone else who feels he or she can contribute constructively may offer an assessment in support (or criticism) of a colleague. Staff may be promoted or demoted by this process, which the Deputy General Manager calls "democratic" (Lei, Nov 18, 2002).

The company offers continuous training programmes for employees who are seen as fading, or under-performing in other ways. The company management believes that a cooperative culture is the key to a successful enterprise.

Little Dragon recognised the inadequacies of former management practices. It now attempts to inculcate "individual discipline, and move human management towards logistic management." With this remark, Lei Yuan believes that managers across China are better off relinquishing an archaic past and embracing a future, albeit one that will suffer growing pains, but which is at least based on sound market analysis. He argues that the market should lead as in a developed market economy, not that production should lead as in a planned economy.

7.4 Continuing the industrial evolution: The imperative of change

The company believes it provides its technicians and engineers with an environment to match the company's technological aspirations. Laboratories in Berlin, Tokyo and Los Angeles have been built to continually upgrade the technology required to maintain and increase the company's competitive advantage in washing machine technology: "The development strategy is specialisation as the key to success." (Lei, Nov 18, 2002).

The company developed strategic alliances with BSH of Germany, Matsushita of Japan, and Motorola and GE from the United States; as well as joint ventures with Bosh of Germany. A home-grown example of an alliance is that the company also includes a pack of P&G detergent with every washing machine sold on the domestic market. The company believes that by combining with other researchers and suppliers in their markets all the parties can benefit from sharing some technologies and information. Little Dragon and P&G conduct market surveys together, and Motorola researches washing programs with the company.

In the late 1990s, Lei Yuan began writing a number of short articles, or position papers, which the Little Dragon Group then placed on the World Wide Web, but only in Mandarin. Without significant exposure to Western industrialists or to Western business philosophies, he revealed a philosophy that espouses many Western business concepts. However, for him the development of his own thought about the strategic direction which his company should pursue, was not so much a coherent philosophy as a series of shared revelations, or epiphanies. The articles were intended only for a Mandarin readership, as a "wake-up call" to industrial peers in the People's Republic. In "Corporations and Markets", he states his belief that despite the problems Chinese industry faces with capital and organizational structure, the "crux of the problem is the problem of management." His initial standpoint is that the era of economic shortages should now be relegated to the past, and that "the market has gone from an emphasis on sellers to an emphasis on buyers ... Nonetheless many enterprises still hold on to the thought that was prevalent in 1998 when China first began moving towards becoming a market economy. They are still hoping that the market will flourish on its own and they are still expecting that the government will turn on the water and raise the fish. These are the troubles left behind by an era of a planned economy." (Lei Yuan, position paper, 2001).

Once Chinese managers understood that the problems of the planned economy gave way to a new raft of problems, Lei Yuan exhorted them to analyse the market: "The front line of the enterprise is the market." He devised an aphorism: "The enterprise is only able to live if the market lives, the market can do without the enterprise, but the enterprise cannot do without the market." (Lei Yuan, position paper, 2001). This counters the still oft-held view that "production is the front line," reminiscent of a planned, but failed, economy. Lei Yuan's focus on the market orientation of future companies was all pervasive: "An important step that enterprises must take is 'all staff must be market orientated.' Above all, enterprises must nurture the potential of young workers and encourage them to be market oriented. About 60 percent of current staff members were selected from the open market. One hundred percent of management staff were selected from the open market. Receptionists, sales people and so on must all be selected one by one. All of the enterprise's resources must be put to good use. Human capital is first, but product development and production must also be closely, if not inseparably, coiled around the market. Little Dragon won segment after segment of market share that way." (Lei Yuan, position paper, 2001).

This is however not an exhortation for a plunge into the market without strategic planning: "Enterprises still need to be creative and apply modern sales theories. In this regard, enterprises need to do some very difficult, very detailed and very sensitive work. It's not sufficient to just say 'the market is the leader' and leave it at that." (Lei Yuan, Nov 18, 2002). Lei Yuan is aware that in a market economy, public perception of a product and service are important. "What you've said to people they won't remember, but the impression of service you bring to them will always be remembered. So learn to serve, because good service will produce more value. This is an important step to [becoming] a successful enterprise. If we consider service as well as trying our best to do our own work , we can determine the future – this is the right attitude towards customers and also a core value [we need] to serve the customer. […] General Director Hing proposed an idea, that of the "consumer standard", [and] this is [a] higher [standard] than any standard target." (Lei Yuan, Nov 18, 2002).

7.5 Future aims

These comments are not borne of traditional Chinese industrial theory; they are the first steps of a nascent industrial culture in which every such step is demonstrative of the courage and the will to be innovative in order to climb out of a time warp. A number of elements of the innovative approach to industrial change are there: The vision that communicates the need to change on a large scale, in this case, the whole HR and managerial position from a planned to a market economy; the need to select the workforce on a merit and equitable basis; the need to adopt an analytic approach toward market forces; and the need to lead toward a new model of management as the bedrock towards achieving a better business model. "The core of administration is to manage operations, but [more importantly] the core of management is to make strategic decisions. This is the new revolution and it has to uplift our foundations." (Lei Yuan, Nov 18, 2002).

Chapter 8

Jiangsu Little Dragon Group

The second set of perspectives covering November 2002-March 2004

8.1 Strategic change and innovation: Breaking with conventions

On revisiting the Jiangsu Little Dragon Group in March 2004, the researcher had the opportunity to again interview Mr Lei Yuan, Deputy General Manager; as well as for the first time conduct an interview Dr Hing, General Manager, and Deputy Chair of the Board of Directors of the company.

While the time that had elapsed between the interview series was less than one and a half years, there was a discernible trend towards change in the direction of expanding domestic and international markets through a extending their washing machine range and increasing production. There had also been considerable change in the governance of the company. In addition, the company was actively exploiting opportunities that arose as environments were changing, and continued to innovate in product as well as process. Clearly, the company was also marked by a new-found corporate confidence since the time of the last interview: Dr Hing in particular, asserted his company's elevation in the fields of advanced technology, market share and productivity. These had been discussed in late 2002, by his second in command in much more tentative terms. The company was maturing with considerable rapidity.

To break a paradigm is a significant form of breaking with conventional methods, and it means removing a set of assumptions so that they might be considered obsolete and no longer relevant in a new environment. Dr Hing's agreement with Toshiba is a case in point. Because Little Dragon was a small company compared to the dominant global players such as Siemens of Germany and Panasonic and Hitachi of Japan, Little Dragon deals with them respectfully. "My opinion is that cooperation in the factory is much better than competition in the market. In every city in every market we compete. But in our workshop, design shop cooperation is much better than to compete." (Hing, March 24, 2004). Hing considered learning from other companies to be important in the evolution of his own. "I'm going to Canada next week, and to a Toshiba factory in Thailand; I've been to a Siemens factory and I can go where I like. We don't have enemies." (Hing, March 24, 2004). It was because of this view that Dr Hing struck an accord with Toshiba of Japan which was not understood nor appreciated at first by his own Board. "No enemies only partners […] That is an important consideration in Little Dragon." (Hing, March 24, 2004).

However, partners can be seen as potential competitors, and it is here that Dr Hing's view of competition showed considerable insight. The Toshiba chairman informed Dr Hing in 2003, that his company wanted to be the number two provider of washing machines in the People's Republic of China. But Dr Hing considered that no company ever aimed to be number two, stating matter-of-factly that this was a "lie", and that "He [Toshiba 's Chairman]'d like to be number one." He interpreted this as potential market encroachment by a high-tech Japanese giant, and contrary to apparent logic, offered Toshiba a partnership. "Last year, we finished more than 20 models for them, the "Three Series", but for their $US 2 million investment they got machines that were better than ones produced in Japan. That was the Chairman's comment." (Hing, March 24, 2004). His view of the competition that Toshiba represented was that, "we [couldn't] stop them from coming onto the market, even if we anticipate[d] them. They had to come into the Chinese market." But he calculated that, "The new presence [would] be good for Little Dragon." He took advantage of the practice of partnership by staking his own company's reputation: "We ha[d] something they need[ed]: Little Dragon has a strong background in design and manufacturing." Dr Hing was aware of the approximate cost of the Japanese investing in plant to set themselves up in competition with a fully established Little Dragon, and with the Little Dragon brand that had wide recognition in its own country. His estimation of the initial cost of a new plant for a newcomer to China like Toshiba, was approximately $US 20 million. He convinced Toshiba that there was "no need for them to invest in fixed assets." The agreement between the partners was that, "[Little Dragon would] assist them; we [would] design for them; we [would] made the machine for them." These washing machines, designed and manufactured by Little Dragon, but branded "Toshiba", were destined for the Chinese domestic market.

However, while it may appear that Little Dragon had agreed to make Toshiba a more powerful competitor in China, Dr Hing maintained that he controlled the conditions. He stated, "We have the value line of their products, and that gives us some rights. We negotiated the transfer price, [so] we gained money from this cooperation. We controlled the speed of many things in their progress in this market. In a far assumption [In an extreme situation – or in a worst case scenario] what will happen? If we stop production they will have nothing to sell onto the Chinese market. That's the power of the production base. So we control the circle [design and manufacturing cycle], and the steps of their presence in this market." (Hing, March 24, 2004). He was also aware that Panasonic had already established three factories in Wuxi for refrigerator and compressor production, and whilst this might not represent head-to-head competition, if Panasonic were to switch to washing machine production, it would lead to head-to-head competition and a price war. Clearly, high-technology companies from Japan would have to be dealt with strategically.

Therefore, Dr Hing positioned himself to partner the entry of Japanese competition into his domestic market, and in so doing, he was able to apply certain controls to the process. However, in re-designing the traditional paradigm of commercial competition, he pushed the partnership with Toshiba still further to the advantage of his own company. Previously, Little Dragon had bought technology from Matsushita of Japan: once for the development of washing machines and once several years later for the development of air conditioners. Asked if he was paid a royalty or a transfer fee in now manufacturing for the Japanese, Dr Hing replied, "At the moment we only charge a transfer fee." But the relationship between Little Dragon and Matsushita had been different from that between Little Dragon and Toshiba. He explained, "But it is different from Matsushita. The design comes from Japan and the manufacturing takes place at Little Dragon in China. But we learned almost nothing from Matsushita. But this time it is different. Little Dragon designed, but Toshiba engineered the process. So we learned a lot from Toshiba. They taught us how to make as good a washing machine as Toshiba needs." He added, "We designed for them and that was not a free service; they paid us 2 million Renminbi." (Hing, March 24, 2004). The contract has a confidentiality provision, however, Little Dragon will still be able to take advantage of the situation. Dr Hing commented, "We have a confidential[ity] agreement with Toshiba. We now know all the tricks of their washers, but we can't transfer [them] to anybody. But there is no need; the other players in the market don't need Toshiba's information from Little Dragon. We will transfer their technology to our [own] Little Dragon machines." (Hing, March 24, 2004). The partnership was therefore more reciprocal than it first appeared. "We needed a teacher, and that's become Toshiba. So in one year, we reached the high target [standard] of Toshiba. And for them, we are an important partner because they could enter the [Chinese] market quickly, in just eight months." (Hing, March 24, 2004). And how would the Chinese consumer benefit from this partnership? "The consumer has a very good design from Little Dragon made by Little Dragon, with the technology from Toshiba." (Hing, March 24, 2004). True to his statements about competition, Dr Hing added, "We could sell [the new composite washing machine] as a Little Dragon product but with their [Toshiba's] technology, and if we did that we would expand our product line. We could exchange products. [Parts could become interchangeable]. This is how we are cooperating with Electronics, Hitachi and other competitors. [But] Toshiba and Siemens are primary brands. We don't change the position of each brand. We create a new composite brand in the factory, not in the market. We don't change the position of the brand in the market – if we do it in the factory, it is much cheaper." (Hing, March 24, 2004). Therefore, Dr Hing's strategy created a new paradigm out of former competition through a joint venture with that competition, which eliminated all rivalry, and which assisted both companies to profit, particularly Little Dragon.

The Chinese government also broke with convention in its social policy in announcing that industry would in future be responsible for funding their employees' pension. Lei Yuan explained that, "Workers who were employed before 1984 will have their retirement pension paid for by the state, but after that it comes from the company. It is the biggest change [in our company]. It puts a lot more pressure on the company. The government has created a social welfare scheme and the companies have to contribute to that every month, and this has to take care of retired workers." (Lei, March 22, 2004).

Furthermore, Little Dragon underwent another major change. Lei Yuan revealed that they had "transferred 65 percent of [their] national shares to a company called Sue Te. Little Dragon would continue to produce washing machines, refrigerators, air conditioners, and now it will also be a part of IT (Information Technology), which is produced by Sue Te. It is a private company. This is called a share-transfer, and Sue Te is now in charge of Little Dragon. It is a big step. They bought Little Dragon." (Lei, March 22, 2004). However, it appears that in the acquisition agreement, Little Dragon was allowed to maintain considerable independence, and change is demonstrable at executive level, but not at operational levels. "They may own a majority of our shares, but we have an agreement that there will be no changes to our brand, nor to our registration, or our main business area. There will be no changes to our lead management team or to our workforce." (Lei, March 22, 2004). However, at executive level, changes occurred: "There are now five directors from Sue Te, and two from the National Capital Commission – although the chairman remains." (Lei, March 22, 2004). The reason for the purchase was "because of [Little Dragon's] brand, because it is run in an excellent way, because it has no debt, and because its net capital is positive." (Lei, March 22, 2004). The acquisition did cause the management concern at first: "Initially, we were worried but once we saw that they were serious about our independent development we were happier about it." (Lei, March 22, 2004).

8.2 Globalization: Exploiting opportunities in new environments

Since China was admitted to the World Trade Organization, there have been six washing machine manufacturers that have requested Little Dragon to assist them with design. Little Dragon are targeting the manufacture of 800,000 machines for export to countries abroad in 2005. The majority of those are going to the USA, Japan, Russia, Mexico and Brazil. Membership with the WTO enabled Little Dragon to produce orders for washing machines abroad in excess of 10,000 units. Most of those are being manufactured in China.

In expanding its markets, Little Dragon continued to work on the design and production of their washing machines, and instances of innovation and change included a multi-voltage capacity so that consumers may use them instantly without the need for adaptors, regardless of the voltage in the country in which they reside. The company also negotiated a ten-year contract with American General Motor on a quota system, to produce washing machines with a 10 kg load capacity. Whereas a capacity of 5 kg was sufficient for a Chinese household, the American domestic market required a 10 kg load for the machine to be competitive in the market. Mr Lei stated that the world's annual purchase number of new washing machines was 55 million, and that presently they would produce 800,000 units of that total. He believed this output was realistic, because Little Dragon now had a number of plants in China: four in Wuxi, one in Zheijiang, two in Hubei, one in Changhua; and two abroad: one in Indonesia and the other in Argentina, both of which also represent sizeable domestic markets.

Dr Hing also referred to the importance of international partnerships and markets. Like Mr Lei, he placed considerable emphasis on the company's relationship with General Electric of the USA. Unlike the joint venture with Toshiba, the basis of the partnership with GE was "Collegial. This is to create a new generation of washers. With GE we have another important branch called Mabe – Little Dragon is making washers for the American internal [domestic] market." (Hing, March 24, 2004). This was the contract that Mr Lei had referred to in a previous interview, but Dr Hing added more details. "For Mabe we are making top-loaders. We are doing the design, manufacture and service." (Hing, March 24, 2004). This marked considerable expansion since the 2001 interview: "The China market is big. We have our own [dedicated] sales sites, 3,500 of them. But in the world, we don't have [dedicated] sites. In China we have 1500 service centres, and we export to more than 70 countries, with 200 overseas sales agents." (Hing, March 24, 2004).

However, the challenges that the company faces in the future do not focus only on meeting a numbers target. The company returns about 2-3 percent of total revenue into research in order to produce a technology to achieve performance in a washing machine which saves water and electricity. These two elements, which exist in abundance in many parts of the world, are both in short supply in China, which is ranked thirteenth in water shortage in the world and has electricity quotas in its industries. Whilst the researcher was in China in March 2004, most industries had electricity cuts of one day per week, when production would come to a complete standstill and employees went home. It took three years for the company to develop dedicated software in partnership with AEG of Germany. "Fuzzy" control now regulates the wash cycle depending on load weight, water volume and temperature.

Two other partnership which Little Dragon valued highly were with Motorola and PNG. With Motorola, Little Dragon came to an agreement to make control mechanism for appliances. These consisted of the hardware of electronic control panels and the essential software. The cooperation with PNG is related to the new generation washing machine that Little Dragon is in the process of designing for future manufacture. PNG is a manufacturer of detergents, and in partnership with this company, Little Dragon has produced data over the last ten years, on how to maximise performance between washing machine action, speed, timing, temperature and use of detergents.

Dr Hing speculated that Little Dragon might establish a plant in the Americas, because transportation costs were so high from Asia to its foreign consumer markets, and North Carolina, Mexico, and Canada arose as possible sites. Asked what criteria he would use to make a choice, Dr Hing replied that the factor that was so relevant for most companies, the cost of labour, was not as critical for him. "The cost of labour is not necessarily a long-term consideration. Ten years ago, labour in China was very cheap, but in ten years from now, I don't know. Education, political stability, culture, and the ability to control the factory if not the market – those are important. But we need to go step by step. We can't hurry." (Hing, March 24, 2004). However, Little Dragon had invested abroad in another way, by share purchases: "Our partners include Siemens and Bosch, and [we] own 40 percent of their shares." (Hing, March 24, 2004). Within China, Little Dragon bought shares in three companies that will produce the Little Dragon brand, and in so doing, Mr Lei and Dr Hing believed that they were on their way to capturing 10 percent of the 55 million world-wide sales in the future, although without an exact determination of when this might occur.

8.3 Sustainability: Surviving and thriving

The main plant in Wuxi is presently constructing a second New Zealand [Scott] line for folding metal washing machine casings. There is now also a Japan line, and one from Italy. The relationship with high-tech Matsushita continued when the Japanese devised a clutch mechanism and an injection unit which was subsequently constructed by Little Dragon themselves. Little Dragon also made advances in the area of computer simulations to produce designs; this was innovative because it provided three-dimensional perspectives. The company was satisfied that it could "now design all the software and the hardware that [Little Dragon] needed." (Hing, March 24, 2004). He added that at the core of the washing machine was the software, the control mechanism, not the hard shell.

Little Dragon had continued to work with partners to produce research. The company had joint labs with PNG, Motorola and NEC, and had accumulated about 150 patents and other rights on washing machines. Dr Hing was not satisfied however, with the research outputs, although Little Dragon was advanced in the area of design. "We have a very small research [capability] and we need a bigger design capability. So our R&D is really a small "r" and a big "D", and that is my concern. Directors don't like to make big decisions when it comes to research [...] we don't have enough research." (Hing, March 24, 2004).

However, he devised an innovative training scheme that he believed enabled partners to enhance their communications. "We train our engineers with the engineers and staff of our suppliers. This is an innovation. I don't think we can go forward without the help of our suppliers. So we train together. The result is good. You know we have more than 100 suppliers here in Wuxi. Most of our suppliers are small here, except Motorola. Most don't know what we do, or what we do with their products." (Hing, March 24, 2004). He also pointed out that the average age of a Little Dragon engineer was 32 years, and that they had the capacity to learn English: "Then we can speak the same language as General Electric." The management of Little Dragon also underwent Six Sigma training, one week every month, for twelve months, and staff went to night classes for English tuition.

Dr Hing made a number of comments regarding his management style, particularly those he found successful. He has an Honours degree in engineering and a MBA from Shanghai University, and a PhD in mechanical engineering from France. He maintained that he discussed engineering matters a lot with other engineers. "I have never made a decision by myself. I like to explain my thinking to others before I finally decide." (Hing, March 24, 2004). He believed that his earlier teaching and research experience at his former university helped him to become more consultative. He also stated, "I like teamwork." As far as learning was concerned, he is already on record as having increased the educational demands on his management team, but stated, "I realize that you never stop learning. I used to like games and simulations when I was still at the University of Shanghai studying for my MBA. As a result, I think I can talk to everyone on the shop-floor." (Hing, March 24, 2004).

When asked about the nature of the culture at the plant, Dr Hing remarked that this was changing "from the inside and the outside. We're learning from the Japanese and the Americans – each is a different mirror to see our own face." In a country renowned for rigidity and regimentation, Little Dragon's culture was becoming flexible and more open: "We're becoming more cooperative [collaborative]; we're talking, even admitting our own faults; we're reading reports seriously; and our 'languages' are becoming common – the market is driving that." Finally, with optimism in the future, Dr Hing added that "we're dynamic and young [and] we're using partners as our international platform." (Hing, March 24, 2004). He was evasive on what the future might hold, though, but he asserted that the company's future lay in "learn[ing] how to play internationally. Eventually, we are aiming for a new brand, new channel [distribution], new products, all for new markets. We want to innovate products and change the rules of the game. We are working on new products now. The new brand we want is not Little Dragon, but at the moment that is a dream." (Hing, March 24, 2004).

Chapter 9

The Little Dragon Company

Preliminary Analysis

9.1 Congruence and ambidexterity

According to Lei Yuan, Deputy General Manager of Little Dragon, successful innovation in a lead product, namely washing machines, funded the company's development of those secondary products which were expected to have the potential to grow in market importance in the future. At the time of the first interview with Mr Lei in late 2002, Little Dragon was deploying profits from the sale of washing machines to continue excelling in washing machine design, to develop its line in air conditioners and other white-ware appliances. Congruence in its systems had provided ambidexterity. This strategy, combined with the acquisition of high technologies, top engineers, regardless of their nationality, as well as the creation of strategic alliances, encouraged creative windows of opportunity that could exploit a market more quickly than a company that worked in greater isolation. Little Dragon's initial attempt at transforming their innovation model by purchasing washing machine components from Matsushita, thereby planning to break into the white-ware market through the mere act of copying, was a failure.

9.2 Change: Technology and innovation

Francis, Bessant, and Hobday (2003) point out that radical organizational transformation requires multiple changes. Strategies must be re-written, cultures realigned, processes reworked, and value chains redesigned. The authors explain that

151

total organizational transformation is a risky and uncertain venture. They make two pertinent observations from their research:

1. Develop a plan for facilitating radical innovation.
2. Take learning seriously – study what others have done so that potential pitfalls can be avoided.

(Francis, Bessant and Hobday, 2003, p. 29)

Little Dragon's initial foray into washing machines failed because they did not fully understand the industry or the technology. Copying was a superficial strategy that would not allow the company to fully transform itself. They needed to source not only washing machine components but the complete process technology. Ettlie (2000, p. 268) describes the tension that often exists between product and process technology. He points out that process re-engineering is difficult to imitate and that it fails more often than not, as was demonstrated by Little Dragon when they focused on the product rather than the complete production process. Successful technology transformation therefore requires product *and* process re-engineering as well as having the will and determination to learn. After their initial failure, Little Dragon successfully transformed themselves through a total sourcing of technology.

There are generally two schools of thought concerning the sourcing of technology. Tushman and O'Reilly (1997) focus mainly on the principle of a company which initiates and develops innovation in-house. They postulate that companies evolve their products predominantly in an incremental way, although their aim is to achieve periodic breakthroughs in technology that accelerate the quality or performance of the service delivery of which the product is capable. For this reason, they advocate the creation of the "ambidextrous organization", because such an organization operates a conventional division of production as well as a separate but integrated skunkworks facility. Together the concern "can sustain competitive advantage by operating in multiple modes simultaneously – managing for short term efficiency by emphasizing stability and control, as well as for long-term innovation by taking risks and learning by doing." (Tushman & O'Reilly, 1997, p.167). Tushman and O'Reilly promote the concept that the "route to sustained competitive advantage [lies in] producing streams of innovation" in which interlinking cycles of product manufacture as well as

152

intermittent radical new product development can evolve. (Tushman & O'Reilly, 1997, p.165).

9.3 Approach to innovation

Clearly, Little Dragon is a variant because after its initial failure, it has now twice short-circuited this process. They have externally sourced their technology. In purchasing the necessary "breakthrough" technology in washing machines, they controlled its introduction and implementation with a key ready-made innovative component. They then took advantage of market opportunities in air-conditioning in the same way. Little Dragon's own Research and Development Unit then applied itself to the creation of incremental developments in the field, which were less costly than the search for elusive breakthroughs. Tushman and O'Reilly refer to the breakthrough innovation as a "rare, unpredictable event" (Tushman & O'Reilly, 1997, p.160). Two such "rare" events might include 3M's nineteen year research that led to the invention and manufacture of the measured inhaled dose of asthmatic medication; and secondly, the decade of experimentation it took before Seiko perfected the quartz mechanism to effect wrist-watch accuracy upon which they could then create a reputation as an innovative and quality-conscious company. Some breakthroughs are research driven and cannot be purchased. But where they can be purchased, there may be instantaneous results.

Doz, Hamel, and Prahalad (1989) ask a crucial strategic question of firms considering external sourcing of technology. Their concern relates to the ultimate impact of external sourcing. Will it create the capability for future advances to be made internally or will it merely reinforce dependence? Little Dragon has demonstrated that dependency is not necessarily the consequence of external sourcing through its growing list of patents. Ironically, Japanese electronics firms acquired technology from abroad during the 1950's and 1960's to kick-start research programs that resulted in innovation leadership in later years. These same firms are now cooperating with companies such as Little Dragon to provide the same possibilities for growth and leadership by developing their own internal sourcing of technology.

Engardio and Einhorn note that when a whole chain of employees, such as manager, designers, engineers and production staff work in synchronization, there can be a significant acceleration in the speed and efficiency of product development. They also point to the disadvantages of getting the balance in a joint venture wrong, so that the holder of the original intellectual property spawns a new competitors from the ranks of its own suppliers. For example, Motorola hired Taiwan's BenQ Corp. to design and manufacture millions of mobile phones. But then BenQ began selling phones in 2004 within the lucrative Chinese market under its own brand. That prompted Motorola to cancel its contract with BenQ. (Engardio and Einhorn, March 21 2005, p.53). Of course, Little Dragon and Toshiba are potentially in a similar situation, and Dr Hing would have to make a decision whether one instance of commercial gain, as in the case of BenQ, is worth the cancellation of possible future contracts with Toshiba. It is unlikely that he would think so, although that cannot be verified at the time of writing.

Henry Chesbrough distinguishes between "closed" and "open" innovation. He promotes the view that the model of internal technology sourcing is a "closed" approach to innovation, because in this model, the company "generates, develops and commercializes its own ideas. [And continues by stating that] ... This philosophy of self-reliance dominated the R&D operations of many leading industrial corporations for most of the 20th century." (Chesbrough, 2003, p.36). He identifies the following hallmarks of a company which operates the "closed" innovation model: the most capable employees in the field work for the innovative company itself; to profit from R&D, the company must discover, develop and ship it itself; if the company makes an innovative breakthrough, it believes that it will get to market first; if they are the first to commercialize an innovation, they believe they will "win"; if they create the most and best ideas in the industry, they believe they will "win"; and, this company should control their intellectual property so that their competitors do not profit from their ideas. (Chesbrough, 2003, p.38). It appears that Little Dragon has opened a number of "closed" features in the model because of its purchase of proprietary technology and its deployment of strategic alliances (see Figure 1). However, the company is moving more and more toward a hybrid model that exploits the benefits of external sourcing, internal sourcing, as well as the careful nurturing and management of alliances.

Figure 1 attempts to describe the progression of Little Dragon from ceramics and a predominantly seller-based focus, through to the present where ceramics are simply viewed as artefacts from the past for a company that now deals in high technology products. The Y axis in Figure 1 represents Little Dragon's shift from a seller focus through to a market and buyer focus. The X axis represents Little Dragon's significant transformation from a position of imitation and very little innovation through to the development of a large R&D program and the ownership of 150 technology patents in 2002 – evidence of an increasingly high level of innovation.

Little Dragon succeeded in being innovative in part by pursuing an "open" model of innovation. The company's pursuit of innovation to create a competitive advantage also in part allies itself with the Tushman and O'Reilly (1997) model of discontinuous and incremental innovation. In their purchase of technology from Matsushita to establish and continue evolving the washing machine and air-conditioner lines they took the initiative to ignite white-ware production. Chesbrough refers to this as "open" innovation, and the principles which characterise this approach are as follows: The purchase of knowledgeable employees to bring them into the company when at any given time, the company may lack particular expertise; external R&D can create significant value – internal R&D is needed to claim some portion of that value; the company does not have to originate the research in order to profit from it; building a better business model is better than getting to market first; if the company can make the best use of internal and external ideas, they believe they will win; and, the company should profit from others' use of their intellectual property, and the company should buy others' IP whenever it advances its own business model." (Chesbrough, 2003, p.38). Little Dragon over the last decade and a half has been pragmatically deploying whichever methods it deemed necessary to innovate, compete in the market and exploit it commercially with technology and expertise as its two-edged competitive advantage, regardless of its source.

At a time during the late twentieth century when all Chinese industry was subject to the dictates of a central government that took the responsibility for the central planning of its economy, Little Dragon demonstrated courage and insightful strategic planning in purchasing innovative technology from another company, particularly from a foreign one. It developed a human resources policy which has been hiring highly knowledgeable engineers for years, and has constituted a board of governors a quarter of whom hail from abroad, including one vote from an institution sourced from its main international political rival, the USA. Little Dragon sidestepped politics – it was more interested in the contribution that the US Foundation for Education could make to its organizational learning. Little Dragon developed a lead product that met expectations in each of its main markets: the European model is a front loading rotary action, the Asian model is the preferred top-load impeller style, and the American model has an agitator action. From this lead product's profits, the company purchased additional technology in 1999 for a second major line in air-conditioners. It did not invent the technology, but it was clear that it did not need to. The "discontinuous" technological leap of the Tushman and O'Reilly (1997), model could be purchased from Matsushita, rather than be developed in its own laboratories in which the necessary breakthrough might take considerably longer to achieve. Matsushita clearly saw an advantage for itself in not squirreling its IP, and any discussion concerning the advantages of such a purchase for Little Dragon, should include an explanation of why Matsushita might benefit from such a sale.

In the case of Little Dragon and Matsushita there was innovation taking place in the process of purchase and sale which benefited both companies. A specialist in intellectual property strategy comments that more and more companies are engaging in "strategic licensing" meaning that they are sharing core technologies with others, "even [with] competitors", and that contrary to expectations, this "can have significant financial and strategic benefits." (Kline, 2003, p.89). Kline makes the point that "Patent licensing has become a growth business – revenues have skyrocketed from only $15 billion annually a decade ago to more than $100 billion today – as companies have sought to tap the value lying fallow in the 70 to 80 percent of corporate technology assets that typically never get used in core products or lines of business." (Kline, 2003, p.90). It appears that Matsushita realized over a decade ago that the company which invests in the research and creates new technologies is not necessarily the best one to commercialize every product opportunity, and so it may as well be paid for its IP if it has no wish to go into production itself. Little Dragon's approach for purchasing their washing machine technology must at the time have seemed like a mix of good innovation with good business. The results have demonstrated that Little Dragon and Matsushita may have more in common than IP transactions. Doz and Hamel (1997) point out that alliances allow one company to intercept the skills of another and give it the opportunity to close skill gaps much faster than internal development would allow (Doz and Hamel, 1997, p.558), but they also point out repeatedly that such alliances are often more successful if the partners are also strategically, organizationally, or culturally compatible.

Hislop (2003) has argued that knowledge integration for the appropriation of innovation can be facilitated through a number of mechanisms within the firm. He has broadly categorised these as team working, formal education, and the use of documentation (Hislop, 2003, p. 162). The case of Little Dragon clearly demonstrates that innovation can also be successfully integrated into a firm from external sources through direct acquisition, adding a fourth mechanism to Hislop's three categories mentioned above.

Little Dragon has demonstrated that it is possible to successfully make an extraordinary revolutionary shift from one industry into another. Reading between the lines, the organization and its immediate stakeholders showed remarkable tolerance as well as patience, as management realigned the strategic thrust of the company to transform its centre of gravity from ceramics to domestic appliances. Once the decision makers arrived at the conclusion that change was needed, they literally opened the gates to integrate knowledge into their operations through the importation of technology from a foreign competitor no less. Visionary leadership and management have been combined to ensure that Little Dragon did not stop with the acquisition of knowledge, but that this was simply the catalyst for commencement of the firm's own research and development work. While the case has not focused greatly on the leadership aspect of the transition processes, Harborne and Johne (2003) have argued that leadership and the creation of a climate that is conducive to ongoing change is a requisite element for successful product innovation. This is not without risk as has been pointed out by Celeste's study of strategic alliances (1996). Little Dragon's managers committed the firm to a high-risk, long term venture that exposed and altered their core technology. They were also exposed to outside influence and potential tampering as well as potential leaks. Lei Yuan has demonstrated his company's visionary attitude through his thoughts and references to their actions over the turbulent years of the firm. The audacity of the suggestion of an initial alliance between Little Dragon and Matsushita is in itself worthy of the axiom of innovative and visionary leadership.

9.4 Competition

"The important thing is to try to shape the nature of competition, to take control over your own destiny," according Michael Porter, ("Creating tomorrow's advantages" in Gibson, R., 1998, p.31). The leadership at Little Dragon has so far shown great adroitness in shaping the nature of their competition.

By 2004, within 15 months of the first interview with Lei Yuan, he informed the researcher that the company's sales target for 2005 had been set to 20 billion Renminbi. This goal had been communicated to all 10,000 employees by the company broadsheet as well as seminars in strategy and development, conducted by professionals, in order to obtain alignment. The company's strategic mission was to become one of the top five home appliance providers in the world. (Lei, March 22, 2004). There had also been other significant changes: Little Dragon was no longer the 'hunter' looking to hunt in international markets to sell its washing machines and other appliances. It had become the 'hunted' when Japanese high-tech giant Panasonic placed a large capital investment in Wuxi by building a plant to compete in refrigerators within China's domestic market – refrigerators are one of Little Dragon's lesser products. Dr Hing, General Manager of Little Dragon, appeared undisturbed by this apparent encroachment into his company's territory. However, at the same time as Panasonic commenced production in Wuxi, Toshiba, another high-tech giant from Japan, announced its intentions of imminently engaging in head-to-head competition in washing machine production by constructing a plant of its own in Wuxi. It is thereby challenging Little Dragon in its lead product, in its own market, where it has ranked as number one for over a decade.

With increasing globalization, governments and companies have shown concern with the competitiveness of their industries, and how to best respond to challenges which have been generated through opening markets, abandonment of tariffs and other governmental restrictions and have enhanced international currency flows across borders. (Clarke and Clegg, 1998, p.37). Michael Porter's concern is that companies may well have re-engineered, down-sized or reduced their overheads, but he believes, "Companies have to find ways of growing and building advantages rather than just eliminating disadvantages." (Porter quoted in Gibson, 1998, p.32). One of the disadvantages which Little Dragon has experienced is their lack of depth in their research capability, and having to purchase high technology from abroad, as has been previously discussed. Even though they capitalized on these purchases subsequently, Dr Hing lamented that the innovations with which they have been identified were not cultured from within. "We need a bigger design capability. Our R&D is really a small "r" and a big "D", and that is my concern. Directors don't like to make big decisions when it comes to research. Some say, we are making washers, we don't do research." (Hing, March 24, 2004). While Dr Hing clearly saw this lack of aptitude and attitude as disadvantageous, he was still able to turn a shortfall in research competence to his company's advantage, as the partnership with Toshiba demonstrates. But that is only advantageous in the short-term. Dr Hing was referring to the medium to long-term need for his company to create its own innovations because cheap Chinese labour would be insufficient as a bargaining chip on the global market, where most profit is generated by intellectual property advances. Profits follow in the wake of proprietary technological developments, particularly those that have a disruptive capacity. "Replication facilitates borrowing, but not [...] learning." (Govindarajan and Trimble, 2005, p.14). Therefore, autonomous research is not being ingrained in Little Dragon's industrial culture; in a company that prides itself on its achievements, the lack of originality of those achievements compromises its future endeavours.

9.5 Strategy

Porter (1998), as well as Hamel and Prahalad (1994), have provided relevant insights into the need for companies like Little Dragon to respond to Japanese competition by generating a strategic architecture.

> Strategy [is] more than the allocation of scarce resources across competing projects; strategy is the quest to overcome resource constraints through a creative

and unending pursuit of better resource leverage. It is a view of strategy that recognizes that companies not only compete within the boundaries of existing industries, they compete to shape the structure of future industries. It is a view of strategy that recognizes that competition for core competence leadership precedes competition for product leadership, and that conceives of the corporation as a portfolio of competencies [...]. It is a view of strategy that recognizes that competition often takes place within and between coalitions of companies, and not only between individual businesses. (Hamel and Prahalad, 1994, p.32).

Dr Hing was most likely concerned at the arrival of the Japanese companies, both of excellent high-tech repute, as they based themselves in his home town, and began preying for their share of one of the world's largest consumer markets in home appliances. Little Dragon bought their technology on two occasions from Matsushita, because they were insufficiently resourced to create their own. Therefore, the arrival of Japanese competition might register considerable alarm in the Chinese company. But the company's General Manager, Dr Hing, responded in concert with Hamel and Prahalad's precepts of dealing with competition in the future. Dr Hing turned the future into the present. He invited Toshita, his most threatening competitor in the washing machine market, to contract a partnership with Little Dragon so that cooperation would lead to mutual benefits. In achieving this, Hing used his own company's dominant position in the market as leverage to forge a coalition, not just to produce short-term monetary profits, but to generate long-term advantages that would eventually translate into still greater profits. Hing considered learning from other companies to be important in the evolution of his own, with the most effective way being a mix of cordiality and rationality. "My opinion is that cooperation in the factory is much better than competition in the market. In every city, in every market we compete. But in our workshop [and] design shop cooperation is much better than to compete." (Hing, March 24, 2004). It was this approach that allowed him to filter through any home appliance factory in the world where he wished to go: "I'm going to Canada next week, and to a Toshiba factory in Thailand; I've been to a Siemens factory and I can go where I like. We don't have enemies." (Hing, March 24, 2004). And it was this approach that propelled him towards Toshiba – as a strategic partner – not a competitor. This, despite Toshiba's chair of directors planning to become

160

China's number two in home appliance production. "That's a lie." (Hing, March 24, 2004). Indeed, no one plans to become number two in anything, anywhere.

"We couldn't stop them from coming onto the market, even if we anticipate[d] them. They had to come into the Chinese market." (Hing, March 24, 2004). As Porter maintains, "The important thing is to try to shape the nature of competition, to take control over your [company's] own destiny." (Porter quoted in Gibson, 1998, p.32). He built a coalition by staking his own company's reputation: "We ha[d] something they need[ed]. Little Dragon has a strong background in design and manufacturing." In 2003, the company manufactured 3.7 million individual washing machines, with a revenue of $US 1.3 billion, and was placed number three in the world. (Hing, March 24, 2004). Hing was also aware of the approximate cost of the Japanese investing in plant to set themselves up in competition against a fully established company like Little Dragon, and with the Little Dragon brand that enjoyed wide recognition in its own country. His estimation of the initial cost of a new plant was approximately $US 20 million. He convinced Toshiba that there was "no need for them to invest in fixed assets." There was already one agreement in place, "Last year, [2003], we finished more than 20 models for them, the '3' series." This meant that they had already signed one contract, and had delivered on that, establishing trust, communication channels and other processes. The next agreement between the partners was that Little Dragon would "assist them [in penetrating the Chinese market]; we designed for them; we made the machine for them." (Hing, March 24, 2004). These washing machines, designed and manufactured by Little Dragon, with control panel software created by Toshiba, would be branded 'Toshiba', and these machines were destined initially for the Chinese domestic market alone.

With the Board of Directors at Little Dragon at a loss to explain why their General Manager was proposing to come to the aid of Toshiba by enabling it to gain market share, Dr Hing convinced them that, in fact, he was competing for opportunity share. Instead of using strategy as resource allocation he was using strategy as resource accumulation and leverage. (Hamel and Prahalad, 1994, p.24). Hing controlled the conditions. He stated, "We have the value line of their products, and that gives us some rights. We negotiated the transfer price, [so] we gained money from this cooperation, [2 million Renminbi]. We controlled the speed of many things in their progress in this market. In a far assumption, [in a worst case scenario], what will happen? If we stop production they will have nothing to sell onto the Chinese market. That's the power of the production base. So we control the circle [the design and manufacturing cycles], and the steps of their presence in this market." (Hing, March 24, 2004). Hing retained the power to apply certain low-level controls to regulate the newcomer's presence into the market, however, it could not be determined whether he did so. It does not appear that he deliberately slowed Toshiba down. Toshiba's advantage in accepting Hing's offer of partnership lay in the speed of access to Hing's world of burgeoning Chinese markets in white-ware. It took only eight months for Toshiba and Little Dragon's deal to take effect.

9.6 Learning

Whilst Hing re-designed the traditional paradigm of commercial competition, he extended the relationship still further. He became deputy-chair of the Toshiba Board of Directors, and Little Dragon purchased 25 percent of Toshiba's shares. He was also interested in two other matters: learning and technology, and that precluded a repetition of innovation acquisition as it had previously been conducted with Matsushita. The relationship was to be different, explaining, "But it is different from Matsushita. The design comes from Japan and the manufacturing takes place at Little Dragon in China. But we learned almost nothing from Matsushita. This time it is different. Little Dragon designed, but Toshiba engineered the process. So we learned a lot from Toshiba. They taught us how to make as good a washing machine as Toshiba needs." (Hing, March 24, 2004). Hing was not just competing for product leadership, using Toshiba's technology, he was competing for core competence leadership, and maximizing the rate of new market learning. (Hamel and Prahalad, 1994, p.24). Even with a confidentiality agreement in place, Hing could take advantage of Toshiba's technology, which is of a considerably superior standard than Little Dragon's: "We have a confidential[ity] agreement with Toshiba. We now know all the tricks of their washers, but we can't transfer [them] to anybody. But there is no need – the other players in the market don't need Toshiba's information from Little Dragon. We will transfer their technology to our [own] Little Dragon machines." To Toshiba, contracting within eight months with Little Dragon would have been less time than the alternative made of bricks and mortar, let alone the time it would take to establish their own brand. This comparatively instantaneous penetration of China's market must have made the terms of the partnership worthwhile, although the terms appear to favour Little Dragon, particularly regarding Little Dragon's ability to legally replicate Toshiba's technology in a future generation of washing machines. However, there were further advantages from Toshiba's point of view. China became the outsourced base for productivity underpinned by cheap wages, relative to Japan's high wage rates. With Toshiba's technological capacity, it is likely that the technology they transferred to Little Dragon for the composite washing machine, was already dated, yet still more advanced than Little Dragon's own technology. It is possible that Toshiba was already part of the way, or perhaps even close to achieving, the next generation of technology, although the researcher cannot confirm that.

The Hamel and Prahalad concepts of competing for opportunity share and constructing strategic architecture, thereby competing as a white-ware coalition in China, ultimately provided as many advantages to Toshiba as it did to Little Dragon. It was a two-way strategy: there were mutual benefits. Concurrently, Hing introduced a new element to Little Dragon's corporate culture: the nurturing of innovation by challenging long-held assumptions. This created a shift in the nature of business competition because it became underpinned by capabilities-based design and production; by technology and human resources as enablers of competitive performance; by using that performance as leverage to create new alliances; and by using outsourcer partnerships as the basis of competitive advantage for the mutual benefit of the partnership. Porter provides a reminder that, "A good strategy is concerned with the structural evolution of the industry as well as with the firm's own unique position within that industry." (Porter quoted in Gibson, 1998, p.33). Hing contributed to the evolution of his industry by enlarging his market share even if that needed to be shared with Toshiba, as well as securing this own firm's position within that industry by making Little Dragon an indispensable part of Toshiba's strategy.

9.7 Culture

Hing developed a 'commercial symbiosis' in design and manufacturing, and in the process he also helped to evolve his company's culture in innovative ways to support the agreement reached with Toshiba. His new training system connects his engineers with his Wuxi suppliers, of whom there are over 100. Most are small traders, except for Motorola. "I don't think we can go forward without the help of our suppliers. So we train together. Most don't know what we do, or what we do with their products." (Hing, March 24, 2004). His engineering staff also learn English at night-school, so "we can speak the same language as General Electric." (Hing, March 24, 2004). They also had Six Sigma training to achieve error minimization, one week a month for twelve months. Management staff, mainly comprising engineers, can also train in Shanghai, and Dr Hing opened the criteria for staff selection, so that it would not be confined to top leaders. All of this has contributed to a more informed culture which respects learning, even if it has not always come from within China's own borders. Dr Hing pointed out that his company was also "learning from the Japanese and the Americans. Each is a different mirror to see our own face." The result is a culture that involves being, "more cooperative [possibly means 'collaborative']." For an oriental people, conscious of 'saving face,' Hing was pleased that his staff were "talking, even admitting our own faults; we're reading reports seriously; and our 'languages' are becoming common. The market is driving that. We're dynamic and we're young. We're using partners as our international platforms." (Hing, March 24, 2004). Into this scenario he transfers his university learning, maintaining that his attention to detail is beneficial in engineering, but detrimental to marketing. Mr Lei is an adjunct professor at Southern Yangtze University in Wuxi, and also remains in contact with theory as well as practice.

9.8 Leadership

With his advanced knowledge of engineering from France, Hing described his own style as "more consultative" and disposed towards "teamwork." His decision making process consists of sharing this responsibility with other engineers and managers. This openness has made him in his own words, "an effective communicator" who is adept at transferring knowledge to others, suggesting that while he has proven his ability at 'hard competencies' like negotiating and contracting, he can also provide the 'softer' ones of empathy, creativity and trust. (Clarke and Clegg, 1998, p.50/p.201). Neither Hing nor Lei have secretaries, meaning that they impart their decisions and communications without professional assistance. His and Lei Yuan's leadership style has emphasized above all else, the primacy of knowledge acquisition and development. As Peter Drucker argued in *Post-Capitalist Society* (1993), "The productivity of knowledge is going to be the determining factor in the competitive position of a company, and industry, and entire country. The only thing that will increasingly matter … is management performance in making knowledge productive." (Drucker quoted in Clarke and Clegg, 1998, p.225).

9.9 Conclusion

The Little Dragon company has a high level of congruence in its organizational architecture. Its four vital functions consisting of critical tasks, culture, formal organization and people, are coordinated to achieve high levels of alignment and synchronization. The strategic choices are consistently made clear to the workforce, and its processes are being expanded and refined, as can be seen with the completion of the Scott line and the introduction of the Japan and Italy lines. The executive is well educated and visionary. The culture is moving towards open communication, and consists of young personnel who appear enthusiastic about enhancing their education. The human resource system uses various methods of performance evaluation, and is open to recommendations for improvement to enhance staff morale, as evidenced by the move to monthly payment of bonuses instead of accumulating them for an annual payout. This flexibility stands in contrast to the sort of regimentation often associated with a workforce that it is still, at the time of writing in 2004, largely a product of Communist indoctrination and regimentation. The continual process of learning and un-learning is vital to the General Manager's strategy for excellence and expansion; however, being third in the world for washing machine production does not yet meet the company's long-term targets. To meet those, the company continues to look for partnerships and other opportunities with international companies larger, and by Hing's own admission, more technologically advanced than his own.

The Tushman and O'Reilly model, (1997, p.59) rightly points to the need for companies to be aligned in process and product, because congruity leads to equilibrium. However, the model appears relatively static when that is not always an accurate representation of the reality, because companies are constantly assailed with influences and disturbance from the external environment. For example, the model could provide more insight on how a company can maintain its equilibrium when elements of its congruity are put under pressure. In the case of Little Dragon, these include the government's new laws about companies having to contribute to its staff superannuation; the demand by staff for a bonus re-distribution; and its general manager using the competition to increase the production of washing machines when that had not been planned for, entailing considerable pressure on systems. Christensen cautioned against a company aiming to be always a leader or always a follower. "Companies need to take distinctly different postures depending on whether they are addressing a disruptive or sustaining technology." (Christensen, 2003, p.260). Its purchase of washing machine technologies gave it a disruptive first-mover advantages because it created market leadership. Nonetheless, this company is constantly challenged to maintain its systemic equilibrium, and therefore has to re-calibrate its functions continually in order to remain in congruence. Therefore, congruence is not something that can be achieved, and then ignored as if it were 'fixed,' because the environment is an unpredictable dynamic, demanding constant vigilance and re-alignment on the part of the company.

Figure 1   The Jiangsu Little Swan Group Company focus shift since the late
           1950's.

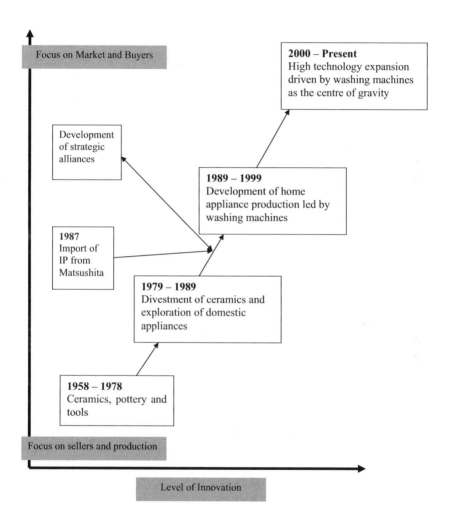

Chapter 10

Alpine Packs the Wilderness Company:
Overview 1973-2004
and First Set of in-depth Perspectives 1973-2002

"When you wear a tie and you've been given a label to put on you saying
'visitor', people here would already know that."

Sandra Gupwell, Co-Director,

Alpine Packs the Wilderness Company, April 4, 2003.

10.1 Overview of the business and change: 1973-2004

In April 2003, co-directors Stewart McBruce, Sandra Gupwell, and the 230 strong
staff of the Alpine Packs Wilderness Equipment Limited celebrated the thirtieth
anniversary of their company, which specialised in designing and manufacturing
outdoors equipment and clothing. It was founded in 1973 through a merger of two
small extant companies, "Alpine Packs", led by McBruce, and "The Wilderness
Company", led by Gupwell.

Their factory is located in Addington, Christchurch, New Zealand, and it is the site of
some of New Zealand's most innovative and functional designs in four outdoor
product ranges: backpacks, clothing, tents and sleeping-bags.

The Company's purpose, as stated on their business cards, was "to inspire people to
explore the natural world." For three decades, this aim was matched by growth in
creativity and practicality as well as in manufacturing processes, and Alpine Packs
achieved increased sales in the domestic market, as well as experiencing some success
in the international markets of Australia, the United Kingdom and Continental

Europe. New product design was coordinated with innovative fabrics, developed scientifically to effect water-proof and heat-retaining characteristics for the lovers of the great outdoors, particularly trampers, campers, climbers and kayakers.

Continual experimentation from the outset in the various fields of production culminated in the company enjoying an enviable reputation for innovative management, robust productivity, stringent quality management, solidarity in teamwork and a strong corporate culture. In addition to those qualities, it also became associated with environmental conservation, an area with which it continues to have a strong affinity.

Then in the 2002 and 2003 financial years, it became clear that Alpine Packs' products were rapidly becoming uncompetitive, and losses of approximately $1,000,000 per year were reported. In view of this, Stewart McBruce and Sandra Gupwell made the decision to outsource production in Asia to increase their margins, not only for sustainability, but to exploit the opportunity to develop the Alpine Packs brand beyond the limits of previous designs and production. Requiring increased resources to enhance and supersede the innovation of their original products in order to regain competitive advantage and increase the sales of the brand internationally, they engineered a down-sizing and restructured the Company within an approximate nine month period, from the planning stage to execution.

In this change-over, the "production" culture which had previously been the dominant one, was replaced with the new dominance of "office" and "design" cultures, underpinned by thirty-five professional staff in relation to only 16 production staff. Present outsource locations include a factory in the Philippines for backpacks; one in North China for sleeping bags; one in Vietnam for tents; and one that manufactures clothes in Southern China. This new equilibrium now controls the destiny of the Company.

10.2 The First set of Perspectives: Products and practices that built the brand

The first twenty years, from 1973-1993, saw much development. From the beginning there was a striving for excellence and a penchant for entrepreneurship and innovation that went on to drive continual experimentation in product diversification and development, as well as experimentation with management techniques and experimentation with the implementation of various human resource practices. Stewart McBruce's approach was entrepreneurial – of a sort: he described entrepreneurship as "not clearly defined". Entrepreneurship refers to "undertaking ventures, pursuing opportunities, innovating and starting businesses." (Robbins & Mukerji, 1994, p.152). Alpine Packs was a dynamic company inspired by an entrepreneurial spirit. McBruce achieved this initially by focusing primarily on his backpacks, and added that even though the element of risk was also often associated with definitions of entrepreneurship, "In the 80s, I changed the whole backpack range but I didn't see it as a risk because I totally believed in what I was doing."(McBruce, April 11, 2003).

Stewart McBruce, saw his role in 2003 as leading the organization and plotting its future direction in rapidly changing markets. A vital part of that was the creation and proliferation of the brand, to focus on entrepreneurial opportunities and to ensure that his team of 230 employees in Addington were focused, or "aligned" on these issues with him. As a 19 year old at the time of the founding of the company, he discovered that he had a flair for designing as well as constructing his products. The product with which he made the company's reputation at the outset was a backpack of superior quality, and the true innovation he brought to its design was the internal light-weight aluminium frame. A frame may have added to the amount of weight that someone could sustain on an outdoor excursion, but its advantage was that it re-distributed the overall weight for greater comfort.

He also believed that innovation played an important part in the company's reputation. "In product innovation, we don't copy other people's products, and we're not fashion driven. We're driven by products that function better."(McBruce, April 11, 2003). McBruce related innovation with profitability: "When we're highly profitable we're more innovative because we have more resources." (McBruce, April 11, 2003). Even in early 2003 when Alpine Packs was already showing signs of financial vulnerability, innovation in design was considered so important that there

170

were nine members in the design team with a budget sufficiently robust to be able to call on outside expertise when required. This included the Wool Research Institute at Lincoln and the Ergonomics Programme Director at Massey University, Assoc Prof Stephen Legg. Rachel Burberry, Head of the Design Team, pointed out that her team tackled "three to four projects per season, [which lasts] six months. The projects that are selected [...] are largely market driven of course, and some of it is our own innovation and our own ideas."(Burberry, April 4, 2003). In 2002, Alpine Packs contracted the services of two additional designers who had previously worked for one of Alpine Packs' strongest competitors, Octerex in Canada; one of them worked for Alpine Packs from his home in Vancouver. Alpine Packs secured the expertise of these designers because their skills in this area were rare and "very specialised", explaining, "There are not very many skilled pack designers in the world let alone in New Zealand. There are more clothing designers in the world than there are pack designers. But technical clothing and people with a passion for the outdoors, there aren't very many." (Burberry, April 4, 2003). It could be said that this was Alpine Packs' first reconnoitre with outsourcing.

Clothing designers, however, played a very important part in the design of outdoor wear for women when Alpine Packs commenced its range for them in the early 'nineties. The Company realized that outdoor pursuits might be male dominated but were not an exclusive male preserve. Alpine Packs created its first "designed by women for women" range, which grew from three products to 45, including packs, sleeping bags and clothing. Concerned with styling, the Company's priority was with functionality because this was at the base of safety. The retention of warmth in alpine climates was important and upper body clothing was designed to effect this but came in women's dimensions: shorter heights, smaller neck, narrower shoulders, chest shape, smaller waist, a narrower back and wider hips. (*Alpine Packs*, Winter 2003, p.32).

10.3   Building competitive advantage: Innovation, management strategies and culture

According to Team Leader, Rachel Burberry, Alpine Packs was always a highly innovative company in which periods of discontinuous innovation propelled it to greater profits. "Discontinuous innovation" means that a company makes large strides forward in one area of design and production, and that it works on different streams of innovation at different times so that one stream helps finance the development of the other.(Tushman and O'Reilly, 1997, p.157).   Her Research and Development budget was among the top five in New Zealand/Australia for this industry, which made it a large budget by New Zealand standards.   Burberry and her design team were motivated to continue the trend towards further innovation to retain the company's competitive advantage, although she knew that every design could be copied offshore within a period of about twelve months of the original's release on the market.

Co-director Sandra Gupwell explained that the materials they used and developed, underwent abrasion tests, waterproof tests, and had been subjected to friction against rough surfaces, and had been exposed to high doses of ultraviolet radiation to gauge and improve their durability and colourfastness.   While Alpine Packs did not invent all the fabrics they used, they aided their continual development and selected them only on the basis of fitness for purpose.   Furthermore, in collaboration with Associate Professor Stephen Legg of Massey University, Alpine Packs designed pack harnesses which provided better ergonomic support for the adventurer. Alpine Packs' Quantum Theory promulgates that when the bearer places a heavy pack on his or her back, the weight pulls the bearer backward, and that this alters the centre of balance.   Then to counteract this backward pull, the bearer bends forward to correct the centre of balance.   As that takes place, the natural S-shape of the spine "changes to a less efficient crane shape, [with the result that] muscles now need to work harder to absorb shock, the bearer tires more easily, [finding] it more difficult to balance during forward motion, [and making the bearer] more susceptible to injury." (*Alpine Packs* Summer 2003, p.32). Therefore, Alpine Packs invested in research, innovative and creative thinking as well as real-user feedback so that the outcomes of each could be integrated into the design process to scientifically improve the product.

To understand the innovative nature of Alpine Packs' products, it is necessary to focus on just a limited selection of them. The Company's defining product was the pack frame, and modern versions are "contoured internal vertical frame bars [that] distribute the load weight from your shoulders and spine down to your lower lumbar area. They also give the sac form and rigidity. The back extension changes shape as you move by stretching and compressing with your spine. This prevents the hip-belt from riding up off your hips." (*Alpine Packs* Summer 2003, p.33). The Quantum harness therefore enables the bearer to carry heavy loads, in excess of 20 kilograms, reduces the rate of fatigue, and allows the bearer to proceed with a natural posture. (*Alpine Packs* Summer 2003, p.32).

Alpine Packs also catered for adventurers in warm environments and other specialised conditions, such as mothers who need to carry their infants. The AirSupply Harness has a smaller capacity compared to the Quantum, and the lumbar pad provides back support and encourages the bearer to stand upright, while highly breathable AirMesh fabric reduces accumulation of perspiration against the bearer's back, which aids dryness and comfort.(*Alpine Packs* Summer 2003, p.33). Finally, the Bambina is a pack to carry an infant, contoured with a 'Y' back to prevent slipping, two-way seats to allow the infant to see in or out, a quick-release system and fleece-lined surfaces which are easy to wash.

McBruce and Gupwell also made improvements to the "pup" tent from the early days when these confined, triangular tents were the only small tents available. Their new design was a different model in which the adventurer could just thread the hoops through and pop them out the ends. This "captive pole-sleeves and open eyelets" (*Alpine Packs* Summer 2003, p.39) construction was very quick, provided more headroom for the same floor space and the hoop tent could be moved around the campsite very easily. In windy conditions, the poles are held rigidly in place on the inside of the pole sleeve, and this reduces the chances of weaknesses developing, while preventing the fly from deforming in high winds.

Furthermore, it was important for trampers to be dry. One fabric that the company uses is UV40 because of its high UV-resistance, high waterproof quality, durability

173

and strength as well as lightweight nature. It is used as fly fabric because of it resistance to cold, wet and windy conditions and was tested in the two sites of New Zealand's most extreme weather: the Southern Alps at snow level, and in Fiordland, which can see 200 mm of rain in one dumping. The exterior of UV40 is fire retardant and has layers of polyurethane, so that water runs straight off the tent surface. (*Alpine Packs* Summer 2003, p.39). Alpine Packs use polyester in tents as well instead of nylon because it has less stretch as fibres absorb far less water, and for that reason their tents avoid sag and contact between the fly and the inner. (*Alpine Packs* Summer 2003, p.39).

The company also began designing and manufacturing waterproof sleeping bags, to high specifications of performance, using substances like Dacron and other waterproof "breathables". A "breathable" is a fabric that allows body moisture from perspiration out through its molecular pores, but not in – just like an air valve in a bicycle tire. The performance ranges from summer lightweights to "expedition" versions suitable for adventurers climbing to 6,000 metres and above, or working in polar regions. All sleeping-bags are layered for warmth, water-resistance, comfort and are lightweight and compact. (*Alpine Packs* Summer 2003, p.37). The fibre that is used in the outer layer is Nextec which is composed of 100 percent polyester micro-fibres which are enclosed in very thin silicon-polymer film. It repels water and has "breathable' characteristics. The interior, or fill, of all sleeping bags is down, rather than a synthetic that is often cheaper but does not perform as well. Down keeps the occupant of the bag warm by trapping heated air emanating from the body; the plumules form pockets of warm air. (*Alpine Packs* Summer 2003, p.37). Alpine Packs use 100 percent silver goose down sourced from cold regions of Europe where evolution has maximised warm retentive quality. They also customised their bags for people with specific needs: women's bags are more contoured than their male counterpart, are shorter and have increased legroom with more down in the foot section. Males too can purchase the latter option with down-packed sleeve in the foot of the mummy to prevent heat loss in the extremities, with an option to unzip this on a warmer night. Further enhancements included an anatomically shaped hood to retain head warmth, and left or right zips depending on the proclivity of the sleeper. (*Alpine Packs* Summer 2003, p.36).

Following this, the company added a new range of synthetic fibre underwear. New Zealand adventurers in particular, believed that warmth could only be provided by wool. But Alpine Packs changed the standard in dryness and heat-retention. The "Alpine" range of clothes for both men and women includes jackets, mountain bibs and pants, headwear, snow gaiters, underwear, mittens and down booties. Gore-tex is used on the exterior wherever there is high exposure to wind and rain, as its membranes allow for the transpiration of body moisture, and repel outside rain and frost. The Gore-tex membrane contains approximately 1.4 billion microscopic pores per square centimetre. A fabric which Alpine Packs also uses and developed itself was Reflex, designed to meet the demands of the New Zealand adventurer who ventures into the very wettest and most rugged environments. It has an ultra-thin and flexible hydrophilic membrane that repels rain and wind, and disperses body vapour build-up via molecular pathways within the membrane. (*Alpine Packs* Winter 2003, p.32)

By 2003, packs constituted 45 percent of production, clothing constituted 35 percent and tents and sleeping bags together comprised 10 percent. In 2003, each minute of manufacturing represented $53,000 for Alpine Packs. (Smith, March 28, 2003). The Company has about 250 retail outlets around the world, of which about a quarter are located in New Zealand. Its products are of a specialist nature, and are sold in sports stores rather than dedicated stores. McBruce believed that while Alpine Packs could create many outdoor requirements for the serious adventurer, there were limits. For this reason, the company never ventured into footwear, for example. According to Joe Barnard, Head of Sales, "The trick in business is recognising what an opportunity is, rather than constantly inventing new technology. We haven't gone much for product diversification, we've done a little within packs, clothing, tents and sleeping bags but not really anything different. Not say, footwear. Although this has come up, and we could have chosen to do it. Stick to your knitting. There's no point in jumping into a new area unless you expert and have a lot of resources and time to develop it." (Barnard, April 4, 2003). McBruce added that this was also the reason why they didn't have dedicated stores, "You have to have a wide range of products to do that. You'd need compasses and boots and so on."(McBruce, April 11, 2003).

McBruce was aware that entrepreneurs take risks and persevere to beat the odds. For him, however, the "safety" of his company and his staff was paramount, and while he had supreme confidence in the superiority of his designs and their success in the market, he was investigating outsourcing to improve his margins without disturbing Alpine Packs' internal order. His and Gupwell's management skills were being tested at the time of the first round of interviews in 2003, because their company had been hard hit by two unrelated factors. The first was the high New Zealand dollar in comparison to the American; and the other was the fallout from the attack on New York in 2001. So-called quality advantages such as the "Made in New Zealand" label were rapidly becoming less of an advantage because of the cost differential. By April 2003, the New Zealand dollar was buying approximately 55 cents American, up from 45 American cents six months earlier. Furthermore, McBruce explained that the consumers he manufactured for were people who took risks by leaving their urban comfort zones and braving the unpredictable and its challenges in the outdoors: "The emotion they [the adventurers] attempt to conquer is fear, because the pioneering spirit is about searching within oneself and testing oneself by pushing out personal limits," (McBruce, April 11 2003). But 9/11 had an impact on that because it was a body blow to the Western spirit as a whole. "Outdoor activity is about transcending fear. [9/11] raised fear, and lowered the freedom [people] perceived they had." (McBruce, April 11 2003). "Outdoor adventure is about travel, and travel, especially air travel, has taken a severe knock." (McBruce, April 11 2003). McBruce estimated that Alpine Packs' sales had dropped between 30 to 50 percent as consumers retrenched, particularly in the lucrative American market.

It was at this very time of difficulty that McBruce's managerial practices and the culture he and Gupwell had evolved over the last thirty years, seemed most likely to reap rewards. In retrospect, McBruce knew by the 1980's that his company needed to expand, and that the model for management that was in place would have to grow with it. He had always disliked the "pathological hierarchies, business models and structures," (McBruce, April 11 2003), which he associated with international big business. He, Gupwell and the management team practised a more egalitarian model in which management and production staff were "a loose friendly family but in order to become big we had to have structures," (McBruce, April 11 2003). McBruce and Gupwell employed a psychologist with a specialisation in communication to produce a company structure in which the long respected notion of sharing, and motivating staff to a common goal, would still be two defining cultural elements at Alpine Packs.

Managerial structures were put in place, and there was now more specialisation: McBruce concentrated more on design and marketing and Gupwell gravitated to human resource management, particularly staff development, which included the profit share implementation
and performance evaluation. (Gupwell, April 4 2003). McBruce commented, "The psychology consultant recommended a human interaction style. I was interested in profit share. We selected a representative group of staff from the business to review my proposal. From the original idea to implementation took about six months. It had a huge impact on the culture of the place. I wanted to reward the effort that people put into their work life. The success of the business was not just created by me." (McBruce, April 11 2003)

Profit share was the obvious reward system to perpetuate in different but no less effective form the family atmosphere that had been created at the set-up stage. McBruce reasoned, "Profit-share and opening the books, with more communication gave us the courage to involve a lot more people to make decisions in the Company. The inherent value at work is 'I come to work to be what and who I am, not just to play a role in the Company'." (McBruce, April 11 2003). Gupwell commented, "When we started, our philosophy was not formal but it was a no ties, no titles, no assigned car-park culture. We treated people the way they should be treated. We developed support programmes. We came up with an ASPIRE programme (Aspiration, Strategy, Participate, Innovation, Reward and Environment). Everyone had aspirations and wanted to help develop the Company. We wanted to reward people – it was a good environment. Around 1986, we developed a profit-share scheme, a bonus scheme, [and] performance reviews for the staff. They developed performance review with us, even though it was unusual for some. It was first done quarterly. Stewart McBruce did mine as managing director, and his was done by the management team." (Gupwell, April 4 2003). Aside from the obvious value such practices might have in bonding employees to each other, the more strategic intent was to enhance quality and quantity of production. Gupwell proceeded to explain further, "Your performance review, PDR, was related to profit-share, so it paid to get a good score. If you got full profit share from PDR based on your last three months' earning, you might get 9 percent of gross earning in that quarter. Or you might get six percent or four percent or none. We used to give staff a full day off, because we weren't financial enough to pay staff in dollars. This was of value to them, and it didn't cost us very much. But later we couldn't get enough staff as were trying to increase our capacity, and we didn't want to go against that, so we changed to cash incentives. We were continuously reviewing our systems so that we were going in the same direction as how and where we were going strategically." (Gupwell, April 4 2003).

These schemes and the evolution of teams over a period of eight years, were highly democratic ways of rewarding staff. In McBruce's own words, "The company was always about sharing, profit was not the most important thing in this business, it was more of a tool. The company is a means for staff to express themselves, and we judge success through designing better products, so the motivation has never been purely material." (McBruce, April 4 2003). This was echoed by Rachel Burberry, Head of the Design Unit, who commented that the spirit of the outdoors brought out "More than profits, because it is about mountains and surf." (Burberry, April 4 2003). She saw Alpine Packs push into globalization as a "jolt into a new reality", and that it would help the company to "confront issues" and "develop technology." (Burberry, April 4 2003)

McBruce referred to the company as "an open and honest culture." (McBruce, April 11 2003). Burberry believed that Alpine Packs was driven by "people, passion, and vision." (Burberry, April 4 2003). Alice Jones, Production Manager, summarised her view of Alpine Packs's culture and put it into the general framework of innovation: "Alpine Packs is successful because of the way it treats people, and are willing to try new ideas, and so we bring good products to the markets. Alpine Packs is innovative in lots of ways. In the way they deal with the staff, in their design and their production methods. [...] It made people grow [...] The company's pretty open and I like that, it's innovative, you can ask anybody anything, and you'll get an answer." (Jones, April 2 2003). This 'openness' referred to many aspects of Alpine Packs' culture: once a month the financial figures were posted on the staff notice-board, with copies going to all teams, and copies going individually to all members of management.

178

Openness was mentioned by all respondents, for example Rachel Burberry commented, "There are opportunities that it brings, I love it, people with talent and skills have a place to grow into. It's about personal and professional growth – definitely. And in the culture, you expect people to deliver and to be expert at what they do. That's accountability." (Burberry, April 4 2003). Pearl Smith commented somewhat more diffidently that even management staff's approximate salaries were common knowledge, "You can just look it up in the book. You'd know that my salary was in the range of $75,000 to $102,000." (Smith, March 28 2003).

The Company had a preference for employing individuals who like the challenge of outdoor pursuits. According to Caroline, Stuart and Linda, "Office staff are mainly the outdoor types. You bring that same passion into the workplace." (Clook, April 2 2003). Sandra Gupwell, manager of human resources, added, "We mainly go for skills and attributes first. Yes, outdoor types are preferred because their values will be more similar [to those of the Company]. It is a prerequisite for sales and marketing employees and customer service staff. Active participation leads to aligned activities, and [an understanding of] skiing and kayaking." (Gupwell, April 4 2003). Joe Barnard's interpretation of this cultural practice was, "Stewart [...] is an outdoor person, and this is a clear point of connection with other people, even if they're from another country. The philosophy is that most outdoor people like what they do. You can't as easily build relationships with people who sell cement." (Barnard, April 4 2003).

Joe Barnard with 12 years experience with the Company, mused that its culture was "the brand, a part of New Zealand heritage [...] and a sense of pride in the product and the company [...] we're a highly technical and performance brand. I tell my staff to say to customers that we're selling the 'complete' brand, and that includes 30 years' experience, with warranty and service." (Barnard, April 4 2003).

Barnard also discussed the innovative distribution methods that the Company developed. Alpine Packs developed the UK market even though it appeared at first that the USA market was larger and more lucrative. However, the latter proved too widespread geographically thereby incurring too large distribution costs. They began with a distributor in the UK who sold to retailers, but in Australia the Company had successfully attempted direct distribution without a "middle-man", and began servicing British retailers the same way, and with the same success. This was in 1995. "We undertook to supply the retailer within seven days of his placing the order, and that was faster than using the distributor [....] we were regarded as the standard in the industry. Alpine Packs acquired a reputation with some retailers saying that we could supply them from New Zealand, when some of their suppliers couldn't do it from 200 miles down the road." (Barnard, April 4 2003). The system worked, and later in the 'nineties, the Company dealt directly with retailers in England, Germany, Switzerland, Denmark, the Netherlands and Belgium. It was a smooth operation whereby one consolidated shipment left New Zealand for a clearing-house in Frankfurt, from which point individual orders were shipped to destinations in Europe. This method also saved the Company considerable funds, because sales-staff continued to reside in New Zealand: "You don't have separate cultures developing around the world. It would have cost us twice as much to employ someone in Germany because the costs are so high, and that's just the salary, that's not even getting him on the road. Tax rates are high; health insurance is high. It was a significant cost-saver for the Company." (Barnard, April 4 2003). As a spin-off from this approach, the sales-staff also learned that they were extra well-received in European retail outlets because they had come from such a distance to do business. To establish further credibility, and shrink the world, the Company adopted the slogan, "While you're sleeping, we're working." (Barnard, April 4 2003). Turning a negative into a positive became a mantra for the Company.

The Company changed to team production in 1996 to further enhance the collaborative atmosphere. Alice Jones traced the teams' evolution with the following comments, "It was well researched: we spent lots of time talking about how we would deal with people and processes, and a lot of time was spent in selling it to the staff. We all went out for a presentation to see how it would work, then the engineers set it up, and we came in the next day, and it was hectic. It was a culture change. We went from supervisors and leading hands to teams which were the authority [in their own right], and [had] responsibility to look after themselves." (Jones, April 2 2003). In fact, the office teams even have responsibility for their own budgets. But as far as the general production staff were concerned, it was "a big change" because "a lot of people come to work and [expect] to be directed to a certain extent, so they found it difficult. We didn't have team leaders at first [so] there was a lack of direction. We've had leaders now [again] for 12-18 months." (Jones, April 2 2003). It appears that the original experiment with teams took a long time to take root in a productive way, but Jones concluded, "We kept working on it and working on it, and being supportive. But there came a time when we knew we had to do something different. There used to be a supervisor managing all the teams, but the problem was that the job was too big. With team leaders it's better." (Jones, April 2 2003). Quality controllers Caroline, Stuart and Linda agreed, "At first, a team was just a collection of people, but now people have specific roles and functions, and that works better." (van der Slee, April 2 2003).

Another aspect of Alpine Packs' culture was "The Quest", a group of teams who ran and kayaked, both day and night, in a competitive spirit. They also were involved in tree-planting and sponsored The Fine Line project, after which the Company supported community-based programmes like Project K. Other community projects in which Alpine Packs was involved included environmental support groups and activities like ROA (the association for conservation professionals), educational programmes such as avalanche awareness, videos and outdoor pursuits centres, expedition teams to the Himalayas, Arctic, Antarctic, Alaska and South America.(*Alpine Packs* Summer 2003, p.153).

Eventually, there was a realisation that a company needed to be profitable to provide a stable place of employment, and in early April 2003, McBruce announced that Alpine Packs would be seeking to manufacture their tents and sleeping bags in Asia instead of in Christchurch. Remarkably there were to be no redundancies in the offing at that time. Staff were to be re-allocated positions within the factory at Addington. Operations Manager, Pearl Smith commented that under present circumstances it had been necessary to effect a "greater urgency." (Smith, March 28 2003).

10.4 Continuing the industrial evolution: The imperative of change

Staff at Alpine Packs had been living with change for many years, and Pearl Smith believed that the company had become more and more "action-oriented" in the last 20 months, although a greater "commercial acumen" still needed to be driven. (Clook, April 2 2003).

Clook believed that one of the reasons Alpine Packs was successful was because of its quality products, and "being prepared to change". He explained that, "The Company was open to change, and [it] explains why we need to change. Some people don't like change here because they don't see why they should change. But you're not scared of change when you have the information." (Clook, April 2 2003).

Staff were aware that there would be more change because Alpine Packs had posted monthly financial statements on the noticeboard for years as part of the openness of their culture. The figures for 2002 told of a discernable trend of profits declining into a loss statement – the first Alpine Packs had ever recorded. The announcement about offshore production was therefore well received: in the face of adverse markets, change was mandatory, and outward appreciation of the staff that their own jobs would be protected as part of the production going offshore to Asia, was immediate. All staff in the manufacturing plant belonged to a team, sometimes as part of cross-functional teams as well. It was anticipated that the unstable markets of the future would enable each team to refine its skills in financial management and production line coordination with other teams so as to carve out greater profitability. Teams had to become intrapreneurial, meaning they would have to recreate the entrepreneurial spirit in a large organization. (Robbins & Mukerji, 1994, p.153). In changing markets, the team culture was expected to develop so that it could play its part in company renewal.

10.5 Future aims

McBruce saw his strengths as the leader of the company as, "a strong vision where we fit in the market, a huge experience to see across the company, and an openness to change to developing things and to get on with people." (McBruce, April 11 2003). He saw the company in the next few years as having to operate in an unstable geo-political climate. Retaining leadership in backpack design and product quality was his primary goal at that time. He endorsed the internationalisation strategy that the company was to embark on, as well as the entrepreneurial spirit that had characterised the company since it was founded. He wished to continue working with Sandra Gupwell and the management team to make Alpine Packs a major player in this market by continuing to advance innovative design, and by means of perpetuating the innovative and entrepreneurial spirit.

Chapter 11

Alpine Packs the Wilderness Company

The second set of perspectives, covering 2003-2004.

11.1 Strategic change and innovation: Breaking with tradition

The financial crisis at Alpine Packs as ascertained in March of 2003 proved to be
more serious than first calculated. Stewart McBruce had made twelve management
staff redundant at the end of 2002, and after that in early 2003, he hoped that this
move and the outsourcing of backpacks and sleeping-bags would provide him with a
"break-even situation, [creating] time to figure out how to become profitable again."
(McBruce, May 21 2004). On July 1 2003, he made the decision that outsourcing
would have to apply to all products and that the factory in Addington would have to
close as soon as the arrangements were in place. He conceded that "the products
[were] far too pricy in the marketplace, were unprofitable and needed to become
profitable [because we were] losing sales. In order to become profitable, we knew we
had to become innovative in our design and development." (McBruce, May 21 2004).
McBruce made the announcement to his staff on 24 July 2003.

McBruce explained that his company had fallen behind, and even though their
insistence on design-led quality products had initially won them respectable market
share, product prices cost them customers. He lamented that, "For some ten years, we
didn't have money to put into development of [all] our products – we didn't have
improvements on our tents for a long time." (McBruce, May 21 2004). This created
a number of contradictions because it meant that in addition to marketing a number of
dated designs in the product range, these products were manufactured locally at high
wage-rates, while the company was aiming to expand its retail abroad in highly
competitive markets. With production staff redundant, he then increased his product

development staff by twice the number employed in 2002, but retaining the company's values was an important consideration in his formulation of new contracts with outsourcing companies.

McBruce, Gupwell and the Management Team decided to sign contracts with four outsourcing plants in South East Asia. There is now a contractual relationship between Alpine Packs and a plant in the Philippines to manufacture backpacks; a contract between them and a plant in Vietnam to manufacture tents; and two contracts in China for the manufacture of sleeping bags and outdoor clothes. The final decision was made by pooling data and evaluations from various sources collated over a period of about six months. They made the decisions by firstly contacting a number of suppliers with whom the company had had long-standing arrangements, and who did business in South East Asia, as well as in the Pacific. On suppliers' recommendations, McBruce and Gupwell made visits to audit them for their various capacities. McBruce insisted that the values by which the Company had begun, ought not to be compromised: "We had no desire to change the quality of the product. We didn't want to downgrade. These people [their would-be manufacturing colleagues abroad] had to be highly responsible employers, who had good working conditions." (McBruce, May 21 2004). The contracts are not exclusive, and the outsourcing companies also had contracts with other onshore companies besides Alpine Packs. McBruce was concerned to choose outsourcing partners, "for their quality and workmanship. We were very particular over all the manufacturing, not just one product, because if one was inferior it would let down the whole brand. So we were equally particular across all products." (McBruce, May 21 2004).

The main movements or phases of change were as follows according to McBruce:
- The first phase was the realisation that the market was adversely affected by the events of "9/11" in New York;
- From that point he began observing the financial situation with close interest;
- He started checking out and investigating alternatives to onshore production;
- He made twelve management staff redundant late in 2002;
- He had hoped to reach break-even point in late 2002;

- He decided to contract out the manufacture of the lesser profit products: tents and sleeping-bags;
- He announced in April 2003 to all staff that two product ranges would be manufactured offshore - no redundancies in the offing;
- He then made the decision that all production would go offshore;
- He announced in July 2003 to all staff that the Addington plant would close, with the exception of office, design and small-run production skeleton staff by end of 2003;
- He closed the Addington plant at the end of October 2003;
- He switched production to South East Asia;
- New products arrived just prior to Christmas 2003;
- Communication, quality assurance and quality control methods changed in late 2003-2004;
- All prior systems geared for workforce of 230 scaled down, heavily modified or newly devised for workforce of 50 onshore staff;
- Physical changes to Addington plant to suit smaller numbers;
- Outsourced consumer goods arrived in New Zealand and Australian stores in December 2003-January 2004.

(McBruce, May 21 2004).

The same events and sequence were corroborated and summarised by Gupwell from a Human Resources perspective: "The preparation, decision making, communications with staff, [a] significant period of support, actual change and people leaving, then work methods changing." She then added that they were now at a stage of having adequate systems in place to start focusing on "Step[ping] up the performance again," because "We're starting to achieve some results. People have changed, processes have changed. We're now operating in our new environment and we have to ask what are our expectations? How are we performing against those expectations, and we now need to look how we're going." (Gupwell, May 28 2004).

McBruce was pleased with the early results. His strategy was to "Work on the existing range of products – we're reinventing this range of products [....] So we are mainly upgrading our products, as well as experimenting with other products."

186

(McBruce, May 21 2004). His evaluation of the situation at the time of writing was that, "The new products are only just hitting the market [...] the quality is as good as before, or in some cases better, but the prices are lower. Markets have been 99.99 percent positive [....] Four out of the last five months have been profitable." (McBruce, May 21 2004).

Every member of the Management Team had one or more specific responsibility in the changeover. These included Stewart McBruce, who drove and coordinated the main changes; Pearl Smith and Sandra Gupwell, who worked on the details of the actual factory closure; Barry Ensor and Joe Barnard who worked on offshore warehousing arrangements; Rachel Burberry, who worked from the design point of view; and Ritchie Adams who worked on production planning. (Gupwell, May 28 2004). However, there was a degree of uncertainty: they could not act from prior knowledge because closure was a new experience for all of them. Therefore, the Team employed three consultancy firms whose role it was to guide them through their legal obligations to the redundant staff, and to devise processes to make closure timely and efficient.

Gupwell recalled that, "They told us what they expected would happen. But some of this did not fit with our culture, so we thanked them, said we don't think this will happen. But if it does, then thanks for forewarning us, and we'll keep an eye out for it. They said the media would be at the gate and the union would be around, but neither of those occurred." (Gupwell, May 28 2004). She was referring to forewarnings, "That staff would hear the announcement [of closure] and would then say goodbye by smashing and stealing things." (Gupwell, May 28 2004). Management's instincts proved to be correct as far as sabotage was concerned because there was none at any time. The "open and honest" culture which had been generated from the company's earliest beginnings produced benefits at the time of its demise: "We thought productivity would go down, and we had to calculate when we were going to run out of work. We wanted to give plenty of notice to find another job. [But] the staff didn't leave, absenteeism almost stopped and productivity went up. Our estimation of productivity was way out. This was a learning element. If there was negativity, it was in using up the sick-pay being used up in that period, which would normally be spread over the whole year. That was fine, because staff were using up their entitlement.

187

Staff also did more wandering around the plant to talk to mates and confidantes."
(Gupwell, May 28 2004). McBruce's version was that he'd made the decision that,
"There would be no secrets in the organization [...] I was advised to go about this the
traditional way, which was to keep it all quiet and give people notice just a few weeks
before the closure. This was because people desert like [rats on] a sinking ship [to]
get other jobs. We decided that we could simply not live with doing that. The value
of being open and honest ha[d] never failed me, [I've] never had a negative result, but
always [a] positive [one]. We didn't know when we were going to close, nor how
many people would leave. [....] The staff were aware that monthly our sales were
down, and that we'd brought in consultants. They were not surprised, we had not kept
them in the dark. They appreciated the openness. And when I discussed this with
Sandra, I put myself in their place and said the one thing I would really like is lots of
notice. In the end, we maintained the relationship we'd always had: open and honest
– we continued the trusting relationship." (McBruce, May 21 2004).

The continuation of business as usual struck Alice Jones as "quite amazing." (Jones,
June 14 2004). She recounted that, "Most people were just getting on with the job. I
don't know that it actually hit for a long time. [...] The atmosphere here was very
positive. [There was] no niggling. It was more a question of 'We've got this time,
let's get on with it.'" (Jones, June 14 2004). In the time between the announcement in
July and closure in October, only one person left for another position. (Gupwell, May
28 2004).

The good faith relationship continued during the time towards closure in a number of
ways. "We were given time to talk after the announcement and were then sent home.
And we [the Management] followed up and talked with everybody to make sure they
were OK. On the day, we made sure that everybody knew what was going on: even
those on holiday or maternity leave. They got their letter and it was explained to them
so they wouldn't find out through the press. On the [next day], we talked to
everybody to try to answer their questions." (Gupwell, May 28 2004). While that may
have sounded definitive and reassuring, Gupwell added caution and admitted that,
"The Team would have been definitive when they could be about what they knew,
and said what they didn't know. It wasn't as if Management had all the answers;
there was a lot that was new. When they had answers they happily talked about them

188

so the staff would know what was going to happen." (Gupwell, May 28 2004). Management continued to provide a caring environment, "We've always been more than just a place of work. So we tried to provide support, to show that we cared. We never tried to screw the staff. We've operated with open book information for years, and so the staff were aware of the struggle in the Company. They had to allow us to make it happen." (Gupwell, May 28 2004).

The staff indeed appeared to given their collective consent, possibly encouraged by a number of measures of assistance that Management provided and supported between the months of July and October 2003. Gupwell took a number of initiatives: she created a "People's People Team" which consisted of two staff members who provided support, whilst she and Pearl Smith were available and gave their home telephone numbers to staff in case they were required to assist with support or advice during non-work time. She invited Work and Income New Zealand to talk to staff about budgeting, updating and formatting their Curriculum Vitae, and discussed post-closure options. Management also contacted other places of work, especially the growing electronics industries such as Tait Electronics, and informed them that about 200 skilled workers would be coming onto the labour market, and if they had vacancies and were prepared to retrain them, they would soon become available. These new vacancies were advertised on a dedicated noticeboard in the factory. With foresight and extra caution, redundancy clauses had also been written into the previous employment agreement: "Because the situation had been steadily getting worse, we wrote redundancy into the agreement because if it ever came to that, we didn't want to have to deal with an emotional issue. [The formula, which applied to everyone, was] Three weeks for the first year, and one week for each complete year thereafter to a maximum of eight weeks." (Gupwell, May 28 2004).

A remnant of the original production staff remained to assist in this profitability. Short runs, prototypes and specialist orders continue to be manufactured by a small team of 12 production staff in the Addington plant in Christchurch, according to McBruce. However, this number had risen to 16 just two weeks later when the researcher interviewed former production manager Alice Jones. Their main working relationship was with the Design Team, in order to ensure that the new designs would be 'manufacturable.' Sandra Gupwell explained that to appoint staff to this

189

production remnant, "We used [their level of] product knowledge, range of skill levels, but aiming at upper levels […] and the other [skill] we used was attitude that they had exhibited as they worked with us over the years." (Gupwell, May 28 2004).

11.2 Globalization: Exploiting opportunities in new environments

Sandra Gupwell identified the "loss of knowledge" as one of the most disturbing aspects of the change. In one of her new-order capacities, Gupwell sold off plant and machinery: "They're going for parts, and in some cases, they could have bought the whole system that we set up, instead of an individual part. That's all part of the loss of knowledge, but now we don't use the old systems and are devising new ones." (Gupwell, May 28 2004) This impacted on results, as Gupwell explained: "People have been working hard, but we haven't necessarily been getting the results. We need to adjust our expectations against our processes. There has been a 'grey' area in operation as we need to work out what we have to do. A lot of knowledge has been lost in the transition. We had to download information for people who were taking on a responsibility for the first time. And we have lost information about the history [of Alpine Packs, and what it successfully developed]: knowing what has and has not worked in the past. We're reinventing the wheel." (Gupwell, May 28 2004). The change-over was generally smooth; in the interim to the new order "approximately $NZ 2 Million - $NZ 3 Million of sales [was] lost, which was not bad." (McBruce, May 21 2004).

Quality control was another new learning experience; the system is "nearly there", according to Gupwell, who was in charge of devising it. "Designers work directly with outsourcing and go over there and work with them until they get it right. They make it up and send it to us as a pre-production sample off the production line and we check that against our QA model. If it's OK we say 'Go for production'. And we go to the factory and do random sampling. It seems to be working. We link these factories together when we go out, as we [now] go four or five times a year. We have a few staff in the QA team who can do this." (Gupwell, May 28 2004). Alice Jones emphasized the personal relationship: "Caroline [van der Slee] has been there and she knows these people, and she communicates with them. The samples determine if they go ahead to production. We have an internationally recognised system of checking before, during and after." (Jones, June 14 2004). Added McBruce: "Formerly, we had a QA system where I read users' letters, and this would go down to the sewers. [But] now we have to specify everything on paper. [....] In the Philippines, the [standard of] English is good. We're fortunate that English is the international business language," (McBruce, May 21 2004), as Design and Office communicate to outsource plants by email and telephone several times a day. "There's several angles: the quality angle, the design one, ordering, logistics, at four different groups. It's a close relationship from a communication perspective." (McBruce, May 21 2004).

Significant changes have occurred to the Sales Team. Joe Barnard recounted some of the most important changes to have taken place since October 2003. The strategy which was formerly employed was direct marketing and supply to retailers. This has now been reversed "in order to expand into foreign markets and increase responsiveness." (Barnard, June 14 2004). The onshore Sales Team now employs a new sales manager for North America, a new appointment has just been made to represent Alpine Packs in the European Union, and the Australian market now has a fulltime sales representative.

Barnard explained that the approach to sales was now in a process of change, because the outsourcing process gave sales less flexibility as it required a longer lead-time. To compensate for that, "we are trying to get a stronger commitment from our retailers. We've had to put in an incentive to make it work. This is an increased margin incentive, so [retailers] will make forward orders, up to six months in advance. We'll give them an increased discount, up to 3, 4, or 5 percent." (Barnard, June 14 2004).

Production could now also be ramped up more so than was possible in New Zealand. The company now has a warehouse distribution centre in Europe, from where Alpine Packs are actively targeting the European [Continental] market. For the first time, Spain, Italy, the Czech Republic and Poland were being targeted. The company is working to meet retail demands in the United States and Canada by the summer of 2005. With the Marketing Management Team responsible for strategic direction setting, the Company is setting up a backpack operation in Europe. Since the transition to outsourcing, sales have lifted: alpine packs have increased, and travel packs sales have improved, particularly in the already more established markets of the United Kingdom and Australia. The strategy was to "price at market price, at the same level as our competitors, [thereby bringing the former price] ten to fifteen percent down. And we gave our retailers more margin. We didn't want to drop the price too much and destabilise the brand. It seems to be working." (Barnard, June 14 2004). He also added that the biggest problem to resolve was the supply line changeover, going from one manufacturing plant to four with a considerable geographic spread, and going from one warehouse to three.

New processes and systems had to be created, and are still being refined. One aspect of this is the lines of communication. In one instance, both Alpine Packs and one of their Australian suppliers were so focused on internal change that each omitted to inform the other that the supply timeline would be disrupted. Because Alpine Packs had been dependent on suppliers since its inception, it had created flexibility around some of their suppliers' inability to deliver regularly and on time. Under the new order, Alpine Packs needed to recreate their schedules for production, and therefore their suppliers should have also done this, but in several instances it was the suppliers who failed in their planning, and Alpine Packs didn't hear about it until it was too late. Alpine Packs has therefore learnt that they must not depend too much on irregular suppliers, because they could not turn manufacturing around to fit in with them. Ironically, one of their suppliers also went offshore for part of their process at the same time as Alpine Packs, but they didn't inform Alpine Packs of that, and this distorted the timeline. As a result, the supplier informed Alpine Packs too late that they would be two months behind schedule with their shipment.

In addition to describing the problem above, Joe Barnard also identified that there was a relationship between competitive advantage and innovation which they still needed to exploit: "We're entering into an environment where we're on a level playing field from a cost structure basis. That will mean that we need to differentiate our products. It's obvious that things are getting more competitive. For example, the UK market didn't have too many competitors in the market, and now there is competition from the US [there]. From the point of view of innovation, we're still looking for the things that make us different. We're trying to design a marketing approach to take advantage of strategic opportunities." (Barnard, June 14 2004).

Those strategic opportunities may lie in the world's wealthiest consumer market, the USA; but Barnard cautioned that, "It's well known to be a graveyard for [foreign] brands," (Barnard, June 14 2004), so vigilance would be required. He considered that the main challenges for the future comprise three main issues: first, to refine Alpine Packs' logistics supply; second, to develop further their products and the brand; and third, to obtain greater control of their distribution. Alpine Packs was looking to manufacture a popular item generating high demand, and so a distribution system would have to be developed to provide adequate supply. The nature of such an item was not disclosed at the time of writing.

11.3 Sustainability: Surviving and thriving

Part of the "open and honest" culture of the old order was having to face long-serving employees, to tell them that they were redundant, and to say goodbye because they had not been selected to be part of the skeleton production staff that would continue. Gupwell's greatest difficulty was, "Face to face telling individual staff members that they didn't have a job after they indicated that they needed one and after they had told you their family circumstances. That I found particularly hard." (Gupwell, May 28 2004). But at the same time, it was symbolic of success: "My greatest success? That people didn't want to go on the last day. And that people had liked the type of culture that we had set up here. We knew we had done something well, and that we'[d] been part of their lives. Some came here as an unmarried teenager and they left [on the last day] married with children. We had married couples working here, and that was fantastic." (Gupwell, May 28 2004). McBruce was surprised: "The staff were absolutely brilliant: there was no negativity. No one complained. I think in a way that staff were relieved that the decision had been made. Only one person left. It was quite incredible." (McBruce, May 21 2004). Barnard commented that the Management Team "thought there might be a mass exodus, but there wasn't. We had the challenge of meeting final orders before outsourcing, and didn't know if staff would stay on to produce it. But it worked very well actually." (Barnard, June 14 2004). Jones added, "Some of the people [the press] spoke to had been here for a

193

very long time, and they said they felt sorry for Stewart. There were one or two other people that were angry. But the biggest majority knew there was no alternative. It was made very clear by Stewart why it was happening. There was no hidden agenda or anything like that. The staff could understand." (Jones, June 14 2004). She maintained that productivity after that was not affected, except on the first day. "The culture assisted the process because things have always been so open and honest, and it brought out the best in people. But I can't explain. When Stewart knew that it was going to close, he wanted others to know as well, even though some people thought he was giving everyone far too much notice. People appreciated that." (Jones, June 14 2004).

Alice Jones then went on to comment that under the restructured order, the culture at Alpine Packs had "changed – it's got better" because "it's a smaller group," so "it's more like family." She remembered that the whole workforce "used to have meetings on Wednesdays, [we] needed the whole cafeteria, but we don't need a microphone anymore." The result was, "we're a lot closer." (Jones, June 14 2004). There was another change that Jones observed: "We're now more directed than we used to be, there's more control – I know that's not a very good word to use at Alpine Packs – but there's more control about what's happening at the factory. Even down from Stewart [McBruce] there's more directive. I think that it needs to be, to get things done and done on time. We've got to be more accountable. There's always been a sense of urgency, but we're being directed more from Shelley and Stewart. This makes us more accountable." (Jones, June 14 2004.) McBruce commented: "We're shifting from a factory culture to an office culture. And now to a design-marketing culture. We've got about 50 office people, and only 16 production staff. We're still casual and interactive. People are still sorting out their areas. We're still hectic. It's still going to take time before we feel that we're working in unison with each other." (McBruce, May 21 2004). Joe Barnard offered a similar assessment: "It's evolving a bit. The factory was a huge big machine, it would quieten down on a Friday afternoon, and that's changed. The focus now is on marketing and design, the big picture of the brand development." (Barnard, June 14 2004).

Chapter 12

Alpine Packs the Wilderness Company

Preliminary Analysis

12.1 Congruence and ambidexterity

Discontinuous changes may be uncommon but they have twice played key roles in Alpine Packs' commercial viability. The first discontinuous changes were Stewart McBruce's invention of the internal frame, providing backpacks with structure for better weight distribution. Then the company invented the hoop tent. Those products marked the fledgling company's entry into the wilderness equipment market as an instantaneous and innovative leader. The second discontinuous change about thirty years later, in 2003, was the company's move towards outsourcing production from New Zealand to Asia, in order to remain viable, thereby extricating itself from an imminent threat of insolvency.

Despite being in an unenviable financial position by March 2003, Alpine Packs' management was a knowledgeable one, and there are abundant examples of congruence. For example, McBruce and Gupwell showed awareness of the need for congruence in its organizational architecture. The owner-operators had been striving to enhance and maintain organizational alignment with its strategic intent as demonstrated by their role functions. McBruce alluded to the practice of aligning disparate elements in the organization when he stated, "My main role in the Company is to lead the organization, and to make sure that we're heading overall in the same direction, and I have to get people to buy into that." (McBruce, April 11 2003). Similarly, Gupwell catalogued a decade long process of evolving human resource management, from Profit Share to ASPIRE to Performance, Development and

Review, and maintained, "We were continuously reviewing our systems so that we were going in the same direction as how and where we were going strategically." (Gupwell, April 4 2003). Tushman and O'Reilly provide an important diagnostic question for analysing congruence: "Given the critical tasks and work flows that must be accomplished, how aligned or congruent are the current formal organizational arrangements (eg structure, systems, rewards), culture (eg norms, values, informal communication networks), and people (eg individual competencies, motives)? Do these organizational building blocks fit with task requirements? Do they fit with each other?" (Tushman and O'Reilly, 1997, pp.62-63). A systematic analysis of these features will show that Alpine Packs was congruent and integrated to a high degree, but it could not make a profit beyond 2001, nor could it be described as an ambidextrous organization. In its lack of preparation for the future, it lacked the capacity to withstand and overcome the fallout from the "9/11" disaster, with which its misfortune became inextricably linked. In Michael Hammer's prophetic words, "When processes are linked, any change to an order ripples through the entire supply chain." (Hammer, Sept. 2001, p.86).

12.2 Change: Unexpected environmental impact

The Company had been losing approximately one million New Zealand dollars per production year since the events of "9/11" in New York in 2001. Once the financial data had been processed in late 2002, Stewart McBruce was able to trace his Company's losses back approximately to that date, explaining that man's adventurous spirit, yearning for challenges in the great outdoors, did not encompass leaving the family behind in urban settings vulnerable to terror attacks by extremists from the Middle East. Nor did it encourage adventuring in isolated regions. "It raised the level of fear. The airlines nosedived and our industry is largely travel based, so it nosedived [as well]." (McBruce, April 11 2003). Was this a credible explanation? CNN have reported that the Boeing Company in Seattle, USA, created 30,000 redundancies since 9/11, (*Business News*, 19 July 2004), which corroborated McBruce's assessment of his own Company's sudden decline. Clarke and Clegg (1998) attempt to explain the world's general economic events as having a cyclical nature, citing first Kondratiev's "long-wave" theory and then progressing to Schumpeter. Kondratiev promulgated the concept of expansion and stagnation alternating rhythmically in half-century cycles that related to massive investment in, and then the subsequent depreciation of, major works of infrastructure such as railways. But Schumpeter believed that cycles were more the product of "clusters of innovation [...] creating new and discontinuous leading edge sectors in the world economy, [periodically] driving macro-economic growth." (Clarke and Clegg, 1998, pp.11-12). However, these do not adequately explain the after-effects of political disturbances such as 9/11. The concept of paradigm shifts may be more enlightening. Significant paradigm shifts may be precipitated by political events, (Clarke and Clegg, 1998, p.13) and those that took place in New York and Washington in 2001, then augured in a war that took place in Afghanistan in 2002, and an invasion followed by an occupation of Iraq in 2003-2005 (and possibly beyond that date). Altogether these events have resulted in new national security measures by a number of governments, particularly in the United States, that now operate under the paradigm that the interests of national security are paramount, regardless of the cost to consumer convenience, the dollar cost to the nation or the cost in lives of their armed forces. It would appear that Alpine Packs became an innocent victim of this shift. "We've been hugely hard hit. For the first time, we've been hit by events outside our sphere of influence." (McBruce, April 11 2003). Even so, it would appear that correctly ascertaining the implications of this at an early stage, and implementing the corrective action by the company, assisted in its reinvention and return to profitability, as evidenced by profit results in the first half of 2004. "Good ideas most often flow from the process of taking a hard look at your customers, your competitors, and your business all at once." (Pearson, Aug 2002).

12.3 Approach to innovation

First it is necessary to go back to the beginning to understand the organizational structures to achieve innovation. From the outset, the company's management created an organization that could be typified as a "social organization" (Jameson quoted in Carnell, 1990, pp. 166-67). McBruce's comments signified his approach to management as a social approach which manifested itself in company structure, communication, and interaction, all of which fits neatly with Jameson's model: "I didn't like the business models that existed with their pathological hierarchies. [...] We had a family style atmosphere [...] a psychology consultant recommended a human interaction style." (McBruce, April 11 2003). Such a company places social values above economics values, and relies on "interdependence, mutual support, caring for others, [and] quality of life. Work is a means to an end, not an end in itself." (Jameson quoted in Carnell, 1990, p 167). This was substantiated by McBruce's social philosophy: "The inherent value at work is, 'I come to work to be what and who I am', not necessarily to play a role in that company. There is a fundamental driver: we do what we like to do, and be respected for that." (McBruce, 11 April 2003). This is predicated on the assumption that when employees are content, they are more cooperative and productive. Jameson's model continues: "Efficiency of output and economic results are to the common good," (Jameson quoted in Carnell, 1990, p 167). This was demonstrated at Alpine Packs largely through the profit share scheme that was designed to, "reward the effort that people put into their work [...] it was a chance to reward the 'more than just effort' they put into the business. [...] The profit motive was not at the top of the list. It was a tool, not a goal." (McBruce, April 11 2003). Under the owner-operator leadership style of McBruce and Gupwell, the Company came to "judge success through better products, and 'wowing' the public; [it was] intrinsic not material [success]." (McBruce, April 11 2003).

This approach created a quality product range of approximately 180 items (Barnard, June 14 2004) from a manufacturing culture which was mutually supportive, open and honest, (McBruce, April 11 2003; Gupwell, April 4 2003; Jones, April 4 2003; Smith, March 28 2003), and one which developed its staff to potential. (Burberry, April 4 2003). These "pragmatic [and] humanist" attributes, according to Jameson, are the result of leadership in which the leaders are "counsellor[s], maintaining work group cohesion and morale, [and who also assume the roles of] innovator, trainer, resource provider and team-worker." (Quoted in Carnell, 1990, p.167). This again fits with McBruce's comment that his main function was to "lead the organization, and to make sure that we're heading overall in the same direction, and I have to get people to buy into that." (McBruce, April 11 2003). Motivating, aligning, supporting and allowing staff to be resourceful and creative fits with Gupwell' human resource management philosophy: "The last six years I've done the HR side [...] profit share [and] performance evaluation [then] we formed into teams eight years ago; we wanted to go into self-management [and] we formed cross-functional teams for decision-making." (Gupwell, April 4 2003). In this environment, the interest of the staff came first in systems that focused on "bargaining, conciliating, planning, [and] administering," (Jameson, quoted in Carnell, 1990, p 167). Staff development was an aspect of education catered for by the purchase of specialist journals on effectiveness of team-work, although Gupwell admitted that since team composition kept changing, team members actually reading them in numbers that would make it effective was not entirely successful. (Gupwell, April 4 2003). These leadership values created a culture "built on trust and just plain people liking them and wanting to work for them. I guess that's really the success of it [...] underscored by an initial [...] innovation, incredible innovation with, in particular, our main product line which is packs." (Smith, March 28 2003). However, most of Smith's colleagues were more enamoured of Alpine Packs' innovation in the systems which placed its employees first, rather than the product.

Tushman and O'Reilly state that, "While market share, return on investment, and performance against budget are useful and important measures for assessing short-term performance, the values and norms that drive behaviour, which combined form an organization's culture, are among the most critical factors in determining long-term strategic success." (Tushman and O'Reilly, 1997, p.100). They also state that, "when a company credibly stands for something of universal value to its employees, the level of commitment or identification is deeper and more enduring." (Tushman and O'Reilly, 1997, p.101). Pearl Smith, Production Manager, offered this opinion: "There have been lots of innovative designs [...] and that has given Alpine Packs the superior branding of quality, performance and trust linked with, I guess, a commitment to protect the environment. So to me that's kind of been the theme of the business, and how it's been successfully going forward." (Smith, March 28 2003). This commitment and enthusiasm was substantiated by the three employees of the Process Improvement Team, who all agreed with one of their number saying, "As a team we discuss problems we've got, and help each other out. We have responsibilities in a team, and support is team support." (Clook, April 2 2003).

199

Alpine Packs then, functioned very much according to the main precepts of Tushman and O'Reilly's congruence model: it was functional, productive, innovative and supportive. Itami points to a related concept, "invisible assets", and these include "technology, consumer loyalty, brand image, control of distribution, corporate culture and management skills. [...] These are the key to adaptability and competitive advantage." (Itami quoted in Carnell, 1990, p.172). Due to a combination of these factors, Alpine Packs made a profit for 28 years of its 30-year existence. However, not all employees were comforted by this relatively meritorious performance. In only the second year of operating at a loss, Pearl Smith commented that in terms of the market realities of the previous year and the present one, the culture could best be characterized as having "a lack of commercial acumen." She went on to explain that it was underpinned by "a lack of the urgency, it is a lack [of awareness] of the consequences." (Smith, March 28 2003).

12.4 Strategy

When Alpine Packs began losing revenue, visionary leadership was required to solve the problem and re-energize the work-force. According to Carnell, (1990), if leaders are to manage change successfully they must demonstrate core competencies in decision making, coalition building, implementing the change plan, and maintaining momentum and effort to realize the plan. Tushman and O'Reilly emphasize "personal actions [by leaders because] they influence their colleagues' values, goals, needs, and aspirations through their relentless attention to shaping interpretations and creating a sense of purpose." (Tushman and O'Reilly, 1997, pp185-6). This is a requisite to continued success in operations, as, in Edgar Schein's terminology, "all involve maintaining the integrity of the system in the face of a changing environment that is constantly causing various kinds of disequilibrium." (Schein, 1997, p.298).

Alpine Packs' management response to the disequilibrium it suffered can be understood by following patterns of behaviour analysed by Schein. He describes "disconfirming data" as "any items of information that show the organization that some of its goals are not being met or that some of its processes are not accomplishing what they are supposed to." (Schein, 1997, p299). Once management recognises failure, the immediate inclination is to preserve the company's reputation, even if it cannot completely adapt to an environmental change. Schein quotes Lorsch (1985) who called this phenomenon, "strategic myopia", which shows how organizational belief systems interfere with leaders' strategies if they do not fit their company's prior beliefs and which had led to prior commercial success. (Lorsch quoted in Schein, 1997, p.300). Management and employees are only prepared to listen to the problem when there are sufficient disconfirming data to indicate severe problems on the horizon, unless a visionary leader can put interventions in place. Schein refers to "cognitive restructuring" (Schein, 1997, p.301) as an aspect from the unfreezing process, meaning that when change is imperative and a new set of assumptions must be created as core to a new culture in order to effect the change successfully. (Schein, 1997, p.301). However, there is a residual aspect to the creation of a new culture: the lingering remnants of the former one. Alpine Packs provided their employees with as much time to look for new jobs as possible. They contacted Work and Income New Zealand as well as other employers who might wish to expand their workforce by hiring ex-Alpine Packs staff; redundancy provisions were already included in the employment contract; and there was the 'People's People Team' to provide assistance and support. There have been precedents for this. Schein explains that when companies that assume that, "they are lifetime employers who never lay anyone off are eventually faced with the economic necessity to reduce payroll costs, they cognitively redefine layoffs as 'transitions' or early retirements, make the transition packages very generous, provide long periods of time during which the employee can seek alternative employment, offer extensive counselling, provide outplacement services, and so on, they preserve the assumption that 'we treat our people fairly and well.'" (Schein, 1997, p.302). Alpine Packs' actions in the process of terminating its production fit well with Schein's description.

Similarly, the choice of outsourcing companies may be explained this way. For Alpine Packs, outsourcing production and refocusing on design and innovation was a critical change. Outsourcing might be regarded as a "cost-centred organizational change methodology, [and] as a strategic direction whereby organizations attempt to concentrate on core activities by releasing capital and management time from non-core functions." (www.massey.ac.nz;~cprichar/303cm). When Alpine Packs'

201

management sought companies in Asia with which to do business, they had "no desire to change the quality of the product – no wish to downgrade. These people had to be highly responsible employers who had good working conditions." (McBruce, May 21 2004). This shows that in spite of major change, "the essence of the new learning is usually some cognitive redefinition of some of the core concepts in the assumption set." (Schein, 1997, p.301).

12.5 Culture

There was surprise that no member of staff, (with only one exception,) resigned from Alpine Packs before the factory closed in late October 2003, (McBruce, May 21 2004; Gupwell, May 28 2004; Barnard, June 14 2004; Jones, June 14 2004). This may be explained in terms of the solidarity within its culture. Like Jack Stack of Springfield Re-Manufacturing, as cited in Tushman and O'Reilly, p.117, Alpine Packs' Director had for many years provided regular monthly statements of financial figures and production performance. This was the foundation stone of its "open and honest" culture. The product improvement staff maintained, "we're all in the same boat. I [Cook] appreciate this information. You can work out for yourself why we do what we do. I [Maynard] definitely appreciate it too. I [van der Slee] also definitely appreciate it. It gives you the wider picture, but some people only come in to do their own work. The percentage that appreciates this information is about 50-50 percent. The production people often look at the figures from the bonus point of view, so it's personal. The office staff look more from the company point of view." (Product Improvement Team, April 2 2003). Tushman and O'Reilly maintain that, "Effective group functioning is enhanced when members like and respect each other, understand each others' perspectives and operating styles, can resolve disagreements, and can communicate effectively." (Tushman and O'Reilly, 1997, p.116). Furthermore, they point to the need "for encouraging support for creativity and risk taking [and] promote a positive attitude toward change." (Tushman and O'Reilly, 1997, p.114). The Product Improvement Team responded unanimously to a question about the reasons for Alpine Packs' success as follows: "The reason for the Company's success is quality products, being prepared to change, that is the people are prepared to change, and explains why we need to change. The Company is open about change, and explains why we need to change. Some people don't like change because they don't see why they should change. But you're not scared of change when you have the information." (Maynard, Product Improvement Team, April 2 2003).

However, Tushman and O'Reilly also mention (1997, pp.115-6) that organizational creativity is a tolerance for mistakes, both of a personal and organizational kind, and Alpine Packs seems to have tolerated for almost eight years, the fact that teams were not as functional as they should have been. Alison Jones recalls, "The main changes included the change to teams about eight years ago. [...] It was a culture change too. We went from supervisors and leading hands to teams which where the teams were their own authority and [had] responsibility to look after themselves, as well as after the team and the product. To a certain extent it worked, but it was a big change from one to the other. A lot of people come to work to be directed to a certain extent, so they found it difficult. We didn't have team leaders at first. There was a lack of direction. We've [now] had leaders [again] for 12-18 months." (Jones, April 2 2003). Finally, therefore, the Company re-instituted individuals into management or supervisory positions, meaning that the Company had come full circle: "The main changes I've seen here is going around in a circle, and we now have the same foundations back to make people accountable. There's a lot more positive people here, even compared to a year ago." (van der Slee, Product Improvement Team, April 2 2003). The company's experiment had not been entirely successful, but it had generated tolerance and patience, making the culture stronger. The fact that the Management Team reverted to instituting supervisory roles meant that employees found a flexibility in their management that is not universally present in managements generally. Because of Alpine Packs' "open and honest" philosophy, culture did not just become embedded in routines and structures. The culture was evolving and stable but it was never fossilized, and so the closure of the Addington plant may have been regarded by employees as the last of a long line of changes – with change being a process to which they were by that time fully accustomed.

12.6 Learning

Many analysts have commented on the need for new learning, as part of the transition process in change, (de Geus, 1999; Clarke and Clegg, 1998; Schein,1997; Tushman and O'Reilly, 1997; Carnell, 1990). Schein makes the point that it is a key element, along with visionary leadership, in the success of the change process: "vision provides some of the key psychological functions of both disconfirming old assumptions and providing enough psychological safety to launch new learning. Visions do not have to be very clear or complete. They have to provide a path and a process of learning to assure the members of the organization that constructive change is possible." (Schein, 1997, p.333). The Alpine Packs employees were informed that a small production team would continue to produce prototypes and small runs, so "closure" was a slight misnomer. There would continue to be a head-office, a marketing and design staff and a production team, therefore the "constructive change" that Schein talks about referred in Alpine Packs' case to an outsourcing future which would entail much change in structure and systems in which learning would play a major role towards future success. Gupwell commented, "It's to do with building up the knowledge again that we used to have. Also upskilling staff and recruiting more knowledgeable staff with a higher skill level in different parts of the world." (Gupwell, May 28 2004). As far as learning was concerned, she also joked that the redundancy aspect of their transition had been the first occasion in which she had participated on such a scale, and with black humour consulted Stewart McBruce about doing it again to obtain economies of scale! Michael Hammer elucidated further:

> Separate processes in separate companies have been connected and combined and now work as one. New technologies may be the glue, but the more important innovation is the change in the way people think and work. Rather than seeing business processes as ending at the edges of their companies, Geon [Hammer's own case-study] and its partners now see them – and manage them – as they truly are: chains of activities that are performing by different organizations. (Hammer, Sept. 2001, p.85).

McBruce focused single-mindedly on systems, and commented: "Changing within the organization means changing systems [...] we need to innovate every single system in the company." (McBruce, May 21 2004). Clarke and Clegg (1998) concluded that, "In knowledge-based business, learning and innovation are the critical drivers of business development." (Clarke and Clegg, 1998, p.431).

With Alpine Packs, that knowledge base will now have to be spread over more geographical miles and diverse individuals than when the Addington plant was in full operation. This is because the knowledge sharing is between individuals across the globe. It is in the process of becoming a "virtual organization", one in which there are few physical structures, but one which has communication and networking systems, state of the art knowledge, and a speed of production, transmission and distribution. Management and quality assurance and control will be networked capabilities, and knowledge will be databased. The glue that McBruce and Gupwell hope will hold it altogether will be shared objectives and the quality and the profitability of future innovations.

An integrated plan for realigning systems with the new vision is exemplified by Joe Barnard's description of the ways in which the distribution system was modified. It is also a good example of new learning leading to adaptation. Whereas prior to October 2003, Alpine Packs operated direct distribution with Australia and Britain, they discontinued this after the new order was established. Even though the old system had served them well, it had to change. In order to impact strongly on the European market, the system now entails dedicated managers in North America, Britain and continental Europe. They are charged with the responsibility of elevating Alpine Packs' profile in countries as diverse as Spain, Italy, the Czech Republic, Poland and Canada. They intend taking market share where they had none previously, and have increased their warehouses from one abroad to three abroad. (Barnard, June 14 2004). This means that design, production and sales are dependent on integrated systems which encompass New Zealand, Australia, the Philippines, Vietnam, China, Europe and North America.

12.7 Leadership

McBruce and Gupwell undertook a great architectural discontinuity in their company. And it must continue to evolve. Much of the success of the transition so far has rested with the quality of their leadership and the devising and implementation of new systems with which they are replacing the old ones. Carnell delivers a personal opinion about the need for leadership to steer change: "The leader needs to cope with change, so do followers. It seems to me that this is the ultimate defining characteristic of effective corporate leaders. They can energise and sustain people to act, to try things out, to get on with the job in hand [...] People need to perceive the credible actions that they can take and that they feel they can control. Thus we bring 'human scale' to leadership and change." (Carnell, 1990, p.183).

At this point, the concept of "resilience" is relevant. Coutu writes on it making the following contribution to an understanding of the situation at Alpine Packs:

> Resilience has three characteristics. The first characteristic is the capacity to accept and face down reality. In looking hard at reality, we prepare ourselves to act in ways that allow us to endure and survive hardships: We train ourselves how to survive before we ever have to do so. Second, resilient people and organizations possess an ability to find meaning in some aspects of life. And values are just as important as meaning; value systems at resilient companies change very little over the long haul and are used as scaffolding in times of trouble. The third building block of resilience is the ability to improvise. Within an arena of personal capabilities or company rules, the ability to solve problems without the usual or obvious tools is a great strength.
>
> (Coutu, 2003, p.80).

All three qualities of resilience are applicable to Alpine Packs. It was true to its earliest and most meaningful value: it was open and honest at all times. For this researcher, there was resilient and effective leadership. The ultimate quality of McBruce and Gupwell's leadership was to achieve total commitment and loyalty in two hundred employees up to the last day of production, when after that, there would be no vision for them, no sustenance and no future but redundancy. The resilience of the company stemmed from the leadership that inspired such loyalty.

12.8 Conclusion

The Alpine Packs case demonstrates that despite having a high degree of vision, congruence, networks of suppliers and direct distribution, quality management and a small number of discontinuous as well as many incremental innovations before the new order was put in place, Alpine Packs failed. It became a victim of its own success as per the Tushman and O'Reilly (1997) model. There are two main reasons for this. Alpine Packs was a social organization, and this meant that its production was geared for acceptable profit instead of maximum profit – the result of operating in a stable but non-urgent environment, (Smith, March 28 2003). Consequently, its margins were sustainable but thin. It was also because it was successful in a stable environment, but an environmental shift had a profoundly negative effect on its ability to compete. Of course, no one predicted the events of 9/11, or its subsequent ripples from the political domain through to the commercial domain, eventually eroding the profits of outdoor equipment industry. Nonetheless, Alpine Packs' management recognised the financial warning signs quickly, and took timely action to create new competitive advantage through a new basis of production in an environment that had undergone a paradigm shift, and that demanded the creation of a new congruence to effect viability.

Chapter 13

Main Analysis

13.1 Introduction

In order to fully understand the social constructs under investigation, Blaikie recommends "immersion", or extensive contact, as the means by which the investigator may fully come to terms with the social actors and their stage. In reality this refers to the iterative process of in-depth interviewing and observing the 'stage', comprising activity on factory floors and in office complexes. The researcher was limited by time and expense, but extensively viewed all three business environments. These are described below; each work environment reflects the nature of the product and the culture.

The visits to each company's premises enabled the researcher to make observations about each company's methods of operations, and to ascertain key elements in company culture. Alpine Packs factory and office environments in Christchurch, New Zealand, were mainly open plan which reflected their key quality as a harmonious and "social organization". The factory had an internal garden to make the place more attractive and to provide a restful place to have lunch.

All of Wave Rider's main office corridors in Torquay, Australia, the lobby and other open spaces were decorated with huge hard-backed action photos of young, energetic sportspeople's extreme feats in the surf and snow, which reflected Wave Rider's core business of manufacturing high quality sporting goods. In one open plan office in the main building, employees were separated from each other by low blue glass partitions between the desks, with the glass being cut in the form of a rolling wave, and comprising bubbles inside the glass to reflect the froth of the surf. Further to the process of immersion, Will Waugh encouraged the researcher to borrow a number of Wave Rider's earliest artefacts from their office archives to take back for student instruction at the Christchurch Polytechnic Institute of Technology, (CPIT). These included the first mono-density wet-suit with over-locked stitching; an early dual-density, psychedelic wetsuit from the 'eighties; the company's first fibre-glass surfboard; the earliest designs in beach-wear; an early backpack; and two first-model tide-watches from the 'eighties. One month later, in December 2001, the researcher received a late model surfboard, a range of late model tide-watches and clothes from Wave Rider's New Zealand manager, Gary Muir in Auckland. All of these were put on display in the CPIT Library as exemplars of evolutionary innovation covering Wave Rider's thirty years business success. This display illustrated the evolutionary nature of innovation in one company. According to the CPIT Head Librarian, this display drew the biggest audiences in the Library's history.

Little Dragon was set in the sprawling urban morass that is Wuxi, renowned for "light industry". Its headquarters were spacious, spartan and functional. Offices were transparent glass cubicles. The ground floor had a display area of their current white-ware. The researcher was shown the operations of the "Scott" line, which was constructed by a New Zealander after whom it was named. It folded metal sheets into washing machine exterior casings with precision and speed, and was semi-automated, requiring just one operator.

Perusal and analysis of relevant company documentation also played a part and sometimes they were useful additions to the overall interview data-generation process. Alpine Packs' production schedules, and Lei Yuan's web sites on the new marketing and management approaches for the company, fall into that category.

This research addresses the question of how three mature industries use processes related to innovation and subsequent management of change to generate sustainable profitability – if not leadership – in their respective fields. The researcher began by posing motives and goals, as well as a number of specific questions, and in this chapter these will be addressed. This chapter should be read in conjunction with the three preliminary analysis chapters, as this chapter attempts to avoid unnecessary duplication, except when it is necessary to provide a context or a particular emphasis.

This investigation was predicated by two main aims. Firstly, to discover the part that innovation and change have played in the success of the chosen businesses pertaining to three companies in different industries, in three geo-political environments.

The second motive was to extend or otherwise modify pre-existing models, because the abductive approach lends itself to that. (Blaikie, 2000, p.126). The ultimate aim of generating new theory derived from the data, is to better inform practitioners engaged in innovation, general management and change management in the future. In keeping with the abductive investigative tradition, this investigation has used Tushman and O'Reilly's, and Christensen and Raynor's research, as sensitising concepts, but has remained open to the concepts of other theorists and practitioners in order to assist in the generation of new theory.

Christensen and Raynor (2003) describe theory building in three stages: describing the phenomenon under investigation, classifying the phenomenon into categories, and expressing a theory that explains what causes the phenomenon to occur and why. (Christensen and Raynor, 2003, pp.12-13). Specifically, a social theories, according to Blaikie, (2000), "are explanations of recurrent patterns or regularities in social life." (Blaikie, 2000, p.143). He goes on to explain that "In the context of research design, a theory is an answer to a 'why' question; it is an explanation of a pattern or regularity that has been observed, the cause or reason for which needs to be understood." (Blaikie, 2000, p.143). However, this is within the general context of Blaikie's reviewing multiple paradigms.

In the case of this investigation, it is more accurate to state that the theory is attempting to answer a 'what' question, rather than a 'why' question, although the latter is also relevant. The main question of this investigation has focused on 'what' as in 'what part have innovation and change played in the success and longevity of three companies?' The results of the interviews with participants depict respondents' own realities in their work environments. The researcher used an interpretivist approach with a relativist ontology with a constructivist epistemology as per the abductive strategy. (Blaikie, 2000, p.241). The task at hand now is to interpret participants' comments and provide meaning by analysing and coordinating their insights and observations.

210

13.2 The radical element

In an early, but valuable contribution to the understanding of innovation, James Utterback's *Mastering the dynamics of innovation* (1994), focused on the process of corporate regeneration, and the part played by "radical" innovation. Having recognised the potentially destructive characteristics of radical innovation to industries that could, at best, only improve through incremental innovations, Utterback came to the conclusion that

> Innovation is not just the job of corporate technologists, but of all major functional areas of the firm. And the support of radical innovation by these areas must be managed with boldness and persistence from the top. Here the responsibility of management is nothing less than corporate regeneration in the face of radical innovation.
>
> (Utterback, 1994, p.230).

However, Utterback equivocated on the ways in which industrialists could take advantage of the potential of radical innovation. On p.227, he put forward three strategies: diversified portfolios of R&D projects and technology; mergers, acquisitions, alliances, and joint ventures; and finally, dual strategies. In recommending each strategy as having a measure of potential for the cultivation of a radical innovation, he then proceeds to dismiss each one as a serious option because each produces too many problems. Around 1994, when Utterback published his research, the issue of radical versus incremental innovation posed problems for him. Having identified the radical as a much more vigorous form of innovation than the incremental, Utterback could only conclude that the radical element was an industrial rogue as well as an industrial wellspring. He wrote, "[It] is so necessary for the regeneration of a corporation's business, yet it is the most painfully difficult to master." (Utterback, 1994, p.221). He concluded,

> The problem is that we cannot judge or predict which of many threats will have such potency, but the cases and examples developed in this work show that even the strongest product and business strategy will eventually be overturned by technological change. The central issue is not when or how this will happen, but

that it will happen for sure. In the final analysis only that understanding will
allow a firm to bridge a discontinuity, because only a total commitment will win
the day.

(Utterback, 1994, p.231).

Therefore, Utterback would have recognised Wave Rider's dual density wetsuit, and
Alpine Packs' internal harness as radical innovations, but he could not have advised
either company how to generate another one of the same magnitude to effect
regeneration on a continual basis. It seemed up to that time, that Utterback's "radical"
innovation, sometimes referred to as Schumpeter's "gale of creative destruction",
(quoted in Rickards, 1999, p.45), was not easily containable, let alone something that
an industry might germinate and cultivate.

Out of the seeds of Utterback's equivocation grew two shoots of theory that attempted
to deal more definitively with the radical element: congruence and disruption.

13.3 Congruence, ambidexterity and disruption

Congruence comprises alignment between the four fundamental organizational
building blocks that are both "hard" (task and structure), and "soft" (individual and
culture). To recap: "critical tasks" comprise component tasks and work processes;
"culture" includes norms, values, communication networks, informal roles and
informal power; the "formal organization" includes strategic groupings, formal
linking, rewards, information systems, career systems, human resources, management
systems; and finally "people" comprises human resource capabilities and
competencies. Also closely aligned are "strategic choices," such as strategy,
objectives and vision; and "executive leadership" which comprises competencies,
demography and group processes. (Tushman and O'Reilly, 1997, p.59).

Managers can lever these to construct organizational capabilities and subsequent
change. (Tushman and O'Reilly, 1997, p.220). They recommend that problem
definition can be analysed by means of a systematic diagnosis in the performance
gaps in the company. This is reinforced by Shapiro (2001), as well as by Bean and

Radford, (2002). The latter state, "alignment is usually used to indicate the convergence of corporate goals and strategies with the actual efforts and activities of employees.   Alignment is a central requirement for stimulating consistently productive innovation in any organization." (Bean and Radford, 2002, p.19). Tushman and O'Reilly define ambidextrous organizations as ones that "celebrate stability and incremental change as well as experimentation and discontinuous change simultaneously. [...] in the most successful firms, managers encourage tight alignment among strategy, structure, people, and culture to ensure today's success and periodically promote revolutionary change for tomorrow's renewal. Ambidextrous organizations create organizational capabilities for excelling both today and tomorrow." (Tushman and O'Reilly, 1997, pp.14-15).   Michael Dell, founder, chairman and CEO of Dell Computers in Austin, Texas, agrees with the concept of ambidexterity, commenting, "You need to encourage innovation when your company's doing well. The last thing you want to do when you're in the lead is become complacent." (*Harvard Business Review*, 2002 Aug., p.41).

The following chart shows the criteria in Tushman and O'Reilly's chart of Organizational Architecture (Tushman and O'Reilly, 1997, p.59). The ticks and crosses indicate whether the relevant features in the case-studies conform to the criteria of Tushman and O'Reilly's ideal organizational architecture. It also contains data on whether each of the companies has at some stage introduced disruptive products. (Christensen and Raynor, 2003). Some of the criteria were observed during factory and office tours in each of the three workplaces rather than as topics of in-depth discussion during interviews. This was part of the "immersion" process, (Blaikie, 2000, p.120 and p.126), and whilst not totally adequate for the observation of all processes, it did give the researcher an impression of the general environment in which employees worked.

Table 8 Comparative features: Congruence, disruption, and ambidexterity

Feature	Wave Rider the Surfing Company (Australia)	Alpine Packs the Wilderness Company (NZ)	The Little Dragon Group Company (PR China)
Strategic choice			
• Vision	√	√	√
• Strategy	√	√	√
• Objectives	√	√	√
Critical tasks			
• Component tasks	√	√	√
• Work processes/flows	√	√	√
Culture			
• Norms, values	√	√	√
• Communication networks	√	√	√
• Informal roles	√	√	No data available
• Informal power	√	√	√
Executive leadership			
• Competencies	√	√	√
• Demography	√	√	√
• Group processes	√	√	√
Formal Organization			
• Strategic groupings	√	√	√
• Formal linking	√	√	√

• Rewards	√	√	√
• Information systems	√	√	√
• Human resource systems	√	√	√
• Career systems	No data available	No data available	√
People			
• Human resource capabilities	√	√	√
• Competencies	√	√	√
Disruptive products			
▪ Introduced **one** or more since company founding	√	X	√
▪ Introduced **two** or more	√	X	√
Ambidexterity	√	X	√

The table indicates that the companies in the case-studies demonstrated a high degree of congruence according to the criteria in the model. However, the chart can not indicate by its very nature, to what degree these criteria were met – simply that to some measure, there were indications that each company already had implemented, or was, systemically implementing ways and means to align the driving mechanisms within the company with its vision. Some of the noteworthy features from the table are commented on in the discussion below, and specific criteria in the body of the text have been highlighted in italics. It should also be noted that Wave Rider and Little Dragon have both introduced at least two disruptive products, with the likely effect that they are in a healthier financial state than Alpine Packs. Alpine Packs did not introduce disruptive products, but did introduce discontinuous innovations in the form of packs and tents which were considerable improvements on existing models available in the market at the time.

13.3.1 Innovation: The Little Dragon Group Company and its pragmatic genius

The Little Dragon Group Company, headed by Dr Hing and Mr Lei, demonstrated congruity and ambidexterity in a number of ways, leading to sustainability and profitability. It is in this company that elements of Tushman and O'Reilly (1997) as well as Christensen (2003) agree, and demonstrate a small problem in Gibson and Birkinshaw (2003). Much of the success of the company can be attributed to a number of key factors: an understanding of the roles of innovation, ambidexterity, proprietary technologies, as well as the introduction of a disruption – possibly more than one – in a market characterised by nonconsumption, a leadership that identifies opportunities and is prepared to take calculated risks.

Little Dragon's lead product is the washing machine. This became a success once the company aligned the technology they had purchased from Matsushita, with the processes required to engineer it, as well as with the willingness to learn how to operate them, and modify them where necessary, for example, to expand production. Successful innovation was therefore an example of a vision followed by the appropriate workflows and competencies. It should be noted that Little Dragon's early washing machine was a disruptive product. The company introduced a superior technology into the Chinese domestic market at a time when that technology already existed in washing machines in Japan. But due to China's isolationist position, Japanese producers could not penetrate the Chinese command economy in the last two decades of the twentieth century, to export their superior technology in fully built-up washing machines. In his first interview with the researcher, Lei Yuan, Deputy General Manager, stated that his company purchased Matsushita's technology in 1989, and then "In 1994, [Little Dragon] reached [production of] 640,000 units of washers and that put [them] in first place, from 24th" where they had been just five years earlier. (Lei, Nov. 18 2002). The company "made a profit of 70 million Renminbi in that year [1994]." (Lei, Nov. 18 2002). The introduction of this technology acted as a disruption in the market, upsetting the market leadership of

216

twenty-three competitors who were placed ahead of Little Dragon. Clearly, the Little Dragon product had "a paralyzing effect on industry leaders [...] who were constitutionally unable to respond." (Christensen and Raynor, 2003, p.35). Christensen and Raynor (2003) maintain that a disruptive innovation "disrupt[s] and redefine[s] that trajectory of introducing products and services that are not as good as currently available products. But disruptive technologies offer other benefits – typically, they are simpler, more convenient, and less expensive products that appeal to new or less-demanding customers." (Christensen and Raynor, 2003, p.34). Little Dragon was a variant on this construct: it had combined low-cost manufacturing with the technology of automation that was much in demand because it reduced manual labour from the domestic washing chore. It is highly likely, therefore that the company tapped into a nonconsuming market, appealing to consumers' need for automation, for the first time. The variant is that the technology was better than competitors' rather than worse, but it had price parity. The company was able to make considerable profit at that price point. Therefore, it still acted as a disruption.

With respect to human resource capabilities, interviews revealed that rewards and career systems were the means that were used to exact maximum profitability from a purchased component. To achieve this they hired top engineers including Dr Hing, a native Chinese with a PhD in mechanical engineering from France. He was subsequently appointed General Manager in order to direct the engineering processes and drive productivity. He was the researcher's second interviewee in this company.

Staff members were paid according to the level of their education and professionalism, with salaries rising to US $100,000 (not including bonuses). It was clear from the interview with Lei Yuan on November 18 2002, that the company had used previously accumulated profits from its lead product, in order to diversify into refrigerators and air-conditioners, and this enabled them to pay Matsushita a transfer fee of US $2.1 Million. Therefore, the company was actively developing a subsidiary product line to complement its primary product line, alluding to the creation of ambidexterity to bolster future product lines.

The successful amalgamation of vision, communication, critical tasks, and work processes were in evidence in the workforce itself. With a workforce of ten thousand in the main Wuxi plant alone, employees were instructed to pursue the company vision and work in collaborative processes on production lines, some of which had many employees, some only a few. Communication took place by means of supervisors' instructions, seminars and a weekly broadsheet published locally in colour, and this led to the evolution of the Little Dragon culture, even one as large as this, becoming consistent in its routine functions. The career path systems ensured that staff had an evaluation system for pay and promotion that was fair and democratic, because it had multiple inputs. Also democratic in its management was the appointment of two members of the American Education Foundation to the Board of Directors of the company, adding a cosmopolitan dimension to management and contributing to the general level of robustness in its systems. It was a bold addition to the governance of a Communist company.

Mr Lei and Dr Hing both gave indications that the former regimentation of their country's workforce under traditional Communism meant that many changes in attitude and work performance had to take place before Little Dragon could compete in an open market. This would become a series of 'defining moments' because it necessitated learning and acquiring new knowledge, encouraging open discussion, engaging in problem-solving and self-diagnosis so that the company might progress as quickly as possible in its own learning processes. (Christenden and Overdorf, 2001, p.104).

As a part of strategic choice, the management had been forging strong links with other technology companies, such as Siemens of Germany, with which it could share research findings. The potential of this company was considered to be so promising and profitable that the Si Wei Te Electronics Company of Nanjing bought a 65 percent share holding in it in 2003, paying the Wuxi Municipal Government, technically Little Dragon's former owner, 568,750,000 Renminbi. (Hong Shi, e-mail 10 Sep 2004). The congruence and performance of its systems had made it attractive as a major company purchase, and in so doing the Si Wei Te Company could take advantage of Little Dragon's brand value to create new value networks for itself, (Christensen and Raynor, 2003, pp.44-45).

This company's congruence was further highlighted by the fact that their processes were aligned to the tasks, and as Christensen and Raynor point out, "processes by their very nature are not meant to change. They are established to help employees perform recurrent tasks in a consistent way, time after time." (Christensen and Raynor, 2003, p.184). Lei Yuan being an adjunct professor, used his company as a case-study with post-graduate students in management, thereby opening its processes and systems to close scrutiny by students. One of those processes was the implication of exercising informal power, which occurred when middle management staff requested their bonus be spread throughout the year, instead of as a lump-sum at the end of the financial year.

Further testimony to the company's conservatism, and hence its support for strong congruency, was its initial concern over Dr Hing's proposal on how to deal in an innovative, if not controversial manner with Toshiba, when the latter threatened to become a major rival in the manufacture of superior-technology white-ware in Wuxi. As a formal link, it is likely that the Little Dragon Board of Directors believed that its essential systemic conservatism would not be able to countenance competition from such a high regarded technology innovator. This raises the issue whether the systemic stability engendered by congruence is able to compete with the impact of innovation whenever a radical form of it occurs in the market. Dr Hing had to defuse the possible impact of such an entrant to 'his' market. According to Leifer et al. the solution to that appeared to be that larger companies must not invest in standard technologies to the detriment of investing in "disruptive technologies." (Leifer et al. 2000, p.3). In other words, congruence could lead to its own complacency, and a workforce must remain vigilant for opportune innovations. However, it is significant that all of Little Dragon's innovative technology was bought from Japan, and that one of the reasons Dr Hing wished to form a closer relationship with Toshiba was because in his vision he wished to access their technology in the future, although he did not specify in what way that might be done. However, by tone of voice and a sweeping hand gesture, he indicated that he was somewhat dismissive of the research capabilities of Little Dragon's own research unit, implying a likely dependency on foreign technological advances in the future, which would likely be purchased for large sums accompanied by complex intellectual property agreements.

This raises a question: how could the Chinese or the Indian societies spanning first to third world conditions within one set of borders, upgrade their education to the extent that they could formulate their own technologies, and then export those technologies embedded in value-added products? It is clear from his association with Toshiba that in Dr Hing's strategy, future technologies would come from the relationship he was cultivating with the Japanese giant – certainly not the other way around. Little Dragon could only offer low cost production on a large scale. Christensen and Raynor comment, "Huge size constitutes a very real disability in creating new-growth businesses. [...] when large corporations keep the flexibility to have small business units within them, they can continue to have decision makers who can become excited about emerging opportunities." (Christensen and Raynor, 2003, p.187). Considering "that organizations develop a capability for sustaining innovation that resides in their processes," (Christensen and Raynor, 2003, p.190), Hing was willing to take the risk that collaboration with Toshiba might eventually mean being subsumed by it, or forced out of the market by it. In offering to design and build Toshiba's proposed product, he would not be improving "product margins from better or cost-reduced products," (Christensen and Raynor, 2003, p.190), unless it were a very long production run, which, with China's population might be possible, particularly since China is experiencing burgeoning growth in its economy. "The World Bank said [in November 2004] that East Asia's economies were expected to grow 7.1 per cent this year, with China recording the fastest expansion at 9.2 per cent." (Malakunas, Dec. 21 2004.)

Hing conceived a bold and innovative strategy: "Instead of one-size-fits-all policies, [he as leader would] spend time ensuring that capable people work in organizations with processes and values that match the task, [creating] a major point of leverage in successfully creating new growth." (Christensen and Raynor, 2003, p.203). However, the question remains how Little Dragon could modify production so quickly to incorporate a new product onto the market. This was resolved in a matter of months: apart from acquiring technology from Toshiba in the product, Little Dragon also acquired the process. It very much followed Christensen and Raynor (2003) model: "*start early, start small*, and *demand early success*." (Christensen and Raynor, 2003, p.246). The Toshiba opportunity allowed the company to a launch new-growth in a subsidiary plant in Wuxi, whilst the main business was ostensibly healthy. It divided business into another unit; and in the same way that the company has always operated, it hungered for profit – its success in the Toshiba collaboration remains to be seen however, as it goes beyond the timeframe of this investigation. However, functioning according to theory, Little Dragon, under the leadership of Dr Hing and Mr Lei had laid the foundations of a virtuous circle of commencing new-growth businesses comprising contracted expertise and low-cost production.

The Chinese example remains in an anomalous category even when compared with a Japanese counterpart that had significant parallels, but could still not be called identical. In 1989, Toyota launched the Lexus as a high-end product, and this product was so successful that within three years it accounted for nearly one-third of Toyota's operating profit while representing only two per cent of its unit volume. Toyota did this because they understood the imperative of creating and re-creating markets to sustain growth in overcrowded and demand-starved economies. (Kim and Mauborgne, *Harvard Business Review*, 2001). This demonstrates that launching a product at the high-end market is not new, but the differences are that Toyota did not compete against nonconsumption. It competed against Mercedes-Benz and BMW; and it did not have to consort with the enemy, so to speak, in order to create its product, and sell it at the high-end under the brand-label of its competitor as Dr Hing did.

The management of the Little Dragon Group Company was not alone in adopting innovative strategies, that entailed change, in Chinese industry. The researcher also witnessed similar innovation in management practices at Sanmao's Huaxia Group and at the Jiangsu Oil Lubricating Company, located on the outskirts of Wuxi. Although they did not become major studies in the way that Little Dragon did, several observations are pertinent. Like Little Dragon, constant flexibility, opportunism and instantaneous adaptability were often the key to the success of these plants. As the Director of Human Resources at Huaxia stated when interviewed by the researcher, "We change every day if we have to." (Jiang Nan, March 24, 2004). This is a significant statement which, while clearly hyperbolic – and meant to be so – has clear application to his company, the Jiangsu Oil Lubricating Company, and Little Dragon. The researcher observed that the employees of all three companies, from manager to operative, worked to capacity, totally aligned to their tasks. In each case, low-cost labour and the willingness to experiment with process and product, enabled these companies to produce, profit, expand and change very quickly, inspite of their size.

This was not only the case with Little Dragon. Another spectacular example was the Huaxia Group which manufactured men's clothing under licence from Pierre Cardin, from whom the company benefited in proprietary expertise and process development. The researcher visited the Huaxia Group twice: once in 2001, and again in 2004, accompanied by Hong Shi, Lecturer at Southern Yangtze University. The following is taken from the Sanmao catalogue, 2001, and comes complete with the authentic English translation, and the original formatting:

> Pierre Cardin came to China for Sanmao. With the accompanying of Zhou Jianping [the founder of the Chinese company], he visited all Sanmao headquarter and reached an agreement with Zhou Jianping: 1. Pierre Cardin would double Sanmao material order within five years. 2. Sanmao Group and Pierre Cardin Company would establish European information station, and Pierre Cardin would help Sanmao train designers and provide advanced technologies in international cloth. [....] In September 1999, Sanmao Group French Branch and Italian Branch were established.
> (Sanmao, 2001, p.4).

In becoming the agent of several international top brands of apparel, the company grew from 18 workers in December 1988 and 300,000 Renminbi of private investment monies, to 13,000 workers in 2004 with a sales volume of 5 billion Renminbi and a tax revenue of 100 million Renminbi. Zhou Jiaping introduced a disruptive innovation onto the Chinese domestic market when he manufactured French-styled clothing by imitation of the original products and without a licence from Pierre Cardin. It was in Christensen and Raynor's terminology, "not as good as currently available products" but the styling was Western and prestigeous, and the alternative was no prestige. He therefore captured a large low-end market of "new or less demanding customers." (Christensen and Raynor, 2003, p.34). It might be more accurate to say that at the end of the twentieth century, Zhou Jiaping did not appeal to less demanding customers, but to customers who wanted difference; even if it did not carry an authentic Pierre Cardin label, it exuded the style. Then, under licence, the

222

company exported Pierre Cardin fashions to France – and to the USA. It entered the low-end of the market because carrying the "Made in China" label would have made it not-good-enough, but compared to not having any Pierre Cardin, it had appeal to the customer who had lesser expectations. Like wearing a fake Rolex, who could tell the difference between the imitation and the genuine article?

The success of this approach is clear: In 2005, the sales volume is expected to reach 10 billion Renminbi, including US $500 million from the USA market. Assets are expected to reach 5 billion Renminbi. The annual capacity for garments is expected to be 10 million units. (*Heilan Group*, 2004, pp.5-6). The pattern comprises technology acquisition (through licensing or purchase), productivity, change through product diversification and then expansion. In short, the disruptive as well as the subsequent sustaining forms of innovation that Huaxia followed, is very reminiscent of Little Dragon's road to profitability. In each case, the innovation was a catalyst from another country that enabled the Chinese firm to hurdle across decades of Western industrial development, and implement it with almost immediate commercial success. This was the Chinese model as the researcher observed it in three companies from three different industries. In this process, foreign companies often became willing players on an industrial stage in which the climactic scene was invariably the generation of greater profits for the Chinese industrialist, who was the lead actor, producer and director at the same time.

Each company had resources as its prime asset, and it was likely that in the future, those with the greatest resources would be bought, as Little Dragon was, to "essentially plug the acquired people, products, technology, and customers into the parent's processes as a way of leveraging the parent's existing capabilities." (Christensen and Raynor, 2003, p.200).

13.3.2 Alpine Packs the Wilderness Company

Alpine Packs the Wilderness Company was a congruent company in many respects, and after its dramatic re-engineering, continued to strive for congruence, even if it departed from the standard model. Led by Stewart McBruce and Sandra Gupwell, its founder-owners, as well as seasoned industrial experts like Pearl Smith overseeing production, and others of more than ten-years standing such as Joe Barnard in sales, the company displayed a strong work ethic and a pervasive culture of love for the outdoors, manifested in the objectives of the company. Its vision was clear, and work flows, managed by division leaders like Pearl Smith, regularly met production targets, according to documents that the researcher sighted. To enhance human resource capabilities, staff were adequately trained to perform critical tasks, and both male and female staff comprised expert sewers of products, although they specialized in a particular product to increase their efficiency. A number of employees had met at the factory and got married from there, continuing to work there once they had a family; and Alpine Packs' emphasis on profit-share and variations on bonus payments schemes developed throughout the years, were just two of the reasons why the company had a nation-wide reputation in New Zealand for being an excellent employer. The company also placed a high emphasis on safety as an aspect of its human resource systems. For example, with respect to a component task, the employee whose job it was to fill sleeping bags with down, operated in a transparent plastic-walled chamber so he could be seen at all times by at least ten other employees, and he was dressed in a suit not dissimilar in appearance to one worn by Neil Armstrong on the moon. His helmet was hermetically sealed to prevent him from inhaling fine-grade down dust. This was just one manifestation of the way in which the company placed social values before profits at all times, according to Stewart McBruce, (11 April 2003) – except when those profits could no longer sustain those values by 2002. Ultimately, the profitability had to be there in order for the company to exist.

The company worked in four main divisions: packs, clothing, tents and sleeping-bags. Each of these divisions was divided into teams, and within the last eighteen months of this research, these teams had appointed team leaders because the last few years' experiment in having everyone within a team take responsibility, was not working well, and the company took a long time – eight years – to come to that realization. This was an example of effecting change through formal links, communicating through informal role-holders, work process assessments and group processes.

The company had forged strong links with its overseas suppliers, including contingency plans when deliveries of supplies were late, and had worked out a well-functioning distribution system for product delivery within Europe and Australia, operated from the company's modern plant in Christchurch, rather than through middle-men residing in Europe itself. Its formal linking included formal staff meetings once a week, where all staff, not just management staff, were encouraged to contribute in any way that was considered constructive. The company operated on an "open and honest" platform where all finances were open to scrutiny by staff once a month, and this became a core ingredient of the company's information systems.

For 29 years of its first 30-year period, the company was profitable. When the disastrous events of September 11 2001 changed people's confidence in travel, and therefore also in the pursuit of outdoor activities, the company suffered losses for the first time. The company lost NZ $1 Million in the first year after the catastrophe in New York. At the same time, the American dollar declined in value relative to the New Zealand dollar. The disruption was therefore not a commercial one. It was at this point that McBruce decided that twelve managerial staff would have to be made redundant to re-align the "people" element in order to balance their precarious finances. Six months later, two hundred more staff were made redundant and the company began arrangements to outsource to Vietnam, China and the Philippines, thereby following a pattern of manufacturing outsourcing that has now become quite common to American and Australian manufacturers. With the Christchurch plant becoming an administrative and management unit, the vision, objectives and strategy had to change.

Alpine Packs was congruent but ceased to be profitable for two consecutive years, nearly leading to its demise. The company could not be called ambidextrous because it did not sufficiently look to developing "innovation streams" for future profits, although its four product clusters were intended to spread risk. Its packs and other outdoor equipment were acknowledged to be of good quality and well received in the market (Smith, Gupwell, McBruce, March-April, 2003) but the market was a niche market, implying the company had a limited number of consumers, and as it happened, their products were easily copied and could be sold more cheaply. The "lack of urgency" to which Pearl Smith referred in her interview on March 28 2003, referred to elements in the company that she considered were complacent and unprogressive. It was likely that this "social" company would have been able to withstand a minor disturbance in the business environment, but a major environmental setback was unforeseen – even though no one could have predicted the magnitude of the one that did them the damage. Nor can a company survive by the reputation it has built through sponsorship such as its support of outdoor expeditions and concern for environmental preservation – although in Alpine Pack's case, such things built them great community goodwill. This may have had an influence on their culture, as will be seen later in this chapter.

In contrast to this, the Wave Rider Company took a more pro-active approach towards diversity, at a much earlier stage of its development as a company. Like Alpine Packs, it too was a company with a limited market – not everyone surfs, any more than everyone backpacks – but whilst Wave Rider went into the production of items that may have been primarily focused on their target market, its vision was wider than Alpine Pack's vision. Strategically, their clothing lines also had popular appeal in the general market, where their youth clothing lines (male and female), sunglasses, watches, caps, and footwear, sold well. These product lines were extensions of Wave Rider's original products, and formed a natural product cluster underpinned by sun and sand. They recognised the portability of their brand and the value that it could add to their company. Their strategy took advantage of the fact that the consumer public was eager for designer labels, and youth had more discretionary spending than ever before. This did not necessarily make them rich, but in the case of purchasing a watch, having more money did make them choosy. Better marketing and distributing overseas is the approach Alpine Packs have adopted now, with dedicated appointees selling and networking for them in Europe and North America, when they abandoned this practice in the late 'eighties as too costly. If this were now the preferred method of distribution, post 9/11, it may be surmised that it might have worked more profitably for them before 9/11 as well. Susan and Stephen Dann state that, "street credibility is easily damaged or lost if the external success of the product is perceived to be the result of the entrepreneur 'selling out' their niche", (Dann and Dann, 2001, p.101), this did not appear to have taken place with Wave Rider, and similarly, it may also have increased Alpine Pack's brand marketability.

226

Nonetheless, before re-engineering, Alpine Packs appeared to be largely congruent in its four critical building blocks. It has to be noted, however, that despite the company being well managed within its self-determined set of perimeters of production and sales levels, and well supported by staff, (as evidenced by their continuing to work unfailingly during the time of its transition), the congruence model does not have an indicator to demonstrate that adherence to the four building block model **and** financial failure can take place at the same time. This is because they appear mutually exclusive. Between 2000 when it was a profitable company, and 2002 when it was not, Alpine Packs did not do anything different in terms of its systems, routines and output – it simply could not sell enough of its products.

Butlin and Carnegie, agreeing with Tushman and O'Reilly, have observed that the main function of the manager is to "align the people, processes and organization of the business in an effective – and above all, profitable – way to implement the strategy. It is easy to lose sight of the requirement to be profitable." (Butlin and Carnegie, 2001, p.113). The Alpine Packs company had the building blocks in place to design new products using incremental innovations relating almost exclusively to style and fabrics improvements, and had the capability to manufacture them. But Stewart McBruce stated that the company's greatest innovations occurred when the research could be funded from abundant profit, indicating that profit generation was an irregularly undulating pattern, and implying that no discontinuous innovations had been created for about a decade. (McBruce, interview, April 11 2003). Butlin and Carnegie support Tushman and O'Reilly when they state that, "The challenge […] is to set the framework for the business to improve what is important, deliver the right bottom line and build capability (and ongoing profits) for the future." (Butlin and Carnegie, 2001, p.113). It is a sobering thought that Alpine Packs had the expertise, experience and systems to deliver its products in times of geo-political stability, but it became an object lesson in financial failure at times of geo-political volatility. However, to be fair to Alpine Packs' management, New Zealand companies, like its people generally, consider themselves uniquely insulated from global vicissitudes because of New Zealand's geographic isolation. Nonetheless, in the twenty-first century, a company that is dependent on foreign sales for overall profitability, will therefore live or die by it, and cannot use geographical location as an excuse for failure.

In relation to that, successful enterprises have been undergoing revolutionary changes to become and remain competitive: neo-classical management orthodoxy has given way to multiple changing management paradigms, and strategic planning and rational strategy have been replaced by strategic thinking, innovation and a focus on core competence. (Clarke and Clegg, 1998, p.6). Alpine Packs is to be credited with the fact that the time between 9/11/2001 and the announcement to outsource in 2003 was only a year and a half apart. Once the new environmental factors were understood, Stewart McBruce's managerial competence made him act almost instantaneously, and just as quickly, he replaced the social company paradigm by a quasi-virtual company paradigm. By resorting to outsourcing production, Alpine Packs underwent a major architectural discontinuity in a very short interval. Yet McBruce had to maintain congruence to complete the last contracts under his old regime, and at the same time plan strategically for total change, minimising his loss of profits in the process. McBruce and the group processes within the management team dismantled the very paradigm on which they had built the thirty-year business that had comfortably sustained them in stable times. Producing that strategic change did not result in the political problems that many authors warn about, but the transition time and the new company architecture after that, caused the management and design staff to think deeply about achieving a new congruence, where new expectations would be underpinned by new objectives and a number of new competencies and processes.

The congruence model now becomes a geographically distended one covering Asia-Pacific to take on another dimension, a "virtual" dimension, with much systemic learning that is now obsolete under the new order, and new learning needing to take its place in order to make partnerships in Asia effective. McBruce and Gupwell (Interviews, May 2004) both noted that under the new order, the investment of time devoted to re-emphasizing innovation and learning through design, reconfiguring systems of communication and quality management, re-organizing logistics management and distribution, was considerable. It can be seen therefore, that congruence is not just a platform for innovation, but also a measure of stability, and that in the new order, McIntyre and his remaining staff were striving for congruence, even though it was bound to take on a new pattern from the one before. Shapiro, 2002, comments that in the new kind of environment that Alpine Packs found itself in, they had to work to make the "flow of information seamless and transparent", adding that "the place where work is done is no longer important, who does it is flexible, and even when it is done it becomes more transparent. Collaboration can now take place with suppliers and customers up and down the value chain." (Shapiro, 2002, p.135). Being an owner-operator meant that McBruce and Gupwell did not have to contend with opposition or other input from the public which could have slowed the transition down considerably. In making a profit again in the early months of 2004, it appears that Alpine Packs staff found the right combinations of "collaboration," or work processes. But Clark and Clegg sound a warning about nascent cultures: "Commitment to the generation and sharing of knowledge can only be inspired in employees, suppliers, customers and others who feel a sense of connection with the company and who share its values and objectives." (Clark and Clegg, 1998, p.431). This raises the question of how 'connected' employees in a virtual organization feel in relation to their parent organization when physical contact is reduced to a minimum.

13.3.3 Wave Rider the Surfing Company

Wave Rider, also owner-operated, was the antithesis of Alpine Packs because it has remained profitable from inception to the present, (except for two years in the late 'eighties). Yet the companies were similar in that Wave Rider also followed a pattern of outsourcing at about the same time as Alpine Packs did. The main difference between the two companies lay in Wave Rider's conservative financial operations, the profitability of their "proprietary technologies" of wetsuits and watches (Christensen and Raynor, 2003), early franchising, which disseminated its brand world-wide, and its profit margins which enabled it to become as ambidextrous a company as the Little Dragon Group Company. In Waugh's own words, "We've in most cases been able to control our expenses therefore we have had some profit. In most cases that has financed our growth and that, to some degree, controls our future." (Waugh, Aug 24, 2001).

One other major factor was important when discussing the differences between Wave Rider and Alpine Packs. Wave Rider produced two disruptive products thus far in its existence, which accounted for very rapid increases in profits. The first was the dual density wetsuit and the other was the tide-watch. The wetsuit was a disruptive product because it drove the heavier O'Neil product, manufactured in the United States, out of the Australian market, except for the purpose of deep-sea diving, which was a very limited market. Wave Rider's product was purpose-made for surfers, had excellent repair/replacement back-up service, and competed against nonconsumption. It succeeded in the latter because it grew the sport of surfing by enticing those consumers who previously would have felt too cold to have braved the surf for even long enough to learn to balance on their boards, let alone enjoy the ride. "Many disruptions are hybrids, combining new-market and low-end approaches," according to Christensen and Raynor, (2003, p.47), and the dual-density wetsuit was a hybrid because it targeted nonconsumers, that is non-surfers, and those who were surfers already and wanted the product's technology against the cold, and yet retain flexibility.

During their interviews on Aug 24 2001, Sinclair and Waugh offered insights into their vision, their marketing strategy, the human resource systems they used to appoint new staff, how they related to staff with whom they created franchises overseas and allowed them to exercise their own creative flair to appeal to nationals in their countries. They also made clear how they innovated, manufactured, controlled quality, distributed, and sold their products. High technical skills may not have been necessary to be part of their workforce, but their employees were good at what they did, learning mainly on the job, and manufacturing quality products.

More complex tasks were involved of course, in the manufacture of the tide-watches, and these became a disruptive technology because they disrupted the watch market, as Seiko did, when for the first time there was a serious watch that had style and 'cool' for youthful consumers. (Christensen and Raynor, 2003, p.63). It was a disruption at the low end of the market because it was marketed at impecunious yet choosy youth, and was differentiated from conventional watches because it had a two-fold capacity: it told time and tide. The latter was a unique feature for those who sought to know the tides as well as those who simply sought a modicum of customization. Its innovative dial-look and multi-functions appealed first to its target market (and later to a wider market). And for Wave Rider, it became a new-growth business. Subsequent improvements to the watch's functions have been sustaining innovations. It was the quality of the watches and the back-up service in Wave Rider's dedicated stores which enabled the watches to climb the upward trajectory. (Christensen and Raynor, 2003). As the two theorists state in the same work, "[The] mismatch between the true needs of consumers and the data that shape most product development efforts leads most companies to aim their innovations at nonexistent targets. The importance of identifying [the desired] jobs to be done goes beyond simply finding a foothold. Only by staying connected with a given job as improvements are made, and by creating a purpose brand so that customers know what to hire, can a disruptive product stay on its growth trajectory." (Christensen and Raynor, 2003, p.95). Wave Rider's two disruptive products accomplished that.

Will Waugh commented that over time, starting with very little in Sinclair's garage, the company slowly expanded from constructing boards to designing and manufacturing wetsuits, before diversifying further. For almost a decade after incorporating the company, the two partners themselves did almost everything that was required to earn a profit, from cutting neoprene to cutting deals with retailers. Therefore, their operations, or congruence, built slowly and steadily, and only later did it involve a larger number of individuals, when explicit care needed to be taken to effect congruence on a wider scale. Surfing was their passion – the business appears at times from both Sinclair and Waugh's accounts to have come second, although that was inferred rather than stated. (Interviews, Aug. 24 2001). Wave Rider's management and employees wanted a lifestyle in which they could surf when surf was up, and work when surf was down, and this became a cultural value, making their component tasks and work processes very flexible. Wave Rider provided them with that opportunity, and the company has been in turn rewarded with staff loyalty.

There are a number of items of evidence that this company was congruent, even if the irreverence of their culture may not always make appear to be so. Evidence of congruence is the expansion of the company from a staff of two to one of 1400 world-wide within thirty years of the company's founding. Furthermore, the company designed and produced incremental and breakthrough innovations at a much more consistent rate than Alpine Packs. The company also expanded into a new, albeit related line of production in the late eighties, when they began manufacturing snow products to cater for the off-season. In doing so, they also had to expand into new premises, building on the prior success of their work processes. Increased production led to increased profits. In terms of clothing, they had to develop new technologies to deal with fabrics that provided warmth and water-repellent characteristics. The critical tasks learned in clothing manufacture were to serve them well since a few years later the company began large-scale youth wear production.

The congruence at Wave Rider may have a 'loose' construction as the staff at Torquay still surf when they can, denoting perhaps a disdain for systems and procedures, but the congruence at Wave Rider is unlike any found at Little Dragon or Alpine Packs. The congruence is cemented by communication networks both on and off the factory floor. As Waugh put it, by employees' "like-mindedness", or passion, for the sport of surfing in which the company's slogan "The Search" became an expression of extreme exhilaration and freedom. As such, it now competes with bunji jumping and high-cliff diving, but Wave Rider made a considerable contribution to the industry of extreme sports, because when it was a start-up, surfing was one of the few extreme sports – the others had yet to be borne.

Sinclair and Waugh spoke with passion about their philosophy and surfing fraternity, and how their innovations catered ever better for the fraternity's needs. Everyone connected with the company was intensely committed to every form of creativity, every system and process, and every innovation that would make the pleasure even just a little bit greater, according to Herbert, Waugh and Sinclair (Aug. 24 2001). Some of those processes involved the production of custom orders for particular clients, particularly surfboards. As Susan and Stephen Dann comment,

> The intimate understanding of the norms and values of the niche gained by being a member of this segment allows for greater creativity in developing marketing strategies and tactics. Street Level Marketers (SLM) know how far to push the boundaries of acceptability within the niche before becoming irrelevant, unfocused or unacceptable to the norms of the market.
> (Dann and Dann, 2001, pp.97-98).

This of course, is not just confined to marketers, as in this case, it is particularly applicable to the manufacturers. In the terminology of Leifer et al., (2000), the management of Wave Rider invented their own radical innovations because they were

232

their own "transition team" and comprised their own "radical innovation hub." (Leifer et al. 2000, p.190). Their versatility and flexibility, as well as the passion they shared for the sport provided them with their own "radical innovation capacity" and this gave them a source of "long-term competitive advantage." (Leifer et al. 2000, p.196).

Core competencies drove product development, (Clark and Clegg, 1998, p.38). With every new product line, from boards to watches to STL Code boardshorts, the aim was to maximise the value and pleasure felt by the consumer – to the point where the physical limitations of the products at all times had to exceed the limitations that the surfer or skier could impose on himself, so that he could remain safe and comfortable. Those product qualities assisted the reputation of the brand. Because Wave Rider claimed that they themselves were the customer, the congruence was strong: the relationship between Payot in France, Tonay in the United States, and Sinclair and Waugh in Australia, ensured effective and efficient sharing of a vision as well as of shared global technology with regional differences in the final product. There was a power balance, trust and collaboration in the executive leadership; there was global purchasing and benchmarking from the outset; and there were marketing skills learned from being surfers and snow-boarders, because they had a close association with them with forty years, testimony to the strength of their communication, cultural norms and strategy.

13.4 Outsourcing

Both Wave Rider and Alpine Packs underwent a significant shift during the time of this investigation, as they looked to Asia for their main production bases, and even Little Dragon began a modest outsourcing programme based in Indonesia (Dr Hing, March 24 2004). James Brian Quinn expressed the shift in this way,

> With rare exceptions, the economic and productive power of a modern corporation lies more in its intellectual and service capabilities than in its hard assets – land, plant and equipment … Virtually all public and private enterprises are becoming predominantly repositories and coordinators of intellect.
> (Quinn quoted in Kiernan, 1997, p.5).

Quinn and Kiernan appear correct that up to the turn of the century, this was the model by which transnationals commonly did business. It can be seen endorsed in Alpine Packs as it increased its domestic design staff. However, Wave Rider commissioned designs from its International CEO, residing overseas, instructing him to create a new discontinuous product with seamless fabric processing. And Little Dragon designed and manufactured the 300-Series for Toshiba. This means that whilst the early model places all intellectual capabilities, such as design, at the company's home-base, there is a change occurring to this model. The change is that overseas employees are beginning to contribute to design. This is the area which Quinn and Kiernan considered the company headquarter's proprietary intellectual property. And this is related to production. As Christensen and Raynor (2003) have commented, "Not all innovative ideas [or existing products] can be shaped into disruptive strategies, however, because the necessary preconditions do not exist; in such situations, the opportunity is best licensed […]" (Christensen and Raynor, 2003, p.55).

A shift in location could effect a shift in culture. With a staff of 170 in Torquay, Wave Rider could maintain its culture because of the multiplicity of critical tasks. Alpine Packs with a staff of about 50 was already witnessing a shift in its cultural norms from manufacturing to design and management. Its information systems and formal linking changed: close working proximity with fewer colleagues in like occupations removed the need for formal staff meetings.

Little Dragon predominantly bought its intellectual property, but now in outsourcing to Indonesia itself, it too became part of this worldwide trend. For this reason, where there is outsourcing or where there are company subsidiaries, the congruence model not only has to adapt to a multitude of re-combinations, but it also needs to have an additional dimension built into it to remain a valid model for manufacturing integration and ambidexterity. It may need to add 'repositories and coordination of IP' as part of its management and design functions. Similarly, disruptive products are a feature of Little Dragon, and outsourcing may affect the model.

The congruence model is the name that stands for stable, well-coordinated production. Congruence between parts is necessary but in all three case-studies, its dynamic has undergone a shift. It is now appropriate to consider also how communication systems may be included as an element in the model that now has elevated status. It is such a critical aspect of multi-national corporate life and can take on so many forms that it may merit a category of its own, like "People" and "Critical Tasks". Culture may also have undergone a change. For example, does the outsource company contracted to manufacture for a mainland company adopt any of the features of mainland culture, or does it retain its own? Or does it combine into a mixture of the two? Both Alpine Packs and Wave Rider spoke of their outsourcing companies as if they were natural extensions of their own mainland congruence. Wave Rider's publicist, Graham Herbert, commented for example, that, "the causes of most problems are easily identified and addressed due to a high level of commitment at both ends," but the most important aspect of the relationship for the company is that "in approximate terms, [they make] 10 gross profit percentage points on most products." (E-mail from G. Herbert to the researcher, 20 Aug 2004). Outsourcing can make an impact on congruence. However, neither Wave Rider nor Alpine Packs had thoroughly evaluated the outcomes for themselves – they were still at early stages. Yet the one factor they were certain about was that outsourcing aided their profit motive. Whether it would aid their ability to innovate had not been determined at the time of writing. When Christensen and Raynor (2003) state that an essential component of leadership is the ability to spot future possibilities for profit, it is equally important to train staff to appreciate the need to cultivate those possibilities. It remains to be seen whether long-distance connections can engender "wisdom and intuition" in a low-economic workforce, which may not have the education to appraise the situation.

The various forms of influence that outsourcing has on its parent company and vice-versa merits further investigation, as does its pervasiveness and importance to the phenomenon of globalization. In early 2005, Engardio and Einhorn published a feature article in *BusinessWeek*, in which they provide a broad canvas of the outsourcing situation. Whilst this is in the form of reporting rather than scholarly exegesis, a number of points can be made. Outsourcing formerly related to manufacturing, but it is now beginning to include innovation and design. Where R&D used to remain in-house, Dell, Motorola and Philips are now reported to be purchasing complete designs of some digital devices from Asia, applying their own specifications and their own brand-names. As this nascent practice is developing, large Western companies save money and gain efficiencies. For example pharmaceutical companies such as GlaxoSmithKline are creating joint ventures with Asian biotech research companies in order to cut the average $US 500 Million cost of bringing a new medicine to the market. Procter & Gamble Co. says it wants half of its new product ideas to be generated from outside by 2010, compared with 20 percent at the present time. (Engardio and Einhorn, March 21 2005, pp.52-53).

13.5 Leadership and creativity

Tushman and O'Reilly (1997) believe that leadership is crucially important because leaders must have a vision for their innovation that may surpass the understanding and expectations of their consumers; it may even surpass the value network of their employees. This is because "products that do not appear to be useful to our customers today (that is, disruptive technologies) may squarely address their needs tomorrow." (Tushman and O'Reilly, 1997, p.258). Executives' resource allocation must extend their company's profitability, and it is their leadership that "requires that employees continue to hone and exercise that wisdom and intuition," (Tushman and O'Reilly, 1997, p.258), so that the workforce may remain receptive to innovation which is rarely a product of mainstream thought processes.

Tushman and O'Reilly (1997) typify the manager who leads innovation and change as an "architect, network builder and juggler." In turn, the function of each role is to "build [a] fit," "manage strategic change" and "host contradictory strategies, structures [and] competencies." (Tushman and O'Reilly, 1997, p.225). These are reminiscent of Mintzberg's ten managerial functions (cited in Robbins & Mukerji, 1994, p.9) but they are less compartmentalized. For example, Tushman and O'Reilly's model assumes the capacity for the contemporary manager to work simultaneous complexities, particularly under the role of juggler: "Hosting contradictory strategies, structures, competencies, and cultures in service of incremental, architectural, and discontinuous innovation, as well as integrating these contradictions with a clear vision." (Tushman and O'Reilly, 1997, p.215). Butlin and Carnegie underscore these functions with a requirement for contemporary leadership to the build "capabilities in enterprises to institutionalise the capacity to innovate [which] is really about creating new value for money. To do this well, the best innovators focus on the right type of business model." (Butlin and Carnegie, 2001, p.110). A key part of that model as shown by all three cases is the need for management to communicate effectively with their staff and treat them as the professionals they are. Creativity and innovation cannot thrive in an environment that has strong restrictions. So Dr Hing at Little Dragon had to actively drive his staff towards openness, because it was not an integral part of work behaviour in China. His initiatives in having his management staff learn English and gain experience in Six Sigma practice assists this openness. It does this in two ways: Firstly, it enables contact with foreign experts in the field who are contracted to instruct; and secondly, it enables the Little Dragon staff to travel and communicate in English outside of China, with greater facility and confidence. This is an aspect of learning consistent with the strategic direction of the company.

13.5.1 Little Dragon Group Company

The leadership of Little Dragon can be best characterized as one of invention particularly in the area of strategy and innovation. Mr Lei, Deputy General Manager, was a product of Communist regimentation for most of his working life, but his fresh approach to advancing his company's interests lay in his ability to identify with present as well as future market realities. This was exemplified by his writing of occasional papers on the Internet, and reaching out to Japan, arch-foe of World War II, to purchase advanced technology there. In both interviews he seemed completely confident about his company's robust future by capturing bigger markets domestically and internationally.

Likewise Dr Hing, General Manager, believed in innovating his way into bigger markets, and doing so with the expertise of other technology companies with whom he could forge alliances and partnerships. Both he and his older colleague, Mr Lei Yuan, made the comment a number of times that they wished for harmonious relations with all other companies, and that competition might take place on the shop-floor but not in the market because that was too expensive an undertaking. Both prided themselves on their philosophies of enhancing their company's place in the national industrial order using company size and production output as main data, to prove the point.

Dr Hing's determination to enhance the quality of his technology was demonstrated by his perspicacious view of Toshiba as his would-be partner, rather than his competitor, in the domestic market of China. It is interesting that Tushman and O'Reilly focus on remediating companies which have lost their competitive advantage, (Tushman and O'Reilly, 1997, pp.57-77), but they do not suggest that those companies could be more creative and exploit their opposition's apparent competitive advantage. To the creative mind, this is indeed an option. Dr Hing did this with Toshiba by offering them a deal they could not refuse, much to the advantage of Little Dragon, as well as to Toshiba. To manufacture for the competition, (and in the process for oneself), to win a $2 Million one-of price from Toshiba, and to win the Deputy Chair's position on their Board of Directors shows that Dr Hing was not bound by the bonds of his company's conservative congruence or culture. He realized that he could not stop Toshiba from preying in his market, but he could control much of the process of their entry to 'his' market if he were placed in charge of that process. In persuading his own Board of Directors to relinquish "the wisdom and intuition of their mainstream thinking" (Christensen and Raynor, 1997, p.258), and get them to approve his proposal, Dr Hing was demonstrating vision, willingness to take risks, responsiveness to problems, and a total dissociation with his country's past industrial paradigm that indulged in isolation and self-sufficiency. Hing broke his company's traditional paradigm of how to deal with competition in an aberrant way, because in Toshiba he saw an opportunity to align the technology of his own company with that of a more advanced Japanese company. Importantly, the necessary resources were duly allocated. (Christensen and Raynor, 1997). His strategy architecture was to accumulate knowledge capital for the future of his own company. (Hamel and Prahalad, 1994, p.24).

13.5.2 The anomalous innovation: The Chinese solution

Dr Hing's achievement was out of the ordinary. Christensen and Raynor (2003) call "disruption [...] a relative term", (p.41), and this can be seen as follows: Dr Hing achieved part possession of a Toshiba's washing machine technology creating a product architecture that could neither be called disruptive, nor sustaining, yet at the same time his innovative actions had elements of both. It shares the disruptive characteristic relative to nonconsumption at the high-end margin market because it introduced a new level of luxury, and it shared the sustaining characteristic relative to the improvements they had been making to previous series of washing machines. This makes Dr Hing's actions anomalous. China is only in the beginning of the twenty-first century developing new market growth at the high end because of its economic expansion, and wealth generated by this trickling down to consumers who were nonconsumers of luxury before because there was none. In this instance, contrary to Christensen and Raynor's (2003) main thesis the nonconsumption was taking place at the high-profit end of the market but now there is room for generating commercial growth as China undergoes change. Dr Hing was sufficiently far-sighted to realize that. Whilst Christensen and Raynor state, "It is clear what executives who seek to create new-growth businesses should do: Target products and markets that the established companies are motivated to ignore or run away from. Many of the most profitable growth trajectories in history have been initiated by disruptive technologies." (Christensen and Raynor, 2003, p.43). By targeting the high-end of the unexploited domestic market, Dr Hing was consolidating his company's position right across the value chain: no other established company could be motivated to enter this market because the Little Dragon and Toshiba consortium now had a tight grip on the entire market between them.

13.5.3 Alpine Packs the Wilderness Company

If the leadership of Little Dragon may be typified as one of acquisition, the leadership of Alpine Packs may be typified as one of adaptability. In the first interview, Stewart McBruce seemed pleased with all that he and his business partner Sandra Guppwell had achieved. In 2002, the company had only suffered one year's loss following 9/11

(2001), and even though the financial signs were ominous since that loss amounted to NZ $1 Million, there was observation of that fact, but there was no panic, (interview with Stewart McBruce, 21 May 2004). Both McBruce and Guppwell were clear in their different functions and responsibilities as leaders, and upon interviewing Alpine Packs' staff, it became clear to the researcher that the company's employees held the leadership of the company in very high regard. While there was a slight possibility that staff complimented the leadership because they thought that word might get back to the leadership if they did not do so, or perhaps that this was expected of them and would reflect negatively on their loyalty to the firm, it seemed to the researcher that their comments about "fairness" and "great [company] atmosphere," were genuine and sincere.

In Tushman and O'Reilly's description, Stewart McBruce would be an "architect": he built "congruent structures, [dealt with] human resources and cultures to execute critical tasks in service of strategy, objectives and vision." (Tushman and O'Reilly, 1997, p.225). But then, like Dr Hing, he broke his own paradigm. Only this was a paradigm he had carefully nurtured and cultivated over the years himself – it was not one he had inherited as a cultural norm, as in Dr Hing's case. Every action McBruce took as leader of his company was formerly directed at achieving an equal distribution of resources, opportunities, and profits for the whole staff. (McBruce, 11 April, 2003). He realized however, that his organization had to undergo radical change or thirty years' work would dissolve into bankruptcy.

The undoing of the company was primarily its lack of strategic vision, probably because it did not feel the need for one. Christensen and Raynor comment that,

> established organizations typically face the opportunity to create new growth businesses – and the consequent requirement to utilize different resources, processes, and values – at a time when the mainstream business is still very healthy – when executives must not change the resources, processes, and values that enable core businesses to sustain their success. This requires a much more tailored approach to managing change than many managers have felt necessary [...].
>
> (Christensen and Raynor, 2003, p.189).

Inspite of having a capable research unit, the company operated at too low margins, and therefore, "their processes and values constitute[d] *disabilities* in their efforts to succeed at disruptive innovation," (Christensen and Raynor, 2003, p.190). As a result, the company was satisfied to design and manufacture sustaining innovations consisting mainly of continual improvement, so that while their brand became synonymous with quality, it was not synonymous with consistent innovation and hence new-growth profitability.

Outsourcing became the solution following 9/11, and this became McBruce's strategic vision. From this it is clear that leadership in the twenty-first century comprises responsiveness to the environment, courage, determination and all the characteristics that Tushman and O'Reilly describe under their headings of "network builder" and "juggler". (Tushman and O'Reilly, 1997, p.225). Within the space of a year and a half, Stewart McBruce was catapulted from being just an "architect", to assuming all, not just some, of the responsibilities of a contemporary leader, including those of "network builder" and "juggler."

13.5.4 Wave Rider the Surfing Company

The leadership of Paul Sinclair and Will Waugh may be characterised by passion. As leaders at the centre of a surfing culture, they spearheaded its acceptance by the general population, driving it away from the public's previous perception that surfing, and in particular, surfers, were anti-authoritarian radical drop-outs. This was the stereotype they broke, and it may have taken years for surfing to become accepted as a respectable sport, but by the 1980s it had achieved that.

In their own passion for surfing, Sinclair and Waugh wanted to excel in all their endeavours to supply others in their fraternity with the best possible equipment. They achieved this in their two lead products, wetsuits and tide-watches. Their sponsorship of both surfing and skiing competitions for almost four decades in various world locations made it into a spectator sport as well as a challenging one in which to compete.It could be argued that the two of them served the functions of architect, network builder and juggler from an early stage in their partnership. They achieved congruence from an early vision of wanting to serve their expanding market well. They became network builders because they expanded their industry to France, then the USA, and later to another ten countries. And then they became jugglers when they began outsourcing, working with incremental as well as discontinuous innovations in expanded lines of production in youth clothing, sunglasses and footwear. As in the case of Alpine Packs, the founder-owners influenced the nature and direction of their industry, they identified the market giving their company the opportunity to thrive, to provide that market with equipment that had integrity and they shared their love for an outdoor pursuit with others.

At Alpine Packs, Stewart McBruce had the strength and daring to break with the past and change the organizational architecture of his company. It is debatable whether in the case of Wave Rider, Paul Sinclair and Will Waugh maintained many past traditions and their organizational architecture with deliberate intent, but it is a possibility. They knew that not being accountable to any shareholders meant that the company could continue to fuel its innovations in the future at its own pace. However, owning a private company also means that years in which there is no growth or where there is private profit taking, can be undisclosed because no financial data needs to be conveyed to the public. In this case, innovation is unlikely to be generated, because funding is low or unavailable. Public expectations of, and demands on such a company are therefore less than on a public company where shareholders demand growth – preferably growth that exceeds market expectations. (Christensen and Raynor, 2003, pp.1-5).

The quality that all three leaderships have in common is their determination to succeed and their unhesitating commitment to their company. Determination is an essential ingredient in leadership, and takes many different forms. It involves long hours in discussion with colleagues, customers and suppliers; researching new learning; developing ingenious systems to cut costs and so on. Having initially ventured into uncharted industrial territory with early disruptors or discontinuous innovations of varying kinds, the leaders then guarded the interests of that territory zealously, but were prepared to break paradigms of a lifetime, if need be, to sustain their companies. Their life's work in innovation became the object of their pride and faith. Lei and Hing formed a symbiotic relationship with their greatest industrial foe, Toshiba, never for a moment did the General Manager believe that this hi-tech juggernaut aimed to "come second" to Little Dragon, (Hing, 24 Mar, 2004). McBruce and Gupwell willingly destroyed their social organization in order to re-forge a phoenix from its predecessor's ashes, into a "virtual" form. And Sinclair and Waugh broke through popular opinion to change surfing's anti-establishment associations, to create a multi-national that became so much a manifestation of their passion for the sport, that even in retirement, they could not release the company to new ownership for fear that it might change Wave Rider's direction, and thereby undermine its bedrock philosophy of The Search.

13.6 Culture and change

13.6.1 Alpine Packs the Wilderness Company and Wave Rider the Surfing Company

The "disconfirming data" in Edgar Schein's terminology, was clear to Stewart McBruce by 2002. It is more common for a culture in this difficult circumstance, to go the opposite way to the one intended to remedy the problem in the company. "The identity that the organization has built up and that has been the source of its success must now be preserved, even if that means ultimate failure to adapt successfully to a changing environment." (Clark and Henderson, cited in Schein, 1997, p.300). In other words, Alpine Packs could easily at this point have become an unrecoverable victim of its own success. (Tushman and O'Reilly, 1997, p.28). McBruce's sole aim became the saving of his company.

Michael Porter wrote,

> Today, the only way to have an advantage is through innovation and upgrading. But this innovation, this upgrading, has to involve a consistent strategic direction. There has to be a strategic vision within which you are innovating. A company has to have something distinctive at the end of the day that it is reinforcing. To

243

me, innovation means offering things in different ways, creating new combinations.

(Porter quoted in Gibson, 1998, p.34).

McBruce and Gupwell achieved that, even though outsourcing was probably a more mundane solution than Porter had in mind, but it offered a life-line. However, this did not happen without the assistance of the culture they had created. It was vital to complete the contracts within the last five months in 2003. Even with all those completed, McBruce estimated that the transition to outsourcing had cost him approximately "two to three million dollars," (May 21 2004). Without completed contracts that same year, his losses would have been considerably worse and may have delayed his efforts to effect a successful transformation so soon in 2004.

How might the exceptional cooperation shown McBruce by his 200 strong workforce in completing all his old contracts be explained? It is partially explained by Schein when he states,

> If the organization is not under too much external stress and if the founder or founding family is around for a long time, the culture evolves in small increments by continuing to assimilate what works best over the years [...]. General evolution toward the next historical stage of development involves diversification, growing complexity, higher levels of differentiation and integration, and creative syntheses into new and higher-level forms. Implicit in this concept is the assumption that social systems do have an evolutionary dynamic. [...] Specific evolution involves the adaptation of specific parts of the organization to their particular environments, and the impact of the subsequent cultural diversity on the core culture.
> (Schein, 1997, pp.305-306).

Alpine Pack's culture was usually considered to be one homogeneous entity by participants involved in this research. Some considered the "office" culture to stand a little apart because its functions were differentiated from the manufacturing one, and because these staff members were expected to be participants in outdoor pursuits, which manufacturing staff did not have to engage in if they did not want to – although the encouragement was there.

244

Similarly, Wave Rider's employees could be differentiated between the professional and manufacturing staff. Even though Graham Herbert considered himself to be at one with the surfers because he was one, his literary skills elevated him in the professional stakes above the educational capabilities of his colleagues in manufacturing. Again, Sinclair and Waugh wore very casual clothes at all times, as did McBruce and Gupwell – wearing a tie made the researcher stand out immediately. Therefore, although there was a differentiation in responsibility in both companies, their respective managements preferred to be seen as socially integrated with the rest of the staff. This did not appear to be the case at Little Dragon, due to the more formal social and work conventions within Chinese society. For example, when the researcher was shown the Scott Line, neither Dr Hing nor Lei Yuan communicated with the operator. Mr Lei spoke to a middle manager, and it was he who instructed the employee to demonstrate its operations.

Likewise, both companies had open-plan offices, no dedicated car-parks for management, and had large foyers where their products were displayed. This last aspect also applied to Little Dragon, which had hundreds of white-ware products arranged in sections and ordered according to function, size and price.

In each of the three cases, the visual surroundings pertaining to the company, its products and culture were immediately obvious to a "newcomer". At Wave Rider, the larger-than-life sized photos of talented sportsmen and women engaged in extreme pursuits were inspiring. There was a sense that the newcomer was engulfed in a world of frenetic energy and exhilaration: it was other-worldly, and an image integral the marketing process. It was also an aspect of what Tushman and O'Reilly call "social learning", (Tushman and O'Reilly, 1997, p.103), because immersion in this world shapes a culture in such a way that it perpetuates the values and norms that are appropriate for the company to achieve its objectives. (Tushman and O'Reilly, 1997, pp.102-104). Further enhancing the possibility of stimulating innovative products from a culture, Tushman and O'Reilly explain that two other cultural characteristics are desirable, "support for risk taking and tolerance of mistakes." (Tushman and O'Reilly, 1997, p.113). In that sort of environment, culture has a strong respect for its leadership, in which they place their confidence and trust. The subordinates interviewed in Alpine Packs, and Graham Herbert, a subordinate to Sinclair and

Waugh at Wave Rider, all showed their admiration and respect for the achievements of their founder-owner-management. The fact that so many interviewees at Alpine Packs had been with their company for many years which was also indicative of trust and general contentment.

Both Alpine Packs and Wave Rider were private companies, Alpine Packs still led by their founder-owners, and principal shareholding by Sinclair and Waugh still giving them effective power, (although this may not have been translated into operational power.) The cultures in each were pervasive and could be called "strong". This meant that they had excellent performance, that they shared a set of consistent values and methods in doing business, and that they were so influential that new employees adopted values quickly, and that management created an unusual level of motivation in employees, making work intrinsically rewarding. (Kotter & Heskett, 1992, pp.15-16). This was also likely to mean that when the leadership wished to make far-reaching changes, the workforce was more likely to be in agreement with them rather than in opposition. The change to outsourcing at Alpine Packs was its greatest change in the history of the company, and according to all participants in the research, the 200 employees who were about to become redundant did not remonstrate with McBruce and Gupwell, nor with their own team leaders.

Likewise, when Wave Rider first floated the idea of offshore production, it was not their employees who raised questions about the wisdom of this, it was one textile union and Paul Robinson reporting disquiet in *The Age*. Eventually, the loyalty between employer and employee became a double bond: Wave Rider did outsource much production, but it also retained its 170-strong staff in Torquay working for the local market. Of course, unlike Alpine Packs, Wave Rider was not financially under the same pressure. It is uncertain for how long Wave Rider could have maintained Torquay as its Australian production base however, because Graham Herbert commented in his last interview that, "Wave Rider would not have been able to keep going if it had not outsourced to Asia in order to save on wages. Our major competitors have also gone that way." (Herbert, Jan. 20 2004).

246

13.7 Change

13.7.1 Overview

Many theorists raise the issue of "change" in relation to innovation: Tushman and O'Reilly, (1997); Christensen and Raynor, (2003); Jackson, (2002); Kiernan, (1997); Peters, (1997); Liefer et al., (2000); Clark and Clegg, (1998); Shapiro (2001); Schein, (1997); and Bean and Radford, (2002) are but a few. Each devotes sections in their publications on a series of calculated steps on how best to deal with culture at a time of change. Their recommendations appear, generally speaking, to either use culture as a lever, or to neutralise entrenched culture because it impedes change. In the case of the "strong" cultures at Alpine Packs and Wave Rider, the respect between employer and employee had made the bonds between them strong enough for a higher-than-usual loyalty to be at work, thereby foregoing the need to apply the strong hand of management to bring potentially diverse employees on side. This makes change much easier to manage. In Alpine Packs, change was a part of the culture – none of the participants had fear of it. At Wave Rider, change took the form of expansion through replication. Once the early Australian market appeared satiated with Wave Rider boards and wetsuits in the late 'seventies, the company replicated itself soon after that in France and the United States. Thereby the company reaped the profits but not the problems, since Payot and Tonay could exercise their own form of management as partner-shareholders.

Christensen and Raynor are equally as pragmatic about change as the Wave Rider founders. They believe that, "Established companies can improve their odds for success in disruptive innovation if they use functionally oriented and heavy-weight teams where each is appropriate, and if they commercialize sustaining innovations in mainstream organizations but put disruptive ones in autonomous organizations." (Christensen and Raynor, 2003, p.203). Focusing more closely at the people they would employ in such circumstances, they make the point that "if executives will spend time ensuring that capable people work in organizations with processes and values that match the task, they will create a major point of leverage in successfully creating new growth." (Christensen and Raynor, 2003, p.203). Managers must be particularly adept at demonstrating adaptability and versatility, which those formerly in conservative positions tend to find difficult to do.

This is why Jiang Nan's comments about the management approach at Heilan are so revealing. In claiming that at his company they can change daily, he is in fact stating his staff's ability to make rapid modifications to process and product, in contrast to others' intransigence or apathy. If change is endemic and useful to a culture's longevity, and/or businesses split off others and become self-sustaining autonomous units, then change is easier to effect than in a culture where change is seen as intrusive and counter-productive.

The uniformity of members' behaviour and thinking in the cultures of both companies is so consistent that it may be possible to speak of it in terms of "memes" as first theorised by Richard Dawkins in *The Selfish Gene*, first published in 1976. A meme is "a social object, such as a concept, image, or habit that has been diffused from one person to another, a bit as a gene self-replicates. (http://perso.wanadoo retrieved Dec 21 2004.) The theory helps explain in this very simple example, why contemporary American youths wear their caps backwards, when for a hundred years they all wore them front-wards. It means that the thought of the individual is stronger than the individual him or herself, and can become totally ingrained.

This sameness would help to explain why a culture that has already been typified as strong, can fall into a still narrower sub-category, where adherents in that culture think exactly alike: it is a form of cerebral duplication, learned from others in a culture, where the idea is stronger than the individuals who think it. That may explain why Alpine Packs' staff continued working unstintingly after the announcement was made that the company was going to come to an end in its present form, with 199 out of 200 employees remaining there and working diligently until the factory closure. The meme concept may also be applied to Wave Rider. It too has a culture with a uniformity that may be explained by the concept of meme. The culture's consistency could be the product of a highly self-replicating thought pattern throughout its membership in which "The Search" – for extreme thrills and the ultimate freedom –is the goal, and surfing is the means.

248

13.7.2 Little Dragon Group Company

Culture at the Little Dragon Group Company was not considered by its management to be a vital element in the operations of the company, although Dr Hing was attempting to effect change. When Lei Yuan was first asked about the contribution of "culture" in the second interview on 22 March 2004, he replied in terms of the way his employees were marching towards the company's production target for 2005. The researcher thought that it was possible that the operative word, "culture," had been mis-translated from English into Mandarin, or that Mr Lei did not really understand the concept, or that perhaps there was no real direct translation of this word intoMandarin. However, on March 24 2004, Dr Hing, a very competent speaker of English, fully understood the term, and from the way the question was answered, it appeared as though he was pleased to be breaking through some of the conservative social and work practices endemic throughout PR China's industry. He spoke of more open communication, self-evaluation and greater rewards earned in the company, with bonuses now being distributed periodically rather than at the end of the work year. He was particularly pleased with that change, which had been initiated by middle management. However, that change applied only to the managerial and engineering ranks in the company.

As observed by the researcher, culture throughout the rest of the plant was typically compliant towards managerial directives, with self-effacing employees fixedly going about their business, as in China this is the most respect that an employee can demonstrate towards his or her job, to work and not engage with visitors or other distractions, in any way. This then, could also be described as a "strong" culture, it too demonstrated commitment, loyalty, respect for the company and the product. Employees' greatest awareness appeared to be for the need to serve, and this may actually be a reflection of the culture of the nation as a whole, still subjugated under a very strict political code.

For these reasons, it is understandable that a ten thousand strong culture that has the unstinting work ethic as its main focus, can be depended upon to work in any way management directs it. It is also relevant to look at management itself. Both Lei Yuan and Dr Hing were gracious, knowledgeable and as passionate about their company as Stewart McBruce or Sinclair and Waugh were about theirs. In an age liberated by relaxation of regulations and affiliation to the WTO, Hing and Lei were achieving what was previously regarded as impossible in their country: They were importing technology, producing quality products, exporting them, creating joint ventures with foreign technology giants, and travelling to other countries to examine work practices there. "Change" to them only meant increased possibilities, that is, more production and learning from industrial alliances with high technology companies. Arie de Geus was correct in stating that it is a world of "shrinking political barriers." (de Geus, 1999, p.235). Hing and Lei had a focus that was very intense and urgent. It meant increasing production and augmenting technology, and hence innovation, as the main priorities.

The Chinese attitude to production appeared to be much the same as the Japanese attitude. If it could be made better and cheaper by means of automation and robotics, then production lines with those features would be installed as soon as the company could afford them. In the future, they will most likely have to import the expertise. The New Zealand engineered folding line, the "Scott Line", was an excellent example of where one employee could oversee a large number of mechanical motions replicated to exact specifications.

13.8 Learning

In all three cases, learning was core to their success, but it was rarely in formal contexts. Of the three heads of companies, only Dr Hing had formal business education: He holds an MBA from Shanghai University. Generally, the executives learned from their clients, suppliers, employees, internal and external R&D, courses conducted by institutions, from their competitors and from general dissemination of information through written media such as the internet. Wave Rider prided themselves on being the consumer and their own test-pilots; Alpine Packs lamented the need for the re-creation of systems and procedures in their new order; and Little Dragon calculatingly bought the best of overseas technology and learning whenever they were ready to proceed with the next product line.

The success of the products of all three companies were underscored by the need to assimilate new information, to process it, analyse it, store it and reproduce it to be applied to their particular requirements. In other words, learning was never learning in the abstract; it had to be manipulated for a purpose. It was this process that gave each a competitive advantage, especially in the early stages of their development, because they had the knowledge before anyone else in the market, and developed ways to commercialize it. The secret to continuing this success was to remain ahead of the competition in terms of technologies and niche marketing. And later, when cheap duplicators entered the market, the secret of retaining competitive advantage appeared to be the amalgamation of those technologies with processes that also fused the earlier product with quality and durability – not just a temporary functionality – and then commercializing the next generation of innovation, whether incremental or discontinuous. The market did not, or could not, always distinguish between the incremental and discontinuous – nor did it matter. Either way they were getting a better product.

As part of the learning process, the uninformed consumer might well ask, what questions would Wave Rider's staff ask about neoprene rubber that they do not already know the answer to? What questions might Alpine Packs' staff ask about water-proof breathables that they do not already know the answer to? And what questions might Little Dragon engineers ask about washing-machines that they do not already know the answer to? To all of those questions, the answer is that each company would ask much. Each continues asking questions, particularly in the area of expertise in which the company has already amassed learning to an exceptionally refined or specialised level, because still greater refinement might provide them with their next generation of material, process or product, that is, the next incremental innovation. It is possible that in continuing to ask questions, it may also lead to the next discontinuous innovation, or even a disruptive product. It is for that reason that it is possible that Wave Rider missed an opportunity when Seachange Technology devised an effective portable and wearable electronic shark repellent. Such a feature would have been included in every Wave Rider wetsuit, had Wave Rider had that technology, even though technology this advanced appears to be out of their range of expertise. One pound of electro-wave producing generator, could be distributed evenly under one wetsuit surface, like the back panel, so as not to interfere with natural body motion. When a company misses out on such a proprietary technology themselves because they have not asked the right questions to go forward with their product, they may no longer consider themselves to be at the spearhead of wetsuit development. But they could ask Seachange Technology whether there is scope for business between the companies. As in the case of the tide-watch, one party has the technology, and the other has an established market. An alliance would make commercial sense, and it is a trend that is occurring more and more, because very few companies have the resources to create everything that consumers want to purchase in that market. The expertise that leads to innovations is increasingly specialized.

It is clear from the interviews, more so in the second round, that each company had come to believe in "metacognition". They focused on the process of learning how to learn for the purpose of gaining or retaining competitive advantage in the future. Learning how to learn is "metacognition." For this reason, Wave Rider is likely to continue learning more about bio-aquatics and bring out a new enhanced neoprene making "SlickSkin" obsolete; Alpine Packs is likely to continue learning more about pack design to bring out a larger, yet better balanced version of the "Air supply harness", making it obsolete; and Little Dragon is likely to keep learning from the Japanese and the Germans, so they can make their 300-series obsolete, by introducing more advanced 'fuzzy logic' that will balance scarce water and electricity supplies with the function of cleaning clothes. This supports Arie de Geus' thesis that the company of the future has its roots in two main attributes: "The company is a living being, [and] The decision for action made by this living being result from the learning process." (de Geus, 1999, pp. 235-236). For Tushman and O'Reilly these company features are inherent in the concepts of congruence and ambidexterity.

13.9 Longevity of companies

Companies can sustain profitability through the introduction of disruptive, incremental and discontinuous innovations in their product range. And even though Christensen and Raynor maintain that new-market disruptions are unusual, their sojourn through Sony's remarkable "disruptive odyssey" under Morita (Christensen and Raynor, 2003, p.80) is indicative that the engineering of disruptive innovation can be an ongoing process just like the incremental and the discontinuous. Companies must continue to ask themselves the right questions and pursue the answers that will lead to the right capital investments, the right lines of enquiry in their R&D, and the procurement of staff that is most adept at thinking innovatively, and in respecting change as a force for betterment.

However, room should also be made for anomalous situations. It is clear that Little Dragon has introduced a product at the luxury, high-margin, nonconsuming sector of the market when there was no other product at that time in existence that could perform the way consumers wanted. This technology will inevitably trickle down into less expensive products manufactured by the same company, and will then be copied by other manufacturers whose overheads are still lower than Little Dragon's, and therefore their products may sell as well if not better. Nonetheless, due to the process it has followed with Toshiba, Little Dragon has increased its market-share, which will likely impact upon company longevity in its favour.

It is clear that the model of innovation as the basis for company longevity is undergoing change. The industrialists who have lent their names and accomplishments to this investigation, began as young individuals with confidence that their commercial inspirations would bring them profit. Each inspiration, or dream, was based on the notion that an experience could be commercially enhanced for a consumer to provide greater freedom, than the technology of the time allowed. Lei Yuan dreamt of manufacturing household products that would make Chinese domestic chores more efficient; Paul Sinclair and Will Waugh dreamt that their brand of aquatic equipment would provide their consumers with the safest and most action-enhancing experience in the surf; and Stewart McBruce and Sandra Gupwell dreamt of manufacturing safe and durable equipment for hikers and climbers, to conquer mountains and rivers. Each of them began small. Each began with either a discontinuous, or disruptive product. But these achievements belong to a largely, although not totally, obsolete model. The model where an innovation is inspired by an individual with entrepreneurial confidence with no or little specialized education; with big dreams, and small capital; with a great appetite for hard labour, and an infinite tolerance for small profit margins, is the innovation model of yesteryear. All of the 'dreamers' in the three case-studies in this investigation have described their earliest experiences in that way. And Alpine Packs' near miss with bankruptcy is demonstrable evidence that this cottage-innovation model for industry no longer works in the twenty-first century.

Wave Rider was the first to understand what does work, then Little Dragon, and finally Alpine Packs – just in time. In the twenty-first century, companies innovate for profits and achieve longevity by re-combining many forms of relevant knowledge from a diverse range of resources, and they manufacture products at the location, anywhere in the world, where they may achieve the highest quality at the lowest price, combining it with the most flexible and efficient distribution and sales networks. Utterback (1994) dismissed alliances and joint ventures as a means to generate radical innovation because of the risk of industrial misappropriation, and he was correct that this is a risk. But he did not make allowance for companies needing other companies, not just consumers, to stay in business themselves. Through mutually beneficial arrangements, Toshiba profits from Little Dragon just as Little Dragon profits from Toshiba. And did Matsushita not benefit from selling its unwanted intellectual property to other companies? These may not be entirely balanced arrangements between partners of equal commercial strength, but each company would be the poorer if it were not for the other. This also applies to Wave Rider and its overseas franchises – the benefits are reciprocal.

To be an innovative company in the twenty-first century with the prospect of lasting into the next century, requires a company to have, or to develop, human expertise, and the manufacturing, communication and managerial resources of more than one or two individuals with a pioneering spirit. That is why Sinclair and Waugh sold franchises in France and the USA as soon as they realized that their own small market in

Australia was saturated; and that was why Little Dragon yearned of electronics beyond their own capacity, and so they bought them from abroad. And that is also why Alpine Packs should have recognized certain danger signals in their profit margins before the onslaught of 9/11. The 'We're one factory, and we're alright' attitude was a rapidly decaying formula in the nineteen eighties and 'nineties, and two companies from the case-studies heeded the signal and made changes. The main signal was that global integration was the only viable formula for future innovation on a scale that could reasonably be expected to provide company sustainability.

Globalization takes many forms, and Little Dragon and Wave Rider judged matters right for themselves. Globalization is "the process in which geographic distance becomes a factor of diminishing importance in the establishment and maintenance of cross border economic, political and socio-relations." (www.globalisationguide.org). Globalization means change – that is inherent in its definition. In practical terms, it means a willingness to countenance a change within the existing company, to its management structures and to its operations. It means a sharing of power and wealth; and a willingness to continue learning, which includes learning to manage by Internet communications to locations far removed from head office. Alpine Packs may have exported products but in a global sense it was marginal, and not integrated with the rest of the commercial world in the same way as Little Dragon and Wave Rider were. Just selling products was a 'one-way street.'

In a research sense, a sample of three case-studies cannot be conclusive; however, it can be indicative of certain trends, and these trends point to a new model for this generation of industrial innovation. The new model requires long-distance reciprocity, for example, resourcing a franchise manager from a different country and culture to invent the next innovation, whether it be seamless board-shorts in the case of Wave Rider, or wiper-less windscreens on the next generation of family saloons in the case of an auto manufacturer. The new formula for innovation still aims to construct the discontinuous and the disruptive. But its processes comprise novel elements and unorthodox emphases. It includes self-determination and greater product differentiation – leading the market, not being led by it. This means involving your outsourcing companies in future designs, if and when they are ready to contribute more to the whole, than just contributing cheap manufacturing. Dr Hing pointed to education and political stability as being more important factors in appointing an outsourcing company abroad, than cheap labour. This leads to reciprocity, recognizing that the world that will give rise to the next innovation must not be limited to just your plant, your city, or even your country. All of those have their limitations. There is strength in the new 'collectives', like Little Dragon which keeps entering into new arrangements with other companies, and this is now particularly applicable to all multi-nationals with a quest for innovation, because it leads to sustainability and their own company's survival. Diversity is now a strength, just as homogeneity was once considered to be a strength. The new model is competency-building, imagination-enhancing and these lead to resilience, because its proposals for the latest innovative products derive from a wider pool of shared resources than ever before. These resources, particularly multiple forms of expertise, capital and technology, treat national borders, and even cultural barriers, as though they do not exist.

The pursuit of congruence, ambidexterity, and exploiting non-consumptive markets through disruptive innovations are still relevant ideas within the new industrial innovation model, in which company resilience may be considered paramount. In the nineteen-nineties, Alpine Packs danced with death, but it was not alone. Apple Macintosh Computers Inc., a company with initial success in personal computers in the 'eighties, faded after being eclipsed by IBM and Microsoft – although it was not completely removed from the competition. However, it was collectively determined to reinvent itself drawing on all its resources, and it has in recent times brought onto the market the highly sophisticated and successful iMac and iPod. Re-implementing its electronic expertise in the latter case, meant a shift into a different direction – music. It took up where Sony's Walkman left off. Few expected this company's come-back, but it demonstrates how powerful the characteristics of the new model can be in combination: Wide resourcing, self-determination, expertise, product differentiation and resilience, can produce resurgence. Of course, when it comes to expectations, few people in Western electronics R&D would have predicted that Wipro designers in Bangalore are now developing GPS systems for European sports cars. (Engardio and Einhorn, 2005 March 21, p.52). If the new model for innovation asks more questions than the former one, the question to ask now is: Why not?

Chapter 14

Conclusions and Recommendations

14.1 Conclusions and findings

Each of the three case-studies has a dedicated concluding chapter that needs to be read in conjunction with this chapter. It is acknowledged that three case-studies cannot lead to definitive or universal conclusions, but they can be indicative of trends perceived in this investigation. The research question attempted to address the question of how three mature companies use processes of innovation and the subsequent management of change to generate sustainable leadership in their respective fields, as originally set out in Chapter 1.

The data collected from the three case-studies in three countries between 2001 and 2004, provide insights to the specific questions below, which were originally formulated in Chapter 3 Method, and are repeated here along with the findings:

1. What is the nature of, and the importance of, innovation in industry?

2. How do industrialists from three diverse cultures interpret and implement "innovation?"

3. Are there different forms of innovation towards which each company has a particular inclination?

4. How do the three companies determine which innovations to pursue for commercialization?

5. Is change management a complex strategic undertaking? Why?

6. What is the extent to which the congruence model has applicability and validity in relation to the three cases cited?

7. In which way(s) may the Tushman and O'Reilly (1997) Model be extended or otherwise modified by the data to account for each company's market leadership?

8. In the opinions of senior staff, CEOs and other staff, which management practices have been perceived as being most successful in accounting for the sustainable prosperity of each of the three companies in question?

9. Has private ownership provided advantages over public ownership in the implementation of innovation and change?

10. Have their nations' general political and economic situations helped or hindered the success of each of the companies comprising the case-studies?

11. How do the findings relate to the literature that was originally discussed in Chapter 2?

14.2 Key findings

14.2.1 Question 1.   What is the nature of, and the importance of, innovation in industry?

Innovation is perceived to be important to the companies in the three case-studies because it comprises the commercialisation of their creative ideas. Innovation in the form of dual-density wetsuits, automatic washing machines and ergonomically framed back-packs, supplies the consumers with what they demand. Generally speaking, consumer demand may be for products that are better or cheaper, or that are entirely novel, serving an unmet need for the first time. These companies then exploit demand, and generate sales. These three case-studies illustrate that companies which can conceptualize, design, manufacture, market and distribute and sell innovative products, gain a competitive advantage over those in the same industry who cannot do this, or who do this less efficiently. For example, the Little Dragon Company moved up from twenty-fourth sales position to first in the Chinese domestic market in a very short time. Therefore, through greater sales, firms with a competitive advantage create a better brand and generate greater profits, which in turn may fund the next generation of innovative products. The latter concept became the "ambidextrous organization" theory in Tushman and O'Reilly, 1997, pp.155-179, supported by evidence in the cases of Little Dragon and Wave Rider.

14.2.2 Question 2. How do industrialists from three diverse cultures interpret and implement "innovation?"

The industrialists from the three diverse cultures in question interpret and implement innovation in different ways. It is an adaptive process, as each is acutely aware of innovation as a major factor contributing to competitive advantage in their particular field. Wave Rider of Australia keeps in close contact with the opinions and feedback from its customers through dedicated retail outlets, by means of staff being actively engaged in surfing, and by sponsoring competitions that have a high profile in Australia, France and North America, particularly the Rip Curl Classic staged in Hawaii. It is mainly from within the professional circuit that the refinement of the products take place. Wave Rider believes that its active customers and members of staff, regardless of age and experience, form the most knowledgeable base for future innovations because they consciously form opinions of the company's product when they use them. Because the bond between the company and its devotees is so strong, they communicate in a language that must result in improved products. It also means, of course, that the company's ability to meet the ever-increasing demands of their consumers is as demanding, indeed possibly even more demanding, than staying ahead of the standards set by their competitors. Either way, there is no room for complacency, particularly since every new generation of surfer generates its own brand loyalty, and the brand loyalty of one generation should not necessarily be assumed to be the brand loyalty of the next one.

The Little Dragon Group Company of PR China generated some of its major innovations in the last two decades by conceptualising its end-product first, then purchasing its key technology from Japan, and managing to change its assembly lines to amalgamate hi-tech Japanese expertise with Chinese diligence and exactitude. It has strong alliances with Matsushita and Toshiba, as well as with General Electric from the USA, and Siemens headquartered in Germany. These relationships provide some of the inspiration for incremental innovation, and the process that is put in place to commercialise these is linear and prepared – the company is expecting a certain level of productivity from the factory floor, in which the new technology has been incorporated to construct the next product. Whilst being a company of stretch-target sales underpinned by careful strategic planning, it also shows considerable flexibility and opportunism, illustrated by its exploitation of Toshiba's expansion into the domestic washing machine market in China, by designing and manufacturing machines at the high end of the market where up till now, there has been non-consumption.

Alpine Packs of New Zealand, like Wave Rider, before re-structuring, had a high proportion of staff who actively pursued the great outdoors, and prior to their re-structuring, they sponsored high-adventure expeditions and environmental schemes with funding and with donations of their products. In association with a wide variety of customers and stakeholders, they evolved together, by learning about changing demand in a changing environment. They had a Research and Development Section which employed ten staff before the change to outsourcing, and employed about twenty afterwards in order to emphasize the need for their next generation of innovations to be underscored by design innovations and rigorous testing to ensure that concept and practice combined into a viable commercial product.Management dealt with change by negotiating modification in structure, processes, manufacturing and distribution.A part of managing the change was negotiating redundancy packages.

The case-studies demonstrate that innovation can be sourced through purchasing vital technology and adapting them to make the product functional. It can be commissioned and funded. It can be borne out of desperation, such as the immediate threat of competition; and it can be provided or solicited in the form of advice through users who know their needs well through their long-standing experience. In the case of

Wave Rider, consumers can cast their imagination forward to envision what they would like to utilize in the sport in future – thereby turning the manufacturer and consumer into a pseudo-partnership.

14.2.3 Question 3. Are there different forms of innovation towards which each company has a particular inclination?

Each company is inclined towards a particular form of innovation. It is necessary to distinguish between the three main types of innovation encountered in this investigation – the incremental, the discontinuous and the disruptive – and the ways in which each has benefited the manufacturer's profit-base. In the three cases, analysis showed that Alpine Packs inclined mainly towards the incremental, Wave Rider towards both the incremental as well as the discontinuous, and Little Dragon did not fall easily into a category, because it had introduced the disruptive, the discontinuous and also incorporated the incremental. This showed Little Dragon to be aggressive and to adapt technology towards an ever-increasing number of products in the domestic appliance range. Neither of the other two other companies demonstrated such versatility and urgency towards expansion, possibly because they were privately owned and operated. Since Wave Rider and Alpine Packs catered essentially for niche sporting markets, rather than for the more expansive markets of domestic products, it is understandable that there were limitations on their ability to increase their consumer base. However, Wave Rider's overseas sporting franchise method did steal the march on Alpine Packs, whose commercial vision was always circumscribed.

14.2.4 Question 4 How do the three companies determine which innovations to pursue for commercialization?

Each company attempts to make full use of its existing competencies in pursuing innovations. Each had initially established a customer base that was attracted to one or more of its early products, and then it sought to widen and deepen that base by producing goods that complemented the existing range by creating a greater cluster of products. This cluster was designed to improve on the benefits of the early innovation, and to enhance the overall experience for the consumer, especially in the cases of the two sporting companies.

The Little Dragon Company added other household appliances to their original product, the washing machine, to include driers, air-conditioners and heaters. They also expanded into commercial versions of the same, thereby attracting the corporate purchaser as another category of client. These disruptive innovations created new and profitable markets.

Alpine Packs expanded their innovative range of products to give the serious outdoors adventurer the capacity to tramp further and climb higher – without compromising comfort and safety. Originally manufacturing only packs, the company then began designing and developing outdoor clothing, tents and sleeping bags, manufactured from ever-better performing materials, such as water-proof breathable materials like gortex. The reputation of the original product was the recommendation for consumers to purchase the next innovative product from the same company.

By remaining within its original domain of design and manufacture, each company developed a brand that created a reputation for quality. Once that was established, the market often felt it owed a loyalty to the company and that their next innovation was worth a try because that company had proven experience in the field and by short logic, their next product had to be even better than the previous one. The longevity of each company demonstrates that this consumer behaviour basically followed that logic.

14.2.5 Question 5 Is change management a complex strategic undertaking? Why?

The management of change is considered a complex strategic undertaking for most industries, according to a preponderance of research in this field. This is because it necessitates a shift in vision, objectives, strategy, learning, the manufacturing process, quality management, distribution as well as the human resource management and general management processes to maintain control of it all and drive it to its next commercial destination. Frequently, culture can act as an anchor preventing the ship from attaining forward propulsion; the inertia of a resistant movement can have devastating consequences on change. The relationship between management who desire change and a work culture that desires stasis can be critical to the success of the endeavour. The Literature Review cites many authors who provide lengthy discourse on the problems which managers are likely to encounter in attempting to effect change, and even lengthier recommendations for overcoming this problem. Following many circuitous routes in an attempt to retain quality employees, these authors then often concluded that resistance may be eliminated by dismissing the recalcitrants involved.

However, in the case of the three industries under investigation, it was clear that whilst all had undergone change on varying scales, the processes involved were not so complex and time-consuming. Wave Rider and Alpine Packs are private companies, and have been led and managed by their owner-founders for many years. This means that the cultures were to an extent the product of their management styles, personalities, passions and charisma, which over the years generated respect and loyalty. It would be appropriate to say that Stewart McBruce and Sandra Gupwell in Alpine Packs generated more than respect: respondent after respondent intimated an affection for them; the same could be said of Paul Singer and Will Waugh – Graham Herbert indicated that the two were Australian sporting icons. In such circumstances, a workforce is willing to be led into change, and in the case of Alpine Packs, the measure of the extent to which a culture will change is that it allowed itself to go inexorably towards its own demise when the factory closed without any noticeable resistance.

Change in the Little Dragon Group Company, comprised consistent expansion: it increased in size from one plant in Wuxi to four within the three years that this investigation was conducted. By 2004, Wuxi's Number One Plant was outsourcing to Indonesia. With this company, the difficulty with change was not its development towards expansion as much as its rate of expansion. Its revenue target for 2005 stands at ten billion Renminbi. This sum will likely be achieved because of an opportune windfall contracted in 2003: the collaboration with Toshiba to design and manufacture for this brand in Wuxi, the market area of its commercial rival.

In each case, the strategic implications are challenging because there are elements of risk involved, and these must be minimised. They may include the need to decide who will be the next strategic partner for Little Dragon; the next line of development for outdoors people for Alpine Packs; and how far and fast the product range for the female surfer should be commercialized, for Wave Rider.

All three companies took pride in their latest innovation, be it incremental, like Wave Rider's SlickSkin wetsuit; discontinuous, like Little Dragon's joint venture with its competitor's next-generation technology; or architectural, like Alpine Pack's re-structuring. This was because each one took another step forward in meeting the needs of its market, thereby extending its own longevity as a trader. Therefore, innovation is the demonstrable driver of competitive advantage, and innovation itself, is underpinned by the learning and the technology that are required to make the product functional to the next level of consumer expectation. Little Dragon may actually surpass that expectation at the top end of the domestic market, because Toshiba's technology surpasses anything that Little Dragon has incorporated in its previous models. From Toshiba's point of view, is it possible, even probable, that Little Dragon might become a competitor in the same way that BenQ as a supplier to Motorola became one? Whilst Toshiba ponders this risk, Little Dragon ponders its next move that might exploit Toshiba's technology without endangering its source of that very technology.

At present, Little Dragon, Alpine Packs and Wave Rider provide the intellectual capital and resources for the next innovation. Outsourcing is characterized by a physical dislocation between the place where knowledge resides, and the place where that knowledge is put to work. But all three have to heed the warning that outsourcing requires the company to be clear about the line that separates cost-saving from outsource production, from its intellectual property that is the source of its competitive advantage. That way the outsource manufacturer will be kept in a commercially subordinate position instead of becoming a market rival.

"Executive leadership" plays a critical role in directing competencies and processes in the Model, but the data indicate that most successful leaders do more than that. They have a vision and the strength to drive the necessary changes to achieve success. In the case of Alpine Packs, driving the change towards factory closure appeared to contradict a life-time's way of working, but McBruce and Gupwell achieved it in order to save their company. To leaders who are passionate about their company, surmounting adversity and challenge is the key to the survival of the company. Survival and sustainability are paramount, but the business model must change. In their newly re-structured company McBruce and Gupwell are unlikely to change their maxim of "open and honest", but it now has to be translated into Mandarin, Spanish and Vietnamese.

14.2.6 Question 6 What is the extent to which the congruence model has applicability and validity in relation to the three cases cited?

The findings in relation to this question have been placed in 14.2.11 on the connection between the findings and the literature explored in Chapter 2.

14.2.7 Question 7 In which way(s) may the Tushman and O'Reilly (1997) model be extended or otherwise modified by the data to account for each company's market leadership?

The findings in relation to this question have been placed in 14.2.11 on the connection between the findings and the literature explored in Chapter 2.

14.2.8 In the opinions of senior staff, CEOs and other staff, which management practices have been perceived as being most successful in accounting for the sustainable prosperity of each of the three companies in question?

Each case-study has been given a dedicated sub-section to respond to this complex question.

14.2.8.1 Little Dragon

The Senior Management at Little Dragon plans for innovation and profitability with clear, workable strategies and linear processes that anticipate the introduction of purchased innovative technologies. Dr Hing and Mr Lei communicate the company vision and objectives to employees and other stakeholders in a number of ways, including meetings and weekly broadsheets, to ensure everyone understands what they are charged to contribute to.

In the multi-national innovation model, they formulate strategic alliances and joint ventures with other companies in the same field to share research findings and reduce costs. By doing this, they engender and cultivate relationships for reciprocal benefits; it avoids conflict and makes competitive tension. They remain alert for opportune moments when collaboration with another company may provide innovation, of which the best example is their collaboration with Toshiba. This shares a market, rather than competing within it. Therefore, they contract with others to commit towards a new industry structure where there is mutual sustainability, with each partner making an equal contribution towards successful outcomes.

Alliances can be two-edged swords. Dr Hing is therefore prepared to take calculated risks, even if it means having to argue his case strenuously to his sceptical board. It means that his vision must continually be ahead of the more mundane vision of his own colleagues, and it has thus far, made his company more resilient.

Little Dragon continues to research and develop incrementally to create new technologies as the basis for future innovation. However, Dr Hing appeared to think that this was an exercise with severely circumscribed limitations, and that only relationships with advanced companies would lead to greater technological leaps because of the more advanced levels of education in Germany and the USA compared to China. Dr Hing lamented that the innovations with which they had been identified were not cultured from within. He was referring to the medium to long-term need for his company to create its own innovations because cheap Chinese labour would be insufficient as a bargaining chip on the global market, where most profit is generated by intellectual property advances. Profits follow in the wake of proprietary technological developments, particularly those that have a disruptive capacity.

There has to date been no discontinuous or disruptive innovation generated from within the company itself. What made Little Swan so successful in such a short period of time is its versatility and flexibility: they could purchase innovation , so there appeared to be only one successful way to obtain the technology that the company required. Therefore, the Japanese culture of creating innovation had not carried over to produce a Chinese culture of innovation of its own - the Chinese still expected to be able to purchase an innovation. Dr Hing and Mr Lei have high expectations of their management team, and provide them with the training to do their job properly, even if it costs highly in time and money. Doing the job properly to Dr Hing means looking strategically to the future, rather than looking at the immediate needs of the company. In having his staff trained in Six Sigma and English communication, he is anticipating that each senior member will, at some point in the future, contribute significantly to the company's strength, by understanding finance and English in depth to forge new and profitable alliances with the western world. To Dr Hing and Mr Lei, politics were completely subordinated to commercial success.

14.2.8.2 Alpine Packs the Wilderness Company

Alpine Packs had a less ambitious goal target than Little Dragon. Senior Management kept staff informed of the state of the business at regular monthly intervals, and appeared to make change just as much part of the routine, so that employees never felt threatened by it – it was merely another way of performing better with the same inputs.

McBruce and Gupwell treated their staff with respect and courtesy, aiming to involve them as much as possible in matters that affected their performance and degree of work satisfaction. They did this mainly through the creation of multiple cross-functional groupings charged with the responsibility to arrive at optimum solutions. They trusted their work-force and supported them, as well as their ideas. Staff were invited to commit themselves to the company. McBruce, especially, believed that as a general manager, he might have to modify staff ideas and suggestions if need be, but that the most important way of harmonizing 230 employees was to give them a measure of ownership in the decision-making process.

The management was considered to be fair and reasonable in all staff performance evaluations and promotions, and remunerated or otherwise rewarded staff appropriately. The Management Team were aware of their employees' value, not just because of their specialized expertise in the manufacturing process, but because they encouraged them to be active participants in the domain where their products and services must perform to know whether they were coming up to consumers' expectations. Therefore, Management sponsored and supported expeditions, sports and community concerns to enhance its value network, and to show their products in action.

McBruce believed in creating an overseas market slowly, and to make time to get the processes of communication, distribution and retailing, correct.

As the owner-operators of the company, McBruce and Gupwell had the backbone to face up to the disappointment of failure: They discarded their most trusted work models if it meant they still had one last opportunity to save their company to re-generate profitability.

14.2.8.3 Wave Rider the Surfing Company

Sinclair, Waugh and Herbert showed passion for their business, for their products and made their after-sales services beyond reproach. Sinclair stated that they attempted to meet all customer expectations.

They created strong networks of stakeholders who shared the passion for "The Search". Consumers could advise the company or make recommendations about product performance, as well as the innovations that they would like to see the company make in the future. This closeness to the consumer meant that Wave Rider never stood still, complacently waiting for the next innovation to create itself. They actively pursued the next innovation, and were content to point to a small number of disruptive, and a greater number of discontinuous and incremental innovations as the reason for the company's longevity.

Sinclair and Waugh were financially conservative, and having or accumulating a fund for their next innovation made them an ambidextrous organization. Their funds financed the development of the electro-welded board short.

They introduced new products if they thought they belonged with their product cluster and if it had a good chance of deepening their market. The tide-watch and the back-pack were good examples of this – both of these enhanced the surfing experience.

In the active pursuit of innovation, they dedicated a section, led by a management staff member, to the design and creation of the next innovation, and they funded this party appropriately. Always conscious of quality, they provided this party with time not only to design and manufacture it, but to test it for quality and performance before releasing it on the market. The best example in recent times, was the board-shorts with electro-welded seams to enhance comfort.

Like the management of Little Dragon, they provided their employees with opportunities for educational improvement in an area of expertise where they most wanted to develop extra skills.

Their face to face communication with their customers, led Sinclair and Waugh to experiment with other media, to reach potential customers by talking in their own language whatever that might be: it might be visual as in a website for teenagers, or in print using a more moderate language, as in a written advertisement for more mature audiences.

At all times, like Little Dragon and Alpine Packs, Wave Rider aimed to be the best provider in their industry.

14.2.9. Question 9. Has private ownership provided advantages over public ownership in the implementation of innovation and change?

It appears that private ownership does not provide advantages over public ownership in the implementation of innovation and change. There is some evidence that indeed suggests that the two private companies developed innovations and change at the pace chosen by their owners, rather than by the public wielding power in the form of shares, and thereby demonstrating an impatience for profits. In Herbert, (1999), Paul Sinclair commented, "Money is not why we did it [....] it's not why we do it today and it's not why we want it done in the future either, because if it's done for money and profit, it won't be Wave Rider." Adding to this, Waugh added, "Wave Rider has always been driven by certain fundamental values, among those are making functional, quality and innovative products for surfers and people of like minds." (Herbert, 1999). Alpine Packs shares similar values that have been underscored by innovation and change to drive profits, but not at the expense of sustainable company development in which quality and staff relations come before profits: "In product innovation, we don't copy other people's products, and we're not fashion driven. We're driven by products that function better." (McBruce, April 11 2003). Yet he related innovation with profitability: "When we're highly profitable we're more innovative because we have more resources." (McBruce, April 11 2003).

This may be contrasted with Little Dragon, a public company initially owned by the Municipality of Wuxi City. It used its profit funds to purchase technology for expansion of their product lines, and striving to become number one in the manufacture of washing machines. In achieving this, it created shareholder value through growth. It then sought to create further growth opportunities through the increase in its product range and the quality of its existing product line to capture an ever wider market share. Its CEO, Dr Hing, realized that the domestic market in China was far from saturated, and he developed a strategy with Toshiba so that Little Dragon not only supplied the lower and middle range of the market, but also developed the top end of the market, to take advantage of a rapidly developing Chinese economy that is generating more discretionary spending. In taking this risk, he put his own position on the line with respect to his board. In its development from 1988 to the time of writing (early 2005), Little Dragon's development is characterized by constant change, multiple alliances with off-shore companies, frenetic searches for the appropriate technologies to drive its designs, and constantly increasing

270

productivity for the domestic as well as the export markets. It continues to strive beyond its initial core business, which has not yet fully matured, and has led to fund accumulation to expand other businesses.

14.2.10 Question 10 Have their nations' general political and economic situations helped or hindered the success of each of the companies comprising the case-studies?

The general political and economic situations impacted in varying degrees on business success. In the cases of Little Dragon and Wave Rider, it appears that the political and economic situations assisted their success, because their countries of origin have mainly experienced economic and political stability. However, Alpine Packs was adversely affected by the declining value of the US dollar in 2001 and 2002, which in part accounted for the collapse of its off-shore sales market. Even though Australia and New Zealand have democratic governments, well known for implementing market economies, the Chinese Communist government, implementing a command economy, does not at any time appear to have restricted Little Dragon from creating alliances, purchasing technology or in any other obvious way impeded the growth of the company – as might have been expected of a government of this nature.

One crucial factor for these companies' exports is the value of their respective dollars in relation to the United States dollar. At the time of writing, China maintains its Renminbi to the value of one-eighth that of the United States dollar, creating a considerable imbalance that favours its own exports. Foreign investment in 2003 was about US$53.5 billion. (AP, *Borneo Bulletin*, 20 April 2004, p.37), adding to the World Bank's prediction that the East Asia area generally, including China, could expect "robust economic growth of 6.3 percent in 2004 [....] thanks to rising exports, low interest rates in investment in China, Vietnam and Thailand. [....] Much of the region's growth is attributable to China, which saw imports to fuel its manufactured-goods sector surge by 40 percent in 2003. First quarter 2004 estimates showed a steady upward trend." (AP, *Borneo Bulletin*, 20 April 2004, p.37). During 2003 and 2004 there was upward pressure on both the Australian and New Zealand dollars due to the decline of the American, caused substantially by the American trade deficit of $400 billion, during President George W. Bush's first term of office. These trends would cause Wave Rider's and Alpine Packs' exports to cost the foreign purchaser more, but considering that both companies now manufacture a large percentage of their products off-shore, it is uncertain whether either company has been adversely affected by continued currency fluctuations. Also beyond the scope of this work is whether the cataclysmic tsunamis of 26 December 2004 have adversely affected the production of the outsourced companies in the Indian Rim.

14.2.11 Question 11 Literature and Findings

14.2.11.1 Introductory statement
The literature in connection with innovation and change management has not always been found useful, or applicable, to the three case-studies in consideration. Some was better on the subject of innovation itself than its practical day-to-day ramifications for businesses and their management. Because each company, generally speaking, is a discreet industrial entity, step by step operational guides such as Morgan (2000) found themselves either outdated or having strictly limited applicability in contexts other than those they were specifically written for. However, researchers who approached innovation and change management from the point of view of generating broad conceptual frameworks as well as practicalities, to provide broad understanding succeeded some of the time, but not always. Researchers such as Christensen and Raynor, (2003); Porter, (1996); Tushman and O'Reilly, (1997); Hamel and Valikangas, (2003); Birdi and Walls, (2003); and Govindarajan and Trimble (2005), contributed some relevant and partly testable concepts. Due to the limitations of time and the abductive approach, for all its strengths, not every aspect of their constructs could be assessed, but they provided valuable insights as well as perimeters within which to conduct this researcher's investigation, in which at least some of their theories, or parts thereof, found support.

14.2.11.2 Utterback (1994): Radical innovation
The first researcher to make a solid contribution to this investigation was Jack Utterback (1994). From an industrial point of view, he pointed out that innovation is a

two-edged sword: while an innovative product may find favour in the market, he pointed out in his early study that,

> Renewal of well-established products does not create new industries, nor will it save established firms from decline when their markets are invaded by radical innovations. [....] Simply becoming better and better with current technology will not, in the long run, keep new firms with new technology from absorbing markets and relegating unresponsive established firms to the scrap heap of industrial history. (Utterback, 1994, p.221).

Early in their start-up phase, each company in the case-studies introduced a radical innovation onto the market: the dual density wetsuit, the automatic washing machine, and the framed back-pack for ergonomic support. The outcomes of their ensuing commercial successes, support the concepts and theories that have been discussed in the preliminary and main analyses. But it was Utterback's identification of the "radical" innovation as the nemesis of incremental innovation, that became the theoretical focus of Tushman and O'Reilly (1997) and was then further developed by Christensen and Raynor (2003). All three parties accept the crucial importance of the radical innovation to organizational renewal, and therefore to the organization's longevity. When spun into a continuous thread, it becomes clear that the three parties' concepts may be laid end to end, to form an evolutionary theoretical construct that has contributed much to the understanding of innovation and how it can function to a company's advantage through change.

14.2.11.3 Tushman and O'Reilly (1997): The congruence model

With regard to Tushman and O'Reilly's congruence model of 1997, data indicate that this model has high applicability and validity in two cases. In the cases of Little Dragon and Wave Rider, it was clear that congruence had provided them with ambidexterity, which in turn enabled them to pursue their next innovation(s). Each innovation had a purchase or developmental cost that would otherwise have had to be met by commercial loans, but the funding was instead borne from within.

Alpine Packs was congruent in its systems and processes, as the model postulates, but failed to make a profit in 2002 and 2003 due to a major, and unforeseen change in environmental circumstances, leading to a loss of about NZ $1 Million each year. Due to the unsustainability of these financial circumstances, the company was forced to outsource production and make almost its entire manufacturing staff redundant. In managing the change, it retained its managerial and design staff, and then increased the latter to emphasize design and innovation as the catalysts for future commercial success. But the concept of congruence was not lost in the process of outsourcing – just its geographical separation.

By the time the last interviews were conducted by mid-2004, all three companies were outsourcing some, and up to half, of their production to one or more low-wage Asian economies. This practice had consequences for the applicability of the congruence model because of the challenges involved in controlling off-shore plants by remote control, long distance communication and only intermittent physical presence by headquarter staff. Outsourcing is a fast evolving turbine that drives globalization, as noted by the editor of *BusinessWeek*, March 21 2005:

> Companies […] must decide where they draw the line on outsourcing. In a world that keeps commoditizing core technologies and skills, it takes sophisticated strategic thinking to determine what intellectual property to keep and what to farm out. If too much innovation is outsourced, corporations may find their own suppliers competing with them. One thing is certain – understanding the consumer zeitgeist requires a cultural intimacy that cannot be delegated elsewhere. Intellectual property that enhances customer experience should be held close. Choosing what to let go will be painful.
>
> (Editorial, *BusinessWeek*, March 21 2005, p.64).

The companies in all three case-studies are a part of globalization, although their involvement and impact clearly vary. An outcome of this, is that the congruence model may be modified. During the three years of this investigation, some changes to "market leadership" occurred. Little Dragon cemented its position as the unrivalled supplier of washing machines to China's domestic market and it increased its exports as well. Wave Rider came second in revenue to Billabong, although it retained its position as the number one producer of wetsuits. Alpine Packs lost its position in pack sales, which had previously been its lead product, as retailers could not be guaranteed supplies in the 2003-2004 holiday season, due to the transition to Asian manufacturing and shipping. Alpine Packs was attempting to recover from this situation by May 2004, in order to assure distributors and retailers that the company was now again in a position to guarantee supplies.

The congruence model may therefore be modified by the trend to outsourcing because the companies are geographically divided between head-office and their manufacturing plants. Virtual organizations have been formed in the last three years because company case-study is affected by the need to increase product speed to market, by the imperative to maximize efficiency and minimize costs and overheads. All organizations like this require clear and precise coordination between the 'brain' and 'limbs', precise understanding of the terms of the company vision, its objectives, its manufacturing requirements, and the quality management processes. Skills in problem-resolution and mutual respect for each other's cultures, both national and industrial, are also pre-requisites. Cross-cultural communication, sometimes conducted through an interpreter, and relayed at high speed by fibre-optics, must be accurate and clear. Where offshore outsource manufacturers believe they have mastered sufficient English to obviate the need for an interpreter, there are fertile fields for misunderstandings. Additionally, there must be high levels of mutual trust, cooperation and understanding between employers, employees, suppliers, investors and the communities in which they operate, particularly if the parties envisage a long-term profitable relationship.

Both Wave Rider and Alpine Packs commented that their offshore outsource firms were selected on their ability to perform to requirements and because they shared the company's values. This may be the basis for a common culture that will bind them in future – apart from the obvious commercial arrangements.

These developments have not made the congruence model obsolete. This model is about organizational equilibrium and synchronization to effect alignment between sections of an industry and its employees. To design and produce goods that will continue to make a brand competitive, there is in future likely to be a greater need to generate knowledge, share learning, provide reciprocal communication and supply multifarious input towards the creation of innovative products.

275

Ambidexterity is concerned with developing dual or multiple streams of innovation. Under the model of the virtual organization, it seems that ambidexterity is now tending towards being a necessity as an insurance policy against ever more relentless competitors striving to reach first place. Tushman and O'Reilly's concepts have therefore been beneficial to clarifying the nature of a successful organizational structure to effect innovation and respond to change.

14.2.11.4 Christensen and Raynor, (2003): Disruptive innovation

The disruptive innovation can have a dramatic impact on the market (Christensen and Raynor, 2003), and the company's longevity has greater viability if it can design and manufacture a number of disruptive products, as Sony did between 1950 and 1982 when it successfully built twelve different new-market disruptive growth businesses. (Christensen and Raynor, 2003, p.79). When Wave Rider began selling the tide-watch on the youth market, it too created new growth business. It also became a part of the designer wear market in the Australian youth culture. These watches were outsourced in Hong Kong. Of the three primary case-studies in this investigation, Wave Rider was the first to take advantage of outsourcing, and the first to grow its market through diversification. Furthermore, when GlaxoSmithKline, Procter & Gamble, and Boeing Co. are reported as outsourcing aspects of their innovation to Asia, in addition to increasing amounts of manufacturing, in order to save costs on R&D, manufacturing itself, transport and distribution, they are creating opportunities to become ambidextrous and thereby more profitable. That is, they are aiming to create new products in less time, through cost-saving, thereby enlarging their product range, as well as improving its quality. In the meantime, the Asian companies concerned shelter behind Anglicized names, such as Quanta Computer, Premier Imaging and Wipro Technologies, because, according to Navi Radjou, from Forrester Research Inc, "It is still taboo to talk about outsourced design." (Engardio and Einhorn, March 2005, pp.52-53). Nonetheless, it appears that commercial viability is going to be achieved in the future, more and more through an innovation model that incorporates other companies, often in far-removed places from its headquarters. The companies in the case-studies demonstrate that amply, and this inclination by competitive companies is most likely to increase.

Outsourcing was not a major aspect of the literature in Chapter 2, but as the investigation progressed, it became clear that as a matter of both strategy and operations, commentators such as Engardio and Einhorn, March 2005, had to be incorporated into the discussion to maintain integrity. Outsourcing is now core to all three primary cases, as even China outsources some of its production to Indonesia.

In all three companies, it is clear that much of their brand, expanded range of products and company development are owed to the impetus of disruptive, discontinuous and incremental innovation. The differences between the two private companies and the public one is that the latter is driven to maximum profitability, and the former are more inclined to view sustainable growth, or low-growth core business as their target as postulated by Christensen and Raynor, 2003, p.3.

14.2.11.5 Porter (Nov/Dec 1996): "What is Strategy?"

Michael Porter's 1996 article entitled "What is strategy?" published in the *Harvard Business Review* in December of that year, is useful in emphasizing the role that strategy plays in innovation and implementation.

Each of the companies in the case-studies had operational effectiveness and used innovation as a catalyst for market leadership. Each began with a discontinuous innovation as a launch platform to capture market share. Then Alpine Packs slid into a series of incremental innovations that focused on management to effect operational concerns such as quality, durability and enhanced employee relations. Profitability came with the newly established brand. Little Dragon also expanded by diversifying their range of domestic products, and as in the case of Alpine Packs, growth was driven more for the sake of growth and by operational concerns than strategy for the long term welfare of the company.

Porter argues that a "company needs to establish a difference that it can preserve." (Porter, Dec 1996, p.62). The literature is supported by all three cases-studies with respect to their focus on such managerial undertakings as continuous improvement and institutionalizing learning. But Porter believes that "the essence of strategy is choosing to perform activities differently than rivals do." (Porter, Dec 1996, p.64). This difference is at the core of competitive advantage, which "grows out of the entire

277

system of activities. The fit among activities substantially reduces cost or increases differentiation. Beyond that, the competitive value of individual activities – or the associated skills, competencies, or resources – cannot be decoupled from the system or the strategy." (Porter, Dec 1996, p.73). Did Alpine Packs have a differentiating strategy? With a workforce of 250 it was a medium-sized employer by New Zealand standards, but it did not position itself "based on customers' need, customers' accessibility or the variety of [its] products or services." (Porter, Dec 1996, p.66). It was caught between "straddling" (Porter, Dec 1996, p.68) itself between company profitability and full employment. So there was tension between the need for profit and supplying employment as a social and economic benefit to its host city, Christchurch. As well as this, another tension was exporting to Europe whilst being 13,000 miles away, through agents and agencies, whom it had to pay, and on whom it relied. This is not much different from the position Continental Lite found itself in: it could not appeal on cost while having fat in its workforce. (Porter, Dec 1996, p.69). Its strategy was defective because its chain of value was not designed with one market in mind, and therefore it generated multiple inefficiencies.

The "trade-offs" Porter mentions "create the need for choice and protect against repositioners and straddlers." (Porter, Dec 1996, p.68). Alpine Packs had no wish to become a straddler: It made a conscious decision not to produce footwear for tramping, because it was not their area of expertise, and it would have brought them into too great competition with established footwear producers. Yet it could be argued that Little Dragon did straddle: It paid highly for engineers and scientists in their R&D programme, but it then paid Matsushita even more for their technical innovations, when its own R&D failed to produce the necessary prototypes. It should have focused on one, but not both, according to Porter's thoughts on strategy, in order to have continued being innovative and profitable. It instead failed to create the long-term capacity it was seeking. Therefore it generated dependency, so that their "innovations" with washing machines were actually second-hand imitations and another company's brainchild. In Little Dragon, there was no clear alternative to engineering prowess other than to purchase it from Japan, which meant that their chain also increased its dependency on still more Japanese knowledge and resources. This meant that finally, Little Dragon separated the competitive value of an individual entity, their purchased innovation, from the whole. Its real competitive advantage then, was not the innovation, but its cheap labour. And since "competitive advantage grows out of the entire system of activities," (Porter, Dec 1996, p.73), Little Dragon was not as well served by its purchased technologies as it had originally hoped, because it built no foundation for sustainability.

On the other hand, Waverider sourced sustainable strategy from within itself, by expanding at a sustainable rate where growth did not take place for growth's sake. Also, its wetsuits and watches were integrated in a retail strategy that was aimed at enhancing the beach experience. This company always had a very specific target market, and of the three, it best employed strategy as well as operational effectiveness to maintain its position as a market leader. "Consistency ensures that the competitive advantages of activities cumulate and do not erode or cancel themselves out. It makes the strategy easier to communicate to customers, employees, and shareholders, and improves implementation through single-mindedness in the corporation." (Porter, Dec 1996, p.71).

Porter's work on the value of strategy reinforces and links previous literature by offering a dimension which is not clearly delineated by the other contributors in this thesis.

14.2.11.6 Hamel and Välikangas (Sept 2003): The resilient organization
This investigation has attempted to make a contribution to the knowledge of business innovation and longevity, having been guided throughout by theory. Theory provided constructs that enabled the researcher to analyse and interpret data. In the same way in which Utterback (1994) provided a foundation for Tushman and O'Reilly, (1997) and they provided theoretical constructs upon which Christensen and Raynor (2003) built their theory, they in turn have provided a platform for Hamel and Välikangas' "The Quest for Resilience." (2003 Sept.). The latter theory is proving to be a useful construct to analyse innovation in relation to change, as its particular thrust concerns "reinventing your business model before circumstances force you to." (Hamel and Välikangas, 2003 Sept. p.1). It may be said that Little Dragon and Wave Rider succeeded in this; equally, it must be said that Alpine Packs did not. However, Alpine Packs is testimony to Hamel and Välikangas' contention that drastic change is a periodic necessity, "To be resilient, an organization must dramatically reduce the time

it takes to go from "that can't be true" to "we must face the world as it is." (Hamel and Välikangas, 2003 Sept. p.5).

Furthermore, they contend that "An accelerating pace of change demands an accelerating pace of strategic evolution, which can be achieved only if a company cares as much about resilience as it does about optimization." (Hamel and Välikangas, 2003 Sept. p.11). The resilience in Little Dragon, Wave Rider and the new generation Alpine Packs comes from "perpetual renewal" (Hamel and Välikangas, 2003 Sept. p.12), due to their continued efforts at broadening their product lines, appealing to wider consumer markets and offering their clients the best performing products available.

Whilst this seems sensible under the competitive nature of commerce in the twenty-first century, the question must be asked about the expectations that managers can realistically have of their employees, as change causes them stress. This may be demonstrated by some Alpine Packs staff who still commented ruefully to this researcher in 2003, that their change to teams eight years earlier was change for the sake of change, and therefore destined to be compromised at best and fail at worst. Hamel and Välikangas, therefore, may be in tune with market and managerial forces, but perhaps not so appreciative of the need for stability and predictability on the part of the workforce. Or, if they are, there is no mention in their work of how to deal with it.

14.2.11.7 Govindarajan and Trimble (2005): Ten "rules"

The reason that Govindarajan and Trimble's contribution in their 2005 publication is so significantly different and therefore so valuable to the discourse in this field, is that it focuses primarily on the connection between an innovation and its implementation. It is both a philosophical and practical guide for managers of change. Based on the combined outcomes of research on ten industries, their study provides the reader with perceptive insights on the new managerial capacity that must focus consistently on "forget, borrow and learn," (Govindarajan and Trimble, 2005, p.198). These combine into a formula for strategic innovation. The authors are as aware of the importance of strategy as Porter (1996). But innovation produces unique problems. Whilst it

280

potentially generates great wealth and will likely impose great risks, the authors go further than Porter by combining strategy with an approach to implementation that highlights the need for constant learning and selective borrowing.

Tushman and O'Reilly's model (1997) focuses mainly on an organization's stability and its capacity to respond to change, and this develops into a discourse on the formation of ambidextrous and congruent architectures. Govindarajan and Trimble, 2005, endorse their idea that an ageing organization must become the source of its more innovative offspring, and therefore must initially resource it. This is the imperative of "borrowing," (Govindarajan and Trimble, 2005, p.79). However, they go further than Tushman and O'Reilly: The formula for allowing the offspring, "NewCo", to develop its own identity and create a market share for its own products, is embodied not only in borrowing, but in two additional imperatives: in order to "forget," management must create a new culture; and to "learn" it must resolve critical unknowns and arrive at a working model as quickly as it can. If it cannot forget its parent's success formula, "it will struggle to learn its own." (Govindarajan and Trimble, 2005, p.17). These two authors do not focus on architectural stability as much as Tushman and O'Reilly, (1997), probably because they believe that stability in NewCo is not one of that company's most salient features. Stability of the kind that Tushman and O'Reilly (1997) are talking about will come in time. Strategic innovation is by nature chaotic, and therefore stability is more likely to be effected through employee working relationships than systems, because systems are still in a state of formulation and flux.

It is noteworthy that the notion of forgetting applies only to Little Dragon. When it converted from being a maker of ceramics and tools to being a manufacturer of household appliances, it definitely had to forget the industry characteristics, such as processes, that had made it a semi-profitable enterprise. It is significant that in the case of Wave Rider, the franchise in France worked in the opposite way: There was borrowing of resources and expertise, and a franchise by definition is a type of industry replication. France modelled itself on the Australian parent company, but it did have latitude in its product development to go towards its own design inclinations.

The ten "rules" which the authors present in Chapter 10 of their work focus on both general and specific ways and means with which to implement their three fundamental imperatives. These ten rules are simple statements that can be universally understood, although the authors themselves admit that the rules may not be so simple to implement, because they concede that the "how" of innovative implementation is still nascent. (Govindarajan and Trimble, 2005, p.xxvi). The so-called rules provide a framework that derived from a series of conclusions based on four years' research on a number of companies, of which the most commonly cited is ADI (Analogue Device, Inc). This company manufactures semi-conductors and computer micro-processors and was analyzed by the authors during the mature phase of its life-cycle. At that point, it began work on the highly innovative "MEMS", or "micro-electromechanical system." This system had unique microscopically small moving parts that were designed to be introduced into the market for car passenger safety systems to predict a crash, and therefore MEMS could either prevent or minimize death in the event of a crash. The following ten rules are the result primarily of that case-study, but also of others which the authors studied, like Corning.

Rule 1: In all great innovation stories, the great idea is only chapter 1.
Apart from a highly capable leader, great innovations "require the leverage power of organizational DNA." (Govindarajan and Trimble, 2005, p.185). This is in agreement with Christensen and Raynor (2003), as well as Tushman and O'Reilly (1997). This was borne out with all three companies under investigation. Each one began with an innovation that was commercially profitable, and each has been thriving for about forty years because each also mastered the implementation process after the introduction of the first innovation.

Rule 2: Sources of organizational memory are powerful.
Newco has to separate itself from the orthodoxy of its parent company. (Govindarajan and Trimble, 2005, p.187). This notion is new. Tushman and O'Reilly have a skunkworks embedded *within* the parent organization, and Govindarajan and Trimble maintain that this inhibits the development of independence and therefore early profitability. Therefore, the authors clash on this important point. However, Little Dragon had to consciously "forget" its past when it changed from ceramics and tool production to home appliances. Alpine Packs and Wave Rider had no past that they

282

needed to forget because there was no parent company of which they were the offspring.

Rule 3: Large, established companies can beat start-ups.
They can do this provided they can leverage their assets and capabilities. (Govindarajan and Trimble, 2005, p.187). This is the main thesis of Leifer et al. (2000), and Govindarajan and Trimble utilize it to explain that plant, goodwill, expertise and sales channels can all, or severally, be leveraged or borrowed from the parent company to develop another company, as long as the parent can continue to be profitable enough to continue nurturing its industrial offspring. Therefore, it is not a process of divesting or cannibalizing the parent company. Alpine Packs is an anomaly in this regard because they experienced financial difficulties, but Little Dragon and Wave Rider were profitable in the face of competition. In the case of Wave Rider, it was competing with upstarts like Mambo, and yet Wave Rider's profits were greater: $125 million for Mambo versus $800 million for Wave Rider in 2000. But its profits were not as great as Billabong that year, $1,070 million. Billabong is a big competitor which, unlike Wave Rider, was floated as a public company in the United States. (Stensholt, July 2001). It seems that in surfing, bigger is better.

Rule 4: Strategic experiments face critical unknowns.
"Success depends more on an ability to experiment and learn than on the initial strategy." (Govindarajan and Trimble, 2005, p.188). This echoes Hamel (1997), De Geus (1998) and Pettigrew and Whipp (2001), who also assert the primacy of learning from mistakes. But for Govindarajan and Trimble, learning is not just education in an organized setting. It is also a means of communication between colleagues, as they have to resolve problems through learning and experimentation. This can only take place by means of transparency in constant dialogues at all levels of the organization. Therefore, learning is not a managerial addendum, or something that managers should know the value of: In NewCo, it is fully integrated in every piece of fabric of the new cultural weave that NewCo is attempting to create. One strategic experiment that Wave Rider undertook was manufacturing a zipper-less wetsuit; it was an expensive mistake because surfies could not take them off easily enough because of the water suction effect. The scheme to begin mass production was dropped.

Rule 5: The Newco organization must be built from scratch, with "new choices in staffing, structure, systems and culture [....] to defeat the powerful forces of institutional memory." (Govindarajan and Trimble, 2005, p.191). This notion is reminiscent of Schein (1992) and Hamel and Valikangas (2003). Each of these researchers is emphatic about the need to pursue systemic strength and resilient cultures that imbue employees with flexibility and mental fortitude. In a way, franchising and outsourcing do this to a large extent, but the "blueprint" of the parent company is stamped on the others. In franchising and outsourcing, the "umbilical cord" is never severed.

Rule 6: Managing tensions is job one for senior management.
The relationship between CoreCo and Newco can deteriorate very quickly, mainly due to their respective needs competing for capital. (Govindarajan and Trimble, 2005, p.193). In this instance, the conflict is *between* organizational competitors, and this is a useful insight. Previously, Tushman and O'Reilly (1997), Leifer et al. (2000), and Christensen and Raynor (2003) focused more on the conflict that could arise *within* the older organization, as employees clash over philosophical and process differences, where not everything is firmly established when an innovation is allocated resources. On the other hand, Govindarajan and Trimble make the assumption from the beginning that NewCo's employees do not suffer from such problems, because they were selected in the first place, on the basis of their commitment to an innovation and its development strategy, inside an entirely new organization. This, however, may be an over-simplification on their part. Interdepartmental conflict is probably more common than they have admitted because the compass for a new organizational direction can still have marked lurches between east and west before a company can progress to the north. An example of this is Dr Hing's efforts to pacify his Little Dragon board for their anger in his allying the company with Toshiba.

Rule 7: Newco needs its own planning process.
This is because Coreco's norms for evaluating business performance will disrupt NewCo's learning. These norms cannot apply to NewCo in a different strategic environment. This appears to be correct, but this is not borne out in any of the three companies under investigation. Of course, none was a new company created by an

284

older parent company. Franchises can have their own planning processes, but this is outside the scope of this investigation.

Rule 8: Interest, influence, internal competition, and politics disrupt learning.
"To ensure learning, you must take a disciplined, detached, and analytical approach to making predictions and interpreting differences between predictions and outcomes." (Govindarajan and Trimble, 2005, p.194). They have attempted to place the strategic process on a scientific basis; debate is seen as a sign of alert and healthy minds, as well as of an open environment that encourages divergent opinions. These are the sources of the "lurches between east and west" referred to in the commentary on Rule 6. Learning was an essential aspect of the success of all three companies under investigation.

Rule 9: Hold Newco accountable for learning and not results.
The learning process should be "disciplined" so that accountability in relation to that process can be achieved; but "accountability for results against a plan, while simpler to practice, is counterproductive." (Govindarajan and Trimble, 2005, p.196). This is an advance on DeGeus (1998) and Peters (1997), because they argued that management needed to be aware of what education could do for their organizations in terms of the contribution made by a more informed workforce. But Govindarajan and Trimble specify that learning must be measured against an agreed upon process which has calculated stages of progress. This is a refinement because it is a very particular deployment of the education concept, and it is also less amorphous and haphazard than DeGeus (1998) and Peters (1997). This also combines with the idea that education and learning are a platform for dialogue, as discussed in the commentary on Rule 4. This concept appears to be new and unique to Govindarajan and Trimble; but there was no evidence that the managements of any three case-studies did anything other than plan in the conventional sense: For results rather than learning. In providing journals for employees, Alpine Packs came the closest to educating its workforce for the sake of broader learning, rather than learning as training, which is designed for the purpose of producing immediate short-term commercial results. But according to Sandra Gupwell, not very many employees took advantage of this offer. Evidently, learning as a change mechanism has to be driven to be effective.

Rule 10: Companies can build a capacity for breakthrough growth through strategic innovation.

"Skills in forgetting, borrowing, and learning are the foundation. Managers must start building these organizational skills early in a company's life." (Govindarajan and Trimble, 2005, p.198). In asserting that, the two authors are very reminiscent of Hamel and Valikangas (2003), because in so doing, they also align strategic innovation with the concept of resilience. But Govindarajan and Trimble's approach is more practical. They reduce everything to concrete, day to day actions. For example, under "Recommendations for overcoming the forgetting challenge", in Chapter 3, they write the following practicalities under the most demanding and abstract of their four subheadings, namely culture:

> NewCo must develop a unique culture, starting with a nearly blank slate. It should borrow only the most abstract and universal elements of CoreCo's culture (for example, the value of integrity or teamwork). And it must start with a culture of experimentation and learning, which may directly oppose CoreCo's culture of accountability to plans.
>
> (Govindarajan and Trimble, 2005, p.48)

Govindarajan and Trimble do not ignore the element of risk, nor do they sidestep the fact that industries which engage in strategic innovation are subject to considerable upheaval. Where there is the potential for a great win, there is potential for great uncertainty. That is why Newco must have an initial link to the assets of its parent, but like a teenager who leaves home for the first time, Newco must "forget, borrow, and learn," (Govindarajan and Trimble, 2005, p.198), and so finally it becomes independent, earning its own keep. And then in time, when its profit potential diminishes, it, in turn, has to spawn its own offspring as the source of its income, thereby completing the cycle.

Whilst the cyclical nature of the argument by Govindarajan and Trimble (2005) is very neat, only Wave Rider can approximate it. Wave Rider, "CoreCo" set out to replicate itself in France and elsewhere, and then allowed for individual differences in its offspring companies, so that borrowing and learning were applicable. There was no conscious forgetting under such a commercial arrangement. With Alpine Packs and

Little Dragon now outsourcing, forgetting is again inapplicable as the parent company, CoreCo, wants the offspring company, NewCo, to produce everything to its exact specifications.

Govindarajan and Trimble (2005) have contributed considerably to our understanding of the implementation of change because they focus mainly on practicalities, rather than predominantly on theory, as the other researchers tend to do. Their "rules" are supported by some of the findings of this research. But because of the nature of the three companies under investigation in this thesis, not all of Govindarajan and Trimble's tenets find support, but that does not invalidate their work, nor does it invalidate the work of this researcher. These two researchers do overlap with a number of previously mentioned researchers, and that is consistent with one of the theses of this investigation: researchers continually build on each other's work. They collectively construct ever larger dimensions to the evolution of thought and practice in the domain of innovation and change management.

14.3 Business partnerships

Partnerships have played a significant role in the innovation context, and future research could focus still more on the efficacy of partnerships in commerce. Little Dragon demonstrates that partnerships are one of the pillars of their strength, but there are increasing complexities involved in the process of effecting a successful partnership. These include various countries' views of business ethics, sustainability, the environment and politics. Little Dragon has been successful in transcending the ideological differences between their own communist state and the United States' democratic state; they have been able to maintain low wages for their employees, as well as low levels of industrial pollution; and they have been able to build a plant in Indonesia to reduce levels of wages still further. These features of their commerce, as well as their low currency, have contributed to their profitability, even in the face of some international tensions. Hamel and Välikangas would classify such a phenomenon as comprising "political [and] ideological challenge[s]." (Hamel and Välikangas, 2003 Sept. p.3). Do they have commercial viability when the turbulence of the business, as well as in the political environment, mitigate against such arrangements? Are subsidies, tariffs and artificially maintained currency differentials used as political instruments?

Hamel and Välikangas' model of organizational change itself needs further investigation. In the three cases in this research, change appears to have produced little friction, yet many commentators see change as the instigator of resistance and conflict between employees and management – and not without reason as evidenced by many large companies' experiences. In a unionized country like New Zealand, Alpine Packs might have expected worse resistance. However, the conclusion was that McBruce and Gupwell were owed a generation of respect through their transparent and concerned social manner of operating their Addington plant since the company's founding. How could such respect be engendered by management in a much larger plant, in which the CEO is further distanced from his or her workforce? And in practical terms, how would "resilience [...] become something like an automatic process [...] when companies dedicate as much energy to laying the groundwork for perpetual renewal as they have to building the foundations for operational efficiency"? (Hamel and Välikangas, 2003 Sept. p.13). For example, is it still possible to attain economies of scale, and its nemesis, customization, when there is constant intervention? And is it possible to have a homogeneous culture, when renewal is "perpetual"? (Hamel and Välikangas, 2003 Sept. p.13).

In summary, researchers such as Christensen and Raynor (2003), Tushman and O'Reilly (1997), Hamel and Valikangas (2003), Birdi and Walls (2003) and Govindarajan and Trimble (2005), contributed some relevant and partly testable structures because their models harmonized with one another as well as with many of the findings of this investigation.

In contrast, Leifer et al. (2000) provided a design to effect organization and structures in order to nurture and grow radical innovation, but their operational management of incubation and the "management hub" are complex, expensive and would require constant vigilance. Their model is top-heavy with managerial proprietorship. While it may be said that this pattern suits a country like China where Dr Hing did indeed exercise such proprietorship, it was due more to the culture of regimentation of his nation than a formula for successful growth of innovation anywhere else. It was not supported by Alpine Packs nor by Wave Rider. Nonetheless, their contention that large and established companies, and not just "upstarts" can produce good innovation, is well supported by all three case-study companies.

14.4 The "virtual" company

In light of their contribution, much in the ever-evolving world of business scholarship may be investigated further to deepen the knowledge about the relationships between resilience, change, innovation, company longevity, and competitive advantage. Like Wave Rider and Alpine Packs, outsourced, or "virtual" companies are likely to increase in number and complexity. Questions must be asked about the virtual company. Generally, such companies could be investigated further for their evolving characteristics and commercial success rates.

Is a virtual company more resilient as a business model? In the case of Dell Computers, this would appear to be so. Can a virtual company create innovations more quickly than the former, one-site, organization? It appears from the "new formula for innovation" discussed in the Main Analysis Chapter, that the more resources a company has, the better these are harnessed, the more effective a company can be in the field of innovation. But more research needs to be done, as these companies are still evolving their own ways of working. How do virtual companies evolve their cultures? Does an outsourced plant maintain its own indigenous culture or does it adopt some or all of its "parent" headquarter in another country? And what role does 'learning' play in a virtual company and how is it conducted? Hamel and Välikangas observed that in "The Cognitive Challenge: A company must become entirely free of denial, nostalgia, and arrogance," (Hamel and Välikangas, 2003 Sept. p.3) in order to be resilient. However, the human emotional dimension comprises a company's culture, and allowance must be made for the strength of culture in the success of any company, as in all three of the case-studies in this research, culture played a very positive role. More than that, it is clear that each of the three professed to know its customer well. And in any future model of innovation, that will still be a prime concern. Comments Azim Premji, "To be a successful product company requires intimacy with the customer. That is very hard to offshore in fast-changing markets." (Premji quoted in Engardio and Einhorn, March 21 2005, p.57).

Whilst all three companies believed that at least part of their continued profitability lay in their strong cultures, they also placed emphasis on their virtual organizational skills. It would be useful for future studies to provide more of the answers to on the relationships between long-distance cultural cohesion, or extension, to enhance the practice of those who will also go in the direction of the virtual organization. This has many relevancies, not the least of which would be an understanding of the ways in which designers, suppliers and manufacturers can work most profitably in unison, rather than becoming each other's competitors, a degenerative characteristic of geographic separation.

14.5 The value of this investigation

The value of this investigation is that it documents three companies from their beginnings 40 years ago to the present time, and shows the means they used to achieve regional, then national and finally international recognition. This investigation has shown that one of the most profitable solutions to business problems is to *be* innovative, and to *remain* innovative and thereby have the competition follow in the market-leader's wake. All three companies therefore cultivate a respect for, and achieved a depth of understanding of, innovation and change management.

To retain or increase their market share, these companies creatively deployed innovative strategies. Their histories show that each company generally sought to distinguish its products and/or services from those of its competitors by creating differences, increasing its competitive advantage, expanding its growth and refining its visionary drive on a continuing basis. However, each company also demonstrated highly individual ways of sustaining growth, including the implementation of disruptive, incremental and discontinuous innovations. They also continued leading their markets by purchasing leading-edge technologies, diversifying their product range, forging alliances, creating franchises, resorting to outsourcing, engaging in creative marketing, educating their workforce, and expanding their advertising approaches to include digital means, in order to enhance their customers' experience.

Finally, each of the three, to a greater or lesser extent, became companies that placed considerable emphasis on targeted learning and selective outsourcing. As such they are tending towards becoming "virtual" companies because their managements found outsourcing to be the next challenge in maintaining their lead in the market.

14.6 Recommendations and implications

A significant point to arise from this research is the difficulty concerning the common understanding of some of the variables. Concepts such as "innovation" and "change" are difficult to define, even in theory, but particularly when seen in the complex and shifting day to day environments of interactive behaviours characteristic of large and/or high performing organizations. In the social sciences, many variables such as "creativity", "innovation", "learning" and "human performance" are difficult and complex because when the abductive method is used, it is dependent on the participants' perspectives. The strength of this is that the researcher can visit the insides of a participant's head. Human behaviour inherently comprises measures of variability, diversity and unpredictability. When a researcher uses an interpretivist approach in which the "actors" describe their own roles and scenes, and define their own actions, discrepancies can occur – but extraordinary insights also occur. Therefore, this researcher recommends that other studies be undertaken of perhaps a statistical, quantifiable nature, so as to compliment this investigation.

Each participant during the time of the research was questioned about "innovation", but the researcher did not define it for the participant, which was in keeping with the abductive method. During the two years when data was generated, only one of the participants asked for a definition – no one else even asked for a loose meaning of the word "innovation". Each in his or her own mind appeared confident that he/she knew what the term meant, perhaps if not in theory then in the daily practice of their work environment. It is noteworthy that for the Wave Rider participants, "innovation" predominantly focused on "product"; for employees of Alpine Packs, it predominantly focused on "people", as in social systems; and for the management of Little Dragon, innovation predominantly focused on "process." The researcher concludes this because in each company, participants naturally gravitated towards either product, or people or process as judged by their own emphasis on certain work practices where innovation had most played a leading role in the success of their company. Therefore, innovation may be characterized as a multi-faceted phenomenon in industry, composed of the many elements that comprise product, people and process. Of course, none of the companies focused exclusively on just one feature. Success was the product of innovative combinations, and re-combinations, of two of them, or of all three.

Clearly, while not all the concepts dealt with in this investigation are empirically testable, an interpretivist approach may still provide many useful, and a number of generalizable insights, although it may also impose limitations on the generation of new theory and therefore other investigations using a quantitative approach may help complete the picture in future. This should include the phenomenon of the virtual company, and ways of educating business people to enhance their use of innovation and change.

14.7 Concluding statement

This investigation has canvassed many elements related to successful innovation and change in industry. The three companies in the case-studies are living testimony to the efficacy of incremental, discontinuous, disruptive innovations, and – at times – resourceful strategy. Under pressure from an increasingly competitive environment, the companies in question have been designing and manufacturing their innovations. They have shown the determination to build business resilience based on strategy, technical expertise, managerial acumen, and responsiveness to a consumer market that is increasingly eager for products and services that are novel, effectively meeting its needs, and that are good value for money.

The concepts introduced by Utterback (1994), Tushman and O'Reilly (1997), Leifer et al. (2000), Christensen and Raynor (2003) and Hamel and Välikangas (2003, Sept) have served to clarify the actions and behaviours of the actors in the commercial drama that comprises the three case-studies under investigation, and have helped to explain their commercial successes and occasional failures. The successes include constructing the capacity to design and manufacture ambidextrously, to identify and exploit non-consumptive markets, to purchase technology and call it their own brand, and to conquer new markets through cheap outsourcing and utilizing the Internet for marketing and sales purposes, so that distance would no longer be the impediment that it once was for commerce. And it is in these latter features of company operations that innovation has found its next hallmark of company design. Wave Rider, Little Dragon and Alpine Packs all began their existence about forty years ago with founders who had sound product concepts accompanied by an entrepreneurial spirit. By 2005, they had innovated their way to market success on a different innovation model, and changed their operations to enhance customer service, widen their product ranges, and to expedite their distribution networks whilst striving for quality at the lowest possible cost to the consumer. Managing all that required that none of these companies could ever become complacent. Forgetting, learning and borrowing were part of the success. Paradoxically, the case-studies also endorse replication. These are integral to the complexities of this investigation.

Innovation and change as products of the vision of lone entrepreneurs have evolved into a different and much more complex shape. Conglomerates now share R&D, resources and expertise to invent technologies, create designs, and devise manufacturing processes through joint ventures and alliances. It now seems uncommon for any one individual, or any one company, to have the monopoly on the expertise required to create products and services which the consumer demands in a particular area. The consumer now wants products that are cheap but excellent with the catch-cry being, "I want it all, and I want it now." This is particularly so with Little Dragon's washing machines, just to choose one example.

Innovation has become inextricably linked with globalization, which is playing a greater and greater role on the commercial stage of the world. The innovation model has made a shift from being predominantly inspired, controlled and operated by relatively few people in one country, to being a concerted combination of many people in many countries utilizing many resources, to collaborate for a common good, on a scale heretofore never envisaged, in order to reach markets they could never reach before. Naturally, start-ups must start small. But the outcomes of this investigation support Leifer et al. in their contention that it is not only small

293

companies that can be innovative and entrepreneurial. This research demonstrates that large companies may have started small, but they build the capacity to innovate, thereby expanding their operations, because they generated the necessary expertise. Of all three case-studies, Little Dragon and Wave Rider are probably the best examples of that. Alpine Packs has restructured itself on this innovation model, but it is still at a nascent stage. It would be interesting to see whether the outsource manufacturing companies in future, will become more equal partners with Little Dragon, Wave Rider and Alpine Packs, if their own learning processes evolve. This is already the case with Wave Rider, and appears to be a contemporary trend with others. Wave Rider's franchises make a holistic contribution, and Little Dragon has already accomplished that in a major deal, the 300-Series for Toshiba. Little Dragon is likely to continue looking to its traditional ally, Japan, for its next technological leap, although sourcing from Germany or the United States cannot be ruled out. "It is hard to find good friends, harder to find good competitors. So we keep on good terms with everyone." (Lei, Nov 18, 2002).

Finally, this investigation has attempted to demonstrate by means of an interpretivist approach, that three companies in three countries have thrived on innovation, and could not have attained their decades' longevity without the profitability that various models of innovation, and subsequent change, generated. This investigation then, offers further evidence of the primacy of innovation in its many forms, in achieving commercial success. Of course, innovation has to be accompanied by prudent and appropriate change management. Successful innovation and the competitive advantage that ensues, make a company more resilient when confronting competition. Therefore, it is imperative for survival that old models which sustained the company in its infancy, evolve into new models which will sustain it far into the future.

Bibliography

"Airbus raises its stakes with A380," (2005, January 20), *Borneo Bulletin*, p.25.

Alpine Packs, (2003, Summer), Information pack, Christchurch, New Zealand.

Alpine Packs, (2003, Winter), Information pack, Christchurch, New Zealand.

Associated Press, (2004, April 20), "Good economic prospects for East Asia – World Bank reports," *Borneo Bulletin*, p.37.

Australian Institute of Management, (2001), *Innovation and imagination at work*, McGraw-Hill, Roseville, New South Wales.

Barnard, J. (2003, April 4), face to face interview at Addington plant, Christchurch, New Zealand.

Barnard, J. (2004, June 14), telephone interview between Addington office, Christchurch, New Zealand, and Bandar Seri Begawan, Brunei.

Bean, R. and Radford, R. (2002), *The business of innovation: Managing the corporate imagination for maximum result,* Amacom, New York.

Bessant, J. (2003, March), "Managing innovation – moving beyond the steady state." Available at: http://www.som.cranfield.ac.uk/som/news/events/downloads/Managinginnovati on.pdf Inaugural lecture, retrieved October 21, 2003.

Birdi, K. and Walls, T. (2003), "Developing an Innovative Culture: Implications from Research," Institute of Work Psychology, ESRC Centre for Organization and Innovation, University of Sheffield, Website, retrieved March 3, 2003.

Blaikie, N. (2000), *Designing social research – The logic of anticipation*, Polity Press, Cambridge.

Blaxter, L., Hughes, C. and Tight, M. (1996), *How to research*, Open University Press, Buckingham.

Boyett, J.H. & Boyett, J.T. (2001), *The guru guide to entrepreneurship*, John Wiley & Sons Ltd., Canada .

Burberry, R. (2003, April 4), face to face interview, Addington plant, Christchurch, New Zealand.

Butlin, M. and Carnegie, R. "Developing innovation in medium businesses: a practical approach," in Barker, C. (Ed.) (2001), *Innovation and imagination at work*, McGraw Hill Publishers, New South Wales.

Carnell, C. (1990), *Managing change in organizations*, London: Prentice-Hall Int. (UK) Ltd.

Celeste, R.F. (1996), "Strategic alliances of innovation: Emerging models of technology-based twenty-first century economic development," *Economic Development Review*, Vol.14, No.1, Winter, pp. 4-8.

Chan Kim, W. and Mauborgne, R. (1999), "Creating New Market Space," in *Harvard Business Review on Innovation,* (2001), pp 1-31, Harvard Business School, Boston, MA.

Chesbrough, H.W. (2003), "The Open-Innovation Model", *MIT Sloan Management Review,* Vol.44, No.3, Spring. Pp. 35-41.

Christensen, C. (2003), *The innovator's dilemma*. HarperBusinessEssentials, New York.

Christensen, C. and Overdorf, M. "Meeting the challenge of disruptive change," *Harvard Business Review on Innovation*, (2001), Harvard Business School, Boston, MA.

Christensen, C. and Raynor, M. (2003), *The innovator's solution: Creating and sustaining successful growth.* Harvard Business School, Boston, MA.

Clarke, T. & Clegg, S. (1998), *Changing paradigms: The transformation of management knowledge for the 21st century.* HarperCollinsBusiness, London.

Clook, S., (2003, April 2), face to face interview at Addington plant, Christchurch, New Zealand.

Coulson-Thomas, C. (1997), *The future of the organization: Achieving excellence through business transformation,* Kogan, London.

Coutu, D. (2003), "How resilience works," *Harvard Business Review on Leading in Turbulent Times,* Harvard Business School, Boston, MA.

Curren, T. (1994), *Wave Rider: 25th Anniversary Catalogue,* (Foreword), Victoria, Australia.

Dann, S. and Dann, S. "Innovation from the ground up: Street level marketing," in Barker, C. (Ed.) (2001), *Innovation and imagination at work*, McGraw Hill Publishers, New South Wales.

Dawkins, R. (1976), *The selfish gene.* Oxford: OUP. From http://perso.wanadoo.fr/pgreenfinch/bfglo/bfgl.m.htm retrieved 21 Dec 2004.

De Geus, A. (1999), *The living company: Growth, learning and longevity in business.* Nicholas Brealey Publishing, London.

Dell, M. (2002, August), "Don't fear failure," *Harvard Business Review,* Harvard Business School, Boston, MA.

Dougherty, S. (2003), *Foreign technology, innovation and productivity effects in mainland China,* from http://www.sean.dougherty.org/econ/papersshanghai.pdf retrieved April 19 2004.

Doz, I. and Hamel, G. (1997), "The use of alliances in implementing technology strategies," in M. L. Tushman, and P. Anderson, (Eds), *Managing strategic innovation and change,* New York, Oxford University Press, pp. 556-580.

Doz, I., Hamel, G. and Prahalad, C.K. "Collaborate with your competitors – and win," in *Harvard Business Review,* (1989 January-February), pp. 133-139.

DPA, (2004, November 5), "China forecasts US$100 billion trade with Asean." *Borneo Bulletin,* p.52.

Drucker, P. in Kotelnikov, V.
/www.1000ventures.com/business_guide/innovtion_mgmt_main.html retrieved February 25 2005.

Dunne, G., (2004, August 20), e-mail reply to Robert Pech.

Dyson, E. "Don't innovate, solve problems," in *Harvard Business Review,* (2002 August), p.49. Harvard Business School, Boston, MA.

Editor, (2005, March 21), Editorial, "Outsourcing." *BusinessWeek,* Asian Edition, The McGraw-Hill Companies, New York.

Engardio, P. and Einhorn, B. (2005, March 21), "Special report: Outsourcing." *BusinessWeek,* Asian Edition, The McGraw-Hill Companies, New York.

Ettlie, J.E. (2000), *Managing technological innovation.* Wiley, New York.

Francis, D., Bessant, J. and Hobday, M. (2003), "Managing radical organisational transformation," in *Management Decision*, Vol. 41, No. 1, pp. 18-31.

Frederick, H. and Carswell, P. (2001), *Global entrepreneur monitor: New Zealand 2001,* New Zealand Centre for Innovation & Entrepreneurship, Auckland NZ.

Ghoshal, S. & Bartlett, C. (1994), "Linking organizational context and managerial action: The dimensions of quality management," in C. Gibson. and J. Birkinshaw, (2003), *Contextual determinants of organizational ambidexterity* in http://www.london.edu/sim/Working_Papers/SIM05.pdf retrieved 20 October, 2003.

Gibson, R. (1998), *Rethinking the future*, Bealey, London.

Glaser, B. and Strauss, A. (1967), *The discovery of grounded theory*, Aldine, Chicago.

Office of the Prime Minister, (2002, February), *Growing an Innovative New Zealand.* Wellington.

Govindarajan, V. and Trimble, C. (2005), *10 rules for strategic innovators – From idea to execution,* Harvard Business School, Boston, MA.

Gupwell, S. (2003, April 4), face to face interview, Addington plant, Christchurch, New Zealand.

Gupwell, S. (2004, May 28), telephone interview between Addington Office, Christchurch, New Zealand; and Bandar Seri Begawan, Brunei.

Hamel, G. (2000), *Leading the revolution*, Harvard Business School, Boston, MA.

Hamel, G. and Prahalad, C.K. (1994), *Competing for the future*, Harvard Business School, Boston, MA.

Hamel, G. and Välikangas, L. (2003, September), "The Quest for Resilience." Reproduced in Reprint R0309C. Harvard Business School, Boston, MA.

Hammer, M. (2001, Sept), "The superefficient company," *Harvard Business Review*, pp. 82-91, Harvard Business School, Boston, MA.

Harborne, P. and Johne, A. (2003), "Creating a project climate for successful product innovation," *European Journal of Innovation Management*, Vol. 6, No. 2, pp. 118-132.

Harvard Business Review, (2001), *Innovation*. Harvard Business School, Boston, MA.

Harvard Business Review, (2002 August), Harvard Business School, Boston, MA.

Herbert, G. (1999), *Wave Rider Company Principles & Values Handbook*, Unpublished history of Wave Rider the Surfing Company.

Herbert, G. (1999), *Wave Rider Company Principles and Values Handbook*, Confidential unpublished history and values of Wave Rider the Surfing Company.

Herbert, G. (2001, August 24), face to face interview, Wave Rider Head Office boardroom, Torquay, Victoria, Australia.

Herbert, G. (2004, January 20), telephone interview between Wave Rider Head Office, Torquay, Victoria, Australia, and Bandar Seri Begawan, Brunei.

Herbert, G. Unpublished papers on the origins of Wave Rider the Surfing Company.of Australia.

Hing, W. (2004, March 24), Face to face interview. Jiangsu Little Dragon Group Company boardroom, Wuxi, People's Republic of China.

Hislop, D. (2003), "Knowledge integration processes and the appropriation of innovations," *European Journal of Innovation Management*, Vol. 6, No. 3, pp. 159-172.

Hong, S. (2004, September 10), e-mail reply to Robert Pech.

http://www.3M.com, retrieved October 12 2003.

http://www.emeraldinsight.com, retrieved December 19 2004 and February 11 2005.

http:// www.massey.ac.nz;~cprichar/303cm, retrieved September 13 2004.

http://perso.wanadoo.fr/pgreenfinch/bfglo/bfgl.m.htm, retrieved September 13 2004..

http://www.alpinepacks.co.nz, retrieved August 9 2004.

http://www.brw.com.au, retrieved June 1 2004.

http://www.globalisationguide.org, retrieved March 22 2005.

http://www.Littledragon.com, retrieved November 16 2004.

http://www.littledragon.com/en/company/aboutus.htm, retrieved January 18 2004.

http://www.spark@cnn.com, retrieved March 6 2005.

http://www-mmd.eng.cam.ac.uk/cim/imnet/papers2002/yifang.pdf, retrieved July 29 2004.

http://www.waverider.com, retrieved August 17 2004.

http://www.waverider.com, retrieved December 15 2003.

Hynd, P., Jarratt, P. and Carroll, N. (1994), *Wave Rider: 25th Anniversary Catalogue*, Australia.

Inkson, K. & Kolb, D. (2002), *Management – Perspectives for New Zealand*, Prentice Hall, Auckland.

Jackson, B. (2002), *Organizational behaviour*, Golden Books Centre, Kuala Lumpur.

Jiang Nan, (2004, March 24), face to face interview in Jiangsu Province, PR China.

Jones, A. (2003, April 2), face to face interview at Addington plant, Christchurch, New Zealand.

Jones, A. (2004, June 14), telephone interview between Addington Office, Christchurch, New Zealand; and Bandar Seri Begawan, Brunei.

Keeley, L. (2002, August), "Abandon the crowd," *Harvard Business Review*, p.42. Harvard Business School, Boston, MA.

Kiernan, M. (1997), *Get innovative or get dead,* Century Business, London.

Kline, D. (Spring, 2003), "Sharing the Corporate Crown Jewels,"*MIT Sloan Management Review,* Vol. 44, No. 3, Spring, pp. 89-93.

Kotelnikov, V. /www.1000ventures.com/business_guide/innovtion_mgmt_main.html retrieved February 25 2005.

Kotter, J. (1996), *Leading change,* Harvard Business School, Boston, MA.

Kotter, J. & Heskett, J. (1992), *Corporate culture and performance*, Harvard Business School, Boston, MA.

Lei Y. (2002, 18 November), face to face interview, at the Jiangsu Little Dragon Group Company in Wuxi, Jiangsu Province, PR China.

Lei, Y. (2001), "Corporations and Markets," unpublished position papers, translated by Hong Shi, University of Southern Yangtze, PR China.

Lei, Y. (2002, November 18), face to face interview, at the Jiangsu Little Dragon Group Company in Wuxi, Jiangsu Province.

Lei, Y. (2004, March 22), face to face interview, at Little Dragon boardroom, Wuxi, Jiangsu Province, PR China.

Leifer, R., McDermott, C., Colarelli O'Connor, G., Peters, L., Rice, M., and Veryzer, R. (2000), *Radical innovation: How mature companies can outsmart upstarts.* Harvard Business School, Boston, MA.

Lewin, S. (May, 1997), "Innovation and authority in franchise systems: Toward a grounded theory of the plural form," PhD thesis in economics, Harvard Business School, Boston, MA.

Lubbers, R. http://www.globalisationguide.org , retrieved April 3, 2005.

Malakunas, K. (2004, 21 December), "Asia's economy on the road to recovery," *Borneo Bulletin*, p. 148.

Maynard, L. (2003, 2 April), face to face interview at Addington plant, Christchurch, New Zealand.

McBruce, S. (2003, 11 April), face to face interview at Addington plant, Christchurch, New Zealand.

McBruce, S. (2004, May 21), telephone interview between Addington Office, Christchurch, New Zealand; and Bandar Seri Begawan, Brunei.

Miles, R. (1997), *Leading corporate transformation – A blueprint for business renewal,* Jossey Bass Publishers, San Francisco.

Montemayor, E.F. (1996), "Congruence between pay policy and competitive strategy in high performance firms," *Journal of Management*, Vol. 22, No.6, pp. 889-908.

Morgan, M. (2000), *Making innovation happen – A simple and effective guide to turning ideas into reality*, Business Publishing, Australia.

Moss Kanter, R. "From Spare Change to Real Change: The Social Sector as Beta Site for Business Innovation," *Harvard Business Review*, (2001), pp 153-179. . Harvard Business School, Boston, MA.

Negroponte, N. (2003, February), *Technology Review*.

Pandit, N. (1996 December), "The creation of theory: A recent application of the grounded theory method," *The Qualitative Report*, Vol. 2, No. 4.

Pech, R.M., Pech, R.J., Wei, G. and Hong, S. (2005 February), "Innovation through acquisition: The Jiangsu Little Dragon Group Company in the People's Republic of China," *European Journal of Innovation Management*, Vol.8, No.1, Emerald Group Publishing, Bradford.

Pearson, A. (2002 August), "The innovative enterprise," *Harvard Business Review*, Harvard Business School, Boston, MA, pp.117-124.

Peters, T. (1997), *The circle of innovation: You can't shrink your way to greatness*, Hodder & Stoughton, London.

Pettigrew, A. and Whipp, R. (2001), *Change management for competitive success*, Infinity Books, New Delhi.

Phillips, E. and Pugh, D. (1994), *How to get a PhD*, (2nd Ed), Open University Press, Buckingham.

Piantanida, M., Tamanis, D. and Grubs, R. (2002), "Claiming grounded theory for practiced-based dissertation research – A think piece." 2002 Conference on Interdisciplinary Qualitative Studies, Roundtable Discussion, Jan 3 – 5, 2002. Athens, Georgia.

Porter, M. "Creating tomorrow's advantages," R. Gibson, (1998), *Rethinking the future,* Bealey, London.

Porter, M. (Nov/Dec 1996), "What is strategy?" *Harvard Business Review*, Harvard Business School, Boston, MA, pp.61-78.

Prahalad, C. and Hamel, G. (1994), *Competing for the future*, Harvard Business School, Boston, MA.

Richards, T. and Richards, L. (1994), "Using computers in qualitative research," N. Denzin, and Y. Lincoln, (Eds), *Handbook of qualitative research,* Thousand Oaks, California: Sage, Chapter 28, pp.445-461.

Rickards, T. (1999), *Creativity and the management of change,* London: Blackwell.

Robbins, S. & Mukerji, D. (1994), *Managing organisations: New challenges and perspectives,* (2nd Ed), Prentice Hall, New York.

Robbins, S. and Coulter, M. (2002), *Management,* (7th Ed), Prentice Hall, New Jersey.

Robinson, P. (2002, May 25), "Rip Curl's winning wave may extend to Asia", *The Age.*

Samuelson, R. (2003, June 30/July 7), "The bad news from Boeing," *Newsweek*, New York.

SanMao China, (2001), *Flying to the new millennium*, Heilan Group, Jiangsu, PR China.

SanMao China, (2004), *Heilan Group*, Heilan Group, Jiangsu, PR China.

Saunders, M., Lewis, P. and Thornhill, A. (2000), *Research methods for business students,* Pearson Education, Prentice Hall.

Schein, E. (1997), *Organizational culture and leadership*, (2nd Ed), Jossey-Bass, San Francisco.

Senge, P.M. (1990), *The fifth discipline: The art & practice of the learning organization,* Random House Australia Pty Ltd., Sydney.

Shapiro, S. (2001), *24/7 Innovation: A blueprint for surviving and thriving in an age of change,* McGraw-Hill, New York.

Sinclair, P. (2001, August 24), face to face interview at Wave Rider Head Office, Torquay, Victoria, Australia.

Singh, K., Pangarkar, N., and Heracleous, L. (2004), *Business strategy in Asia: A casebook*, (2nd Ed.), Thomson, Singapore.

Smith, P. (2003, March 28), face to face interview, Addington plant, Christchurch, New Zealand.

Stenholt, J. (July 2001), "Strategy: Sport-wear goes sky-high" *BRW* Vol. 23, No. 26. Fairfax Business Media.

Strauss, A. and Corbin, J. (1990), *Basics of qualitative research: Grounded theory procedures and techniques,* Sage, London.

Taffinder, P. (1998), *Big change – A route map for corporate transformation,* John Wiley & Sons, New York.

Tushman, M. and O'Reilly, C. (1997), *Winning through innovation: A practical guide to leading organizational change and renewal*, Harvard Business School, Boston, MA.

Utterback, J. (1994), *Mastering the dynamics of innovation: How companies can seize opportunities in the face of technological change*, Harvard Business School, Boston, MA.

Van der Slee, C. (2003, April 2), face to face interview at Addington plant, Christchurch, New Zealand.

Von Hippel, E., Thomke, S. and Sonnack, M. "Creating Breakthroughs at 3M," *Harvard Business Review,* (2001), pp 31-55, Harvard Business School, Boston, MA.

Warren, C. "Qualitative interviewing," in Gubrium, J. and Holstein, J. (Eds), (2002), *Handbook of interviewing research: Context & method*, Sage Publications, London.

Waugh, W. (2001, August 24), face to face interview at Wave Rider Head Office, Torquay, Victoria, Australia.

Wave Rider, (1994), *25th Anniversary Edition*, Special Catalogue.

Wave Rider ATS Tide and Surf Watches Manual (2001).

Welch, J. in file://C:WDOCUME-1WUserWLOCALS-1WTempWtriEOLPG.htm, retrieved May 11 2003.

Williams, A. (1999), *Creativity, invention & innovation – A guide to building your business future*, Allen & Unwin, St Leonards, New South Wales.

Wu, X., Ni, Y., and Cao, Z. (2002), *The factor analysis on China's manufacturing enterprises' technology acquisition performance.* Retrieved April 19 2004, from http://www.ifm.eng.cam.ac.uk/cim/imnet/symposium2002/papers

Yin, R. (1989), *Case study research: Design and methods,* (Rev.Ed), Sage, London.

Yin, R. (1993), *Applications of case study research,* Applied Social Research Methods Series, Vol. 34, Sage, London.

Appendix 1

Plain Language Statement – Individual Interviewee

Dear

I am a Doctor of Philosophy student at the Royal Melbourne Institute of Technology University. I am researching the links between industrial innovation, change management and culture in three industries which have undergone change to continue their sustainability. My research is entitled "Innovation, the Management of Change and Organisational Culture."

It has been suggested that you are a suitable person to interview, because you have some knowledge about the new products and services that your company has brought to the market over the last few years, and how these have impacted on the ways in which your company has changed.

The outcome of all the interviews across these three industries will be a collection of accounts from the actual participants in the processes involved with change. I hope to be able to extract some general principles about change from those experiences.

If you are willing to participate in this study, it will involve either one or two individual interviews where you will be asked questions relating to the key ideas mentioned above. Each interview will be about 90 minutes in length; they may be audio-taped if you agree, and they will take place mainly in 2003, at your place of work during work time.

Your participation is voluntary and you may choose to withdraw from the project at any time. After the interviews if there is anything you said that you don't want me to use then I will respect that and remove that information. Your identity will be protected by the use of a fictitious code in the thesis or any other published materials that arise from this study. If any or all of the three industries wish to remain anonymous their identities will not be revealed, a fictitious code will be used, and a draft copy of any thesis material or other material intended for publication will be provided so that research participants may remove any items which could reveal their identity.

If you are willing to participate, I would like you to do two things. Please email me at pechrm@cpit.ac.nz to indicate that you are willing, and please sign the consent form that accompanies this letter, and bring it to the interview. I will arrange interview times and places with one of your management staff and you will be notified by that person.

If there is anything you want to discuss with me, I can be contacted at the email above or you can telephone me at (03) 940-8550 or fax me at the Christchurch Polytechnic on (03) 940-8648. If you wish to contact my research supervisor, Associate Professor Erica Hallebone, you can reach her by phone in Australia at (61) 3-9925-1348 or write to Erica.hallebone@rmit.edu.au

If you have any ethical concerns as regards the conduct of this project please contact Professor Robert Brooks, Chair, RMIT Business Human Research Ethics Committee, Phone: 61-3-99255594, email: robert.brooks@rmit.edu.au

Thank you for considering this.

Yours sincerely

Robert Pech
MA, MBS.

Appendix 2

Research Questionnaire
Semi-Structured

Interview 1 with Mr Lei Yuan, Deputy General Manager, Little Dragon Company, Wuxi, Jiangsu Province.

To be conducted 18 November 2002.

TO BE TRANSLATED INTO MANDARIN.

Please tell me a little about your company and the most important stages in its development.

....

....

....

....

....

Broadly speaking, what production lines is your company going in now?

....

....

....

....

....

Your company has grown considerably in the last 30-40 years. To what do you attribute its growth?

....

....

....

....

....

How would you describe your target market?

....

....

....

....

....

What part did technology and innovation play in your expansion?

....

....

....

....

....

How did you create or develop the technology?

....

....

....

....

....

As your company developed, what were the main changes that the company underwent?

....

....

....

....

....

Where did your main innovations come from? Or how did they originate?

....

....

....

....

....

If not all innovations came from technology, where did they come from?

....

....

....

....

....

What are the main planks of your company strategy, now and in the medium term?

....

....

....

....

....

Do you believe that you are innovative in dealing with staff? If so, how?

....
....
....
....
....

Do you believe that you are innovative in dealing with other industries? If so, how?

....
....
....
....
....

How much do you invest in research and development?

....
....
....
....
....

Please describe the main features of the culture of your company out of which
innovations have been created or developed.

....
....
....
....
....
....
....
....
....
....
....
....
....
....
....
....
....
....
....

Druck: KN Digital Printforce GmbH · Schockenriedstraße 37 · 70565 Stuttgart